CW01507057

European Communication Research and Education Associ‹

This series consists of books arising from the intellectual work of ECREA members. Books address themes relevant to the ECREA's interests; make a major contribution to the theory, research, practice and/or policy literature; are European in scope; and represent a diversity of perspectives. Book proposals are refereed.

Series Editors
Nico Carpentier
François Heinderyckx

Series Advisory Board
Denis McQuail
Robert Picard
Jan Servaes

The aims of the ECREA are

a) To provide a forum where researchers and others involved in communication and information research can meet and exchange information and documentation about their work. Its disciplinary focus will include media, (tele)communications and informatics research, including relevant approaches of human and social sciences;
b) To encourage the development of research and systematic study, especially on subjects and areas where such work is not well developed;
c) To stimulate academic and intellectual interest in media and communication research, and to promote communication and cooperation between members of the Association;
d) To co-ordinate the circulation of information on communications research in Europe, with a view to establishing a database of ongoing research;
e) To encourage, support and, where possible, publish the work of young researchers in Europe;
f) To take into account the desirability of different languages and cultures in Europe;
g) To develop links with relevant national and international communication organizations and with professional communication researchers working for commercial organizations and regulatory institutions, both public and private;
h) To promote the interests of communication research within and among the Member States of the Council of Europe and the European Union;
i) To collect and disseminate information concerning the professional position of communication researchers in the European region; and
j) To develop, improve and promote communication and media education.

Citizen Voices

Citizen Voices
Performing Public Participation in Science and Environment Communication

Edited by Louise Phillips, Anabela Carvalho and Julie Doyle

intellect Bristol, UK / Chicago, USA

First published in the UK in 2012 by
Intellect, The Mill, Parnall Road, Fishponds, Bristol, BS16 3JG, UK

First published in the USA in 2012 by
Intellect, The University of Chicago Press, 1427 E. 60th Street,
Chicago, IL 60637, USA

A catalogue record for this book is available from the
British Library.

Cover designer: Edwin Fox
Copy-editor: MPS Technologies
Production manager: Bethan Ball
Typesetting: Planman Technologies

ISBN 978-1-84150-621-0
ECREA Series ISSN: 1742-9420

Printed and bound by Bell & Bain, UK

Contents

List of Figures

Notes on Contributors

Ashley A. Anderson (Ph.D., University of Wisconsin-Madison) is a Postdoctoral Research Fellow in the Center for Climate Change Communication at George Mason University, US. She has research interests in public opinion, public deliberation and science communication, in particular in relation to online communication environments.

Pavel P. Antonov is the Editor-in-Chief of *Green Horizon* and journalism trainer at the Regional Environmental Center in Hungary. As a Geography Ph.D. candidate at the Open University, UK, Antonov is carrying out research on the impacts of a neoliberal market imperative on journalism and democracy. He is the former Current Affairs Editor-in-Chief, political reporter and host at Nova TV, Bulgaria, a co-founder of BlueLink.net and the author of articles, documentaries and reports on the state of the environment and civil society in Central and Eastern Europe.

Jarkko Bamberg (Ph.D.) is a lecturer at the School of Management, University of Tampere, Finland. In the last ten years, he has been involved in the development and design processes of several ICT-mediated participatory practices in the city of Tampere. His research interests include a range of topics associated with practices of public engagement, urban planning, knowledge production and multimodal meaning-making. He is also interested in methodological questions and has co-edited a book on case study methodology in Finnish (*Tapaustutkimuksen Taito*).

Dominique Brossard (Ph.D., Cornell University) is Associate Professor and Director of Undergraduate Studies in the Department of Life Sciences Communication, University of Wisconsin-Madison, US, and a faculty affiliate of the UW-Madison Robert and Jean Holtz Center for Science and Technology Studies. Her research focuses on the intersection between science, media and the public and on the understanding of public opinion dynamics in the context of controversial science. She has recently co-edited (with Jim Shanahan and Clint Nesbit) the book *The Media, the Public, and Agricultural Biotechnology* (2007).

Anabela Carvalho (Ph.D., University College London) is Associate Professor at the Department of Communication Sciences of the University of Minho, Portugal. Her research focuses on various forms of environment, science and political communication with a particular emphasis on climate change. She is editor of *Communicating Climate Change: Discourses, Mediations and Perceptions* (2008), *As Alterações Climáticas, os Media e os Cidadãos* (2011), *Communication and Political Engagement with Climate Change* (with T. R. Peterson, in press) and of two journal special issues. She is also Associate Editor of *Environmental Communication: A Journal of Nature and Culture*, is on the Board of Directors of the International Environmental Communication Association, and is a co-founder, former Chair and current Vice-Chair of the Science and Environment Communication Section of ECREA.

Julie Doyle (Ph.D., University of Sussex) is Principal Lecturer in Media Studies in the School of Arts and Media at the University of Brighton, UK. Her research focuses upon climate change communication, the visual culture of science and the environment, and media discourses of the environment. She is the author of *Mediating Climate Change* (2011) and has recently completed a Leverhulme-funded project with the artist David Harradine which explored new visualisations of climate change. She is on the Board of Directors of the International Environmental Communication Association and is a co-founder and Vice-Chair of ECREA's Science and Environment Communication Section.

Anders Horsbøl is Associate Professor at the Department of Communication and Psychology, Aalborg University, Denmark. He studied communication, philosophy and applied linguistics at different universities in Denmark, Germany, Austria and Great Britain. In addition to a doctoral thesis on the discursive construction of a political presidential candidate (2003), he has published especially in the fields of (multimodal) discourse analysis, political communication and health communication.

Maja Horst is Head of Department of Media, Cognition and Communication at the University of Copenhagen, Denmark. She holds a Master's Degree in Communication Studies and a Ph.D. in Science and Technology Studies. Her research focuses on public understanding of science, science communication, research management and sociology of innovation. She has also conducted experiments with research communication installations for which she has been awarded the Danish Science Minister's science communication prize. Among other journals, she has published in *Social Studies of Science, Science, Technology and Human Values, Public Understanding of Science, Science as Culture* and *Science and Public Policy*.

Anna Maria Jönsson is Associate Professor at the Department of Culture and Communication at Södertörn University, Sweden. Her doctoral thesis from 2004 'Samma nyheter eller likadana?' (same news or similar?) analyses diversity in television news against the backdrop of theories about the public sphere and the media. Her research interests are in journalism and the public sphere, environmental governance and environmental communication. Several of her recent research projects and publications focus on public participation in environmental discourse.

Inger Lassen is Professor at the Department of Culture and Global Studies at Aalborg University, Denmark, and is currently director of the doctoral programme on Discourse and Contemporary Culture. She obtained her Ph.D. in discourse in professional settings from Aalborg University. Her publications include a monograph on stylistics, an edited anthology on image and identity, and an edited anthology on gender. She has also published articles in journals such as *Document Design, Discourse Studies, Critical Discourse Studies, Risk Research* and *Environmental Studies.*

Pauliina Lehtonen is a Ph.D. candidate at the School of Communication, Media, and Theatre, University of Tampere, Finland. Her research interests include public participation and democracy, knowledge production and communication, and the uses of communication technology, including social media, in civic action. Her doctoral thesis discusses practices of civic action in the context of urban governance. Her methodological interests focus on case study approaches and action research as means to further the dialogic production and communication of research.

Hedwig te Molder is Professor of Science and Technology Communication at the University of Twente and Associate Professor in Communication Science, Wageningen University, the Netherlands. Her work focuses on how issues of science and technology are handled in people's everyday talk, expert discourse and new forms of science and technology communication informed by discursive psychology. From the American Sociological Association, she received the Distinguished Book Award 2007 for the edited collection *Conversation and Cognition* (2005, with Jonathan Potter).

Louise Phillips (Ph.D., LSE) is Professor of Communication at the Department of Communication, Business and Information Technologies, Roskilde University, Denmark. Her current research is about dialogic and participatory approaches to communication theory and practice, including approaches to collaborative research. Her recent publications include the monograph *The Promise of Dialogue: The Dialogic Turn in the Production and Communication of Knowledge* (2011) and the edited volume *Knowledge and Power in Collaborative Research: A Reflexive Approach* with co-editors M. Kristiansen, M. Vehviläinen and E. Gunnarsson (2013). She was the co-ordinator of the NordForsk Network for the Study of the Dialogic Communication of Research (2008–2012) and is a co-founder, former Vice-Chair, and current Chair of ECREA's Science and Environment Communication Section.

Ursula Plesner is Associate Professor at the Department of Organization, Copenhagen Business School, Denmark. She holds a Ph.D. in science communication and does research on innovation communication. Her work draws primarily on communication

communication in innovation processes and the role of the material in communication processes. She has published in journals such as *Qualitative Inquiry, Public Understanding of Science, Journalism – Theory, Practice and Criticism* and *Convergence – The International Journal of Research into New Media Technologies*.

Annika Egan Sjölander is a senior lecturer in media and communication studies at Umeå University, Sweden. Her doctoral thesis entitled 'Kärnproblem' (core issues) from 2004 is an analysis of the Swedish nuclear waste discourse, applying Michel Foucault's discourse analytical understanding. She recently co-edited the volume *Tracking Discourses: Politics, Identity and Social Change* (2011). Several of her research projects have dealt with dimensions of democracy and the role of the (mass) media in relation to environmental issues such as radioactive waste, chemicals and biofuels.

Dietram A. Scheufele (Ph.D.) is Professor and Director of Graduate Studies in the Department of Life Sciences Communication, University of Wisconsin-Madison, US. His work focuses on public opinion, political communication and public attitudes towards new technologies, including nanotechnology, stem cell research and genetically modified organisms.

Michael A. Xenos (Ph.D.) is Associate Professor in the Department of Communication Arts and Director of the Center for Communication Research, University of Wisconsin-Madison, US. He has research interests in political communication, science communication, democratic deliberation, public opinion and civic engagement.

Acknowledgements

This book is the product of collaboration between the Science and Environment Communication Section of the European Communication Research and Education Association (ECREA) and the NordForsk Network for the Study of the Dialogic Communication of Research (2008–2012).

We co-founded the Science and Environment Communication Section in 2007 with the aim of fostering a strong network of inter- and transdisciplinary research on science and environment communication in the nexus between the fields of communication and media studies, science communication, science and technology studies, and environmental studies. Here, science is understood in broad terms as research that has roots in the social sciences, humanities or natural sciences and technology, and the environment is understood broadly as both the natural and the built milieu. The NordForsk network sought to develop the emergent field of study on the dialogic turn in the production and communication of knowledge by bringing together three dispersed traditions of research (action research, science and technology studies and social constructionist approaches to dialogic communication theory and practice).

Some of the contributions to the book are based on papers presented in a panel on dialogic approaches to research communication (organised by the NordForsk network) in the Science and Environment Communication Section at the ECREA Conference in Barcelona in 2008, and almost all the other contributions originated from papers presented at either the Barcelona conference or the ECREA Conference in Hamburg in 2010. We are grateful to the participants in the panels of the Science and Environment Communication Section at the two conferences who gave feedback to the papers that have developed into the chapters of this book.

We would like to thank the Executive Board of ECREA for selecting *Citizen Voices* for publication, with ECREA's financial support, in Intellect's ECREA Book Series. We would also like to thank NordForsk for funding the NordForsk network (project nr. 080149).

Chapter 1

Introduction

Louise Phillips, Anabela Carvalho and Julie Doyle

The starting point for this book is the *dialogic turn* in the production and communication of knowledge in which practices claiming to be based on principles of dialogue and participation have spread across diverse social fields (Aubert and Soler 2006; Gómez, Puigvert and Flecha 2011; Phillips 2011). One such field is planned communication and campaigns. Here we find that authorities increasingly supplement or replace information campaigns aiming to transmit or diffuse expert knowledge to recipient target-groups with communication initiatives in which experts and target-groups are reconfigured as *participants* in sites of *dialogue* where knowledge is co-produced through mutual learning. Another field is organisational development in which employees are encouraged to participate as agents of change through the collaborative production of knowledge in processes of dialogue, rather than being positioned at the receiving end of organisational changes dictated by management.

Yet another field is politics, and central and local government policymaking across policy areas including urban planning and science and environmental policy. The dialogic turn manifests itself here in so-called *participatory* governance, in which elite, top-down decision-making has been supplemented by *public engagement* or *public participation* activities where citizens participate together with government officials and/or researchers in sites for dialogue. According to proponents of the dialogic turn, these sites for dialogue represent spaces for *citizen voices* articulating potentially diverse perspectives. These perspectives are recognised as legitimate forms of knowledge and harnessed in decision-making about issues that affect the participants. The legitimacy of the knowledge forms is often taken to lie in their roots in citizens' locally anchored and socially and culturally specific experiences and values. 'Participatory' governance thus entails a reconfiguration – and apparent *democratisation* – of relations between policymakers, researchers and citizens. As Felt and Fochler (2010: 221) put it, 'governance' is hailed as a new means of collective decision-making in which different social actors participate in 'network-like constellations', in contrast to decision-making characterised by top-down hierarchical relations between government and relevant social actors.

This book concentrates exclusively on the dialogic turn in the governance of science and the environment. Although practices of science communication and public engagement with science and technology concentrate on the natural sciences and technology, the turn to dialogue in research/society relations has not only impregnated *science*, defined narrowly as research in the natural (including environmental) sciences and technology, but also research in the social sciences and humanities as well. Accordingly, when we write of 'science' in this book, we often use it in this broad sense of 'research', and several of the chapters analyse the production and communication of social scientific knowledge while others focus on knowledge based on the natural and environmental sciences and technology.

We attempt in this book to build bridges across the fields of science and technology studies, environmental studies, and media and communication studies in order to provide theoretically informed and empirically rich accounts of how *citizen voices* are articulated, invoked, heard, marginalised or silenced in science and environment communication. Across a diverse range of national, social and institutional settings and on the basis of diverse theoretical and methodological approaches, the chapters together produce an in-depth, research-based analysis of the different, context-dependent, situated ways in which *participation* is ascribed meaning and practised in the communication of science and the environment.

In this introductory chapter, we first sketch out how *citizen participation* is understood and enacted in the communication processes which are constituted within, and constitute, the 'participatory' mode of governance. A key point here is that, in both academic research and everyday practices, 'participation' and 'dialogue' are buzzwords with multiple, vague and shifting meanings (Carpentier and Dahlgren 2011; Phillips 2011). By virtue of their status as buzzwords with a self-evidently positive value, 'participation' and 'dialogue' legitimate the practices that are constructed in their terms: when their positive value is taken-for-granted, critical questions are not raised, and proponents become oblivious to the tensions, contradictions, dilemmas and power imbalances inherent in all forms of knowledge production and communication (Phillips 2011).

Following this outline of the enactment of 'citizen participation' in 'participatory' science and environmental governance, we describe the routes taken in the book through the interdisciplinary terrain of research on public participation in science and environment communication. Here we draw attention to the different ways of conceptualising 'citizens' and 'participation' and the implications of those different conceptualisations for both theory and practice. We also address how different theoretical fields tackle the tensions, contradictions, dilemmas and power imbalances that arise in relation to the participation of citizens in science and environment communication. Finally, we introduce each of the chapters of the book, locating them in that terrain and indicating their contributions to research.

Conceptualising 'citizen participation' in science and environmental governance

As in other fields of social practice in the dialogic turn, the model of communication underpinning science and environmental governance is *dialogue* in which scientists and citizens engage in *mutual* learning on the basis of the different knowledge forms that they bring with them. The official aim is to involve citizens in processes of decision-making on scientific and environmental issues, including issues relating to the built environment such as urban planning. And it is argued that public participation in decision-making will improve the quality of decisions and policy processes. In relation to science governance, the dialogue model is presented in policy documents as a decisive break from the previously dominant discourse which articulated a 'deficit' model of communication; this model assumed that the public suffered from a deficit of knowledge about scientific developments curable through the one-way transfer, diffusion or dissemination of scientific truths (Irwin 2001, 2006; Irwin and Michael 2003). In relation to environmental governance, landmark agreements such as the Rio Declaration on Environment and Development (1992) and the Aarhus Convention on Access to Information, Public Participation in Decision-making and Access to Justice in Environmental Matters (1998) have stressed the importance of public participation in decision making on, and access to information about, environmental issues.

During the past two decades, dialogue-based public engagement initiatives such as citizen consultations, experiments in local democracy and dialogue-with-the-public activities have burgeoned across Europe and the rest of the world with respect to controversial and politically-pressing questions relating, for example, to nanotechnology, food biotechnology, climate change and sustainable development (for example, the British GM Nation? debate over the commercial growing of GM crops [2003], the British Public Consultation on Developments in the Biosciences (PCDB) [1997–1999], the British Nanodialogues project [2005–2007], the German 'Futur' Research Dialogue [2001–2005], the Norwegian CREATE project [2002–2005] and the Swedish Technology Foresight programme [2001–2002]). In both academic texts and policy documents, public engagement exercises such as the above are interchangeably labelled as exercises in *public engagement* or *public participation*, and in this book we use both epithets. It should be noted, though, that since around 2000 there has been an increasing preference for the term *public engagement*, related to the emergence of the concept of *upstream* public engagement, as Delgado et al. (2010: 2) point out. The concept of *upstream* public engagement stresses the inclusion of the public in the process of determining the direction of scientific research; here, the public shape science 'upstream' of scientific developments (Wilsdon and Willis 2004). A contrast is drawn discursively to practices within the *public understanding of science* tradition. These practices treat the public as the recipients or consumers of completed research results: here, the public 'meet' science 'downstream' of scientific developments.

The forms of participatory democracy practised in science and environmental governance often build on models of deliberative democracy developed within political theory (e.g. Benhabib 1994, 2005; Dryzek 2000; Gastil and Levine 2005; Habermas 1996). Participants are positioned as 'ordinary citizens' with a legitimate role to play in deliberations about scientific and environmental developments by virtue of locally anchored, experience-based forms of knowledge, values and preferences. Expertise can be said to be *democratised* in the sense that scientific knowledge and scientific knowers relinquish their monopoly on expertise (Blok 2007). At the same time, principles of deliberative democracy stipulate the need for expert input in order to supply citizens with expert knowledge about the topic that, together with the other knowledges in their possession, will enable them to exercise the rights of *scientific citizenship* responsibly (Irwin 2001). In exercising those rights responsibly, citizens act as competent *scientific citizens* deserving of the voice they have been given in deliberative processes (Elam and Bertilsson 2003).

Citizen participation in processes of decision-making in relation to scientific and environmental issues has been hailed as the guarantor of better and more accountable decisions by virtue of the properties of deliberation (e.g. Coenen 2010; Dietz and Stern 2008; Fischer 2009; Select Committee on Science and Technology, House of Lords 2000;Wilsdon and Willis 2004). At the same time, however, critical questions have been raised by researchers about the extent and nature of the dialogic turn in scientific and environmental governance (as well as more generally). It is argued, for example, that, in practices framed as instances of participatory governance, 'dialogue' and 'participation' are sometimes heavily circumscribed through the top-down design and management of the process (e.g. Goven 2003; Trench 2008; Wynne 2006). The 'ladder of participation' identified by Arnstein in her seminal article of 1969 is often only partially fulfilled, usually in the form of information or consultation and only very rarely deliberation.

Some of this critical analysis suggests that the concepts of 'dialogue' and 'participation' represent buzzwords serving to legitimate practices and thus operating as technologies of power that mask the dominance of certain knowledge interests and forms of knowledge, values and preferences over others. In the worst cases, the concepts serve as a *technology of legitimisation* (Harrison and Mort 1998; Stirling 2008), functioning instrumentally to pass off 'top-down' decision-making processes as 'bottom-up' democratic ones. This is, as noted earlier in this chapter, because the two concepts have a taken-for-granted positive value that tends to conceal the workings of power and the tensions and contradictions intrinsic to practices based on principles of dialogue and participation. As Carpentier and Dahlgren (2011: 8) point out in relation to the concept of 'participation', 'there is [...] a need for a more cool-headed approach towards participation that does not lose itself in celebratory frenzies'.

The critical science and technology studies literature on public engagement tends to concentrate on the framing and outcomes of participatory public-engagement exercises, including how the design positions citizens in particular ways with particular consequences for the results and the effects. The ways in which citizens actually 'fill out', perform and negotiate those positions in the communication processes at the core of the exercises are given little attention. However, there is a growing body of research that does explore empirically how 'citizens' and 'publics' are constructed in the communication processes central to public participation in science and technology – often together with an analysis of the design. Many cases of such research have been published in journals in science and technology studies and environmental studies (e.g. Felt and Fochler 2010; Kerr, Cunningham-Burley and Tutton 2007; Michael 2009). *Citizen Voices* is distinguished by being the first edited book to examine the multiple meanings ascribed to practices of 'participation' in science and environment communication and to its actors – such as 'experts', 'citizens' and 'publics' – and to consider the implications of those meanings for participants' scope for action in the governance of science and the environment. Thus it goes beyond the buzzword of 'participation' and explores how 'participation' is enacted in different ways in different contexts. Here, we use the term 'enactment' in its everyday sense to refer to how 'participation' is played out in practice rather than in the sense in which it is used in actor-network theory (see e.g. Mol 1999/2005).

Citizen Voices is also distinguished by its interdisciplinary scope, straddling science and technology studies (STS), environmental studies and media and communication studies. Since *science communication* has developed as a subfield of STS with relatively little contact with media and communication studies, the combination of STS and media and communication studies opens up for new opportunities for cross-fertilisation. In drawing both on STS and media and communication studies, and by focusing specifically on science and environment communication, the book contributes to the research area in media and communication studies on citizen participation and engagement in the media. This research area has been neglected in the past but now represents an emerging area (e.g. Carpentier 2011a, 2011b; Carpentier and Dahlgren 2011; Dahlgren 2011; Lewis et al. 2004), connected to the development of digital media which are widely seen to carry the promise of participation and dialogue across differences including those of geography, social class, gender and ethnicity.

One of our primary motivations in compiling the book has been to bring together studies which both critically interrogate *and* empirically investigate the different meanings and enactments of 'citizen participation' in different forms and contexts of scientific and environmental communication. The overall purpose of the book is to provide theoretically informed and empirically rich analyses of how 'citizen voices' are brought into being, articulated, invoked, marginalised or silenced in communication processes in a variety of practices of scientific and environmental governance. Two of the chapters (Chapters 7 and 8) theorise 'citizen voices' along the lines of Bakhtin. Bakhtin understands a voice not just as the medium for speech or the uttered speech of an individual, embodied person but as a discourse, ideology, perspective or theme that transcends the individual (Bakhtin 1981); for Bakhtin, meanings – including understandings of self and other – are generated in the tension between different and often contradictory and opposing voices. Thus a Bakhtinian perspective can form the basis for the analysis of processes of inclusion and exclusion whereby particular voices, articulating identities such as those of 'citizens' and particular forms of knowledge, dominate and others are marginalised or silenced (see Chapter 7). Some of the other chapters use the term 'citizen voices' in an everyday sense to refer to the articulation or representation of the perspectives or viewpoints of citizens. The rest of the chapters use the term rarely or not at all, referring instead to citizens or publics or particular groups.

Yet another key feature of the book is that it explores *public engagement* not just in the sense of organised activities belonging to the dialogic turn in scientific and environmental governance but in other senses of the term too. The term *public engagement* has also been used to refer to practices promoting attitudinal and behavioural change in relation to collective problems, such as climate change (e.g. Whitmarsh, O'Neill and Lorenzoni 2010).

And it can also designate processes of citizen-led involvement with social and political issues, through various forms of activism in which communicative practices in different media (and particularly user-generated content in the social media) are key. In this book, analyses are presented of all these forms of public engagement.

In particular, the chapters focus on three main types of public engagement practice. One type is made up of formal exercises in public engagement with science, technology and the environment that are based on models of 'participatory' democracy and organised by researchers or government organisations as part of the dialogic turn in scientific and environmental governance. This type of practice forms the object of analysis in all four chapters in Part II of the book (Chapters 7–10). The second type of practice consists of activities initiated and organised by citizens themselves, partly or wholly through the online media – what Dahlgren calls 'civic practices' (Dahlgren 2011: 91) (Chapters 4–6). The third group represents practices in which the media construct 'citizens' through representational practices (Chapters 2 and 3).

The above spectrum – encompassing organised public engagement with an element of 'top-down' management, citizen-led initiatives involving online user-generated content, and mass-mediated representations of 'citizens' – allows for the creation, across chapters, of a comprehensive account of 'citizen participation' in science and environment communication. This account captures much of the diversity of local enactments. And by bringing together studies in a number of different countries across Europe, *Citizen Voices* stresses similarities and differences in the performance of citizen participation across national contexts. Thus it aims to demonstrate how designs and frameworks for 'citizen participation' are shaped by sociocultural, organisational and national contexts.

One key parameter distinguishing the practices analysed in the different chapters is whether or not 'participation' is enacted on the basis of models of 'participatory' democracy – that is, models such as those of 'deliberative' and radical democracy which operate with a 'maximalist' understanding of participation (Carpentier 2011b), ascribing an active role to citizens in democratic decision-making beyond the minimalist participation of voting stipulated in models of representative democracy. Another parameter on which the chapters vary is how the chapter authors theorise 'participation' and whether they themselves draw on models of participatory democracy such as models of deliberative democracy or a post-structuralist model of radical democracy, critically analysing practices along these lines. A third parameter on which they differ is whether they use the concept of 'citizen' or other social categories such as 'the public', 'publics', 'lay people' or particular groups such as 'activists', 'patients', 'online media users' and 'bloggers'.

In sketching out the paths that the book carves out across an interdisciplinary terrain of research on public engagement with science and the environment, we concentrate below on two features of this terrain: one feature relates to the different ways of conceptualising 'participation' and the implications of those different conceptualisations for theory and practice; the other feature concerns the treatment, in different theoretical fields, of the tensions and contradictions that arise in relation to the participation of citizens in science and environment communication.

Sketching out the interdisciplinary terrain of the book

Drawing on science and technology studies and environmental studies, many of the chapters build on research focusing on the contradictions and tensions in public engagement that, as noted above, emanate from the only partial nature of the shift to a more participatory, democratic, dialogue-based form of scientific and environmental governance. This research shows that – in spite of the rhetoric of participation and dialogue – much science and environment communication still articulates a diffusion model whereby information is disseminated from scientists to publics, and the scope for action or influence of citizens is heavily circumscribed (e.g. Kurath and Gisler 2009; Trench 2008; Wynne 2006; see also Renn, Webler and Wiedemann 1995).

In particular, the majority of the chapters of the book (Chapters 2, 3, 5, 7, 8 and 9) are based on, or in line with, what Horst (2013) has labelled a *model of emergence,* in which communication is conceptualised, along social constructionist lines, as a constitutive force in the context-dependent, relational construction of objects and subjects (e.g. Felt and Fochler 2010; Horst 2008; Horst and Irwin 2010; Irwin 2001, 2006; Irwin and Michael 2003; Michael 2009). As a constitutive force in the construction of objects and subjects, communication brings entities such as 'science', 'citizens', 'publics' and 'scientists' into being. These chapters present empirically rich analyses of how the category of 'citizen' – and related categories representing 'the people' such as 'the 'public'/'publics', 'lay people' and 'activists' – are brought into being in communication processes within particular social and institutional contexts.

A central theme of Chapters 3, 7 and 8 is the implications of particular constructions of the 'citizen' for the extent and nature of citizens' *participation* and, in particular, their scope for action in relation to scientific and environmental matters. This obviously involves addressing issues of power in relation to participation. Chapter 3 shows, for example, in a case study of a series of investigative reports on ethanol in Sweden how citizens are primarily constructed as taxpayers and are rarely heard in the reports. Drawing on a Foucauldian, discourse-analytical understanding of power, Chapters 7 and 8 address how, in two organised initiatives in public engagement in climate change communication, power operates through processes of inclusion and exclusion whereby 'participation' and 'citizens' are constructed in particular ways which exclude or marginalise alternative ways of knowing and doing.

While not all of the chapters view citizens as categories constructed in communication processes and explore the implications for citizens' 'participation' in science and environmental governance, *all* the chapters attend to the extent to which, and the ways in which, citizen voices are heard, recognised, marginalised or silenced in communication processes. In so doing, they touch on issues of power in relation to participation – and in particular, the issue of the *inclusion* of citizen voices in communication about science and the environment – without necessarily theorising power explicitly. In many cases, the analysis draws on the field of media and communication studies in order to theorise and analyse the communication processes in which citizen voices are articulated and circumscribed.

Drawing on media and communication studies, the chapters make use of a variety of approaches for theorising and empirically analysing communication processes in particular social and institutional contexts that make possible and circumscribe the articulation of citizen voices. Citizen identities, political subjectivity, formal and informal spaces for social intervention and decision-making processes all involve meaning-making practices that can be uniquely analysed and assessed by using conceptual and methodological tools from the field of media and communication studies. In recent years, research in environmental communication and media studies has burgeoned (e.g. Cox 2006; Corbett 2006; Hansen 2010; Lester 2010), demonstrating a growing awareness of the importance of understanding communication and media processes in relation to environmental issues. Contributing to this field, this book offers a more specific and much-needed focus upon citizen voices. In so doing, it adds to the research that has been carried out on citizen participation in the media, which, as noted above, has been limited but is now growing in size (e.g. Carpentier 2011a, 2011b; Dahlgren 2011; Lewis et al. 2004).

For instance, one of the key studies in this research area is Lewis et al.'s (2004) extensive content, analytic study of the construction of 'citizenship' in broadcast news in the US and UK, which showed that citizens tend to be represented not as engaged citizens but as 'passive observers of the world' (2004: 154). Citizens are given the opportunity to express *emotions* and talk about their *experiences* but not to voice *political views* or to demonstrate an *active engagement in politics*. From the study it emerged that the most frequent form of citizen representation was that of the private individual who describes, or is referred to as describing, her experience without expressing an explicitly political opinion (2004: 162). Thus citizens' identities and scope for action as 'citizens' are heavily circumscribed: 'While politicians are often seen telling us what should be done about the world', Lewis et al. point out, 'citizens are largely excluded from active participation in such deliberations' (2004: 163). In a similar fashion, all the chapters in this book attend to the implications of the *specific, context-dependent ways* in which 'citizens', 'publics' and 'participation' are given meaning and enacted.

We also recognise the value of Carpentier's distinction between the concept of 'participation', on the one hand, and the concepts of 'interaction' and 'access', on the other (2011a, 2011b). According to Carpentier, there is a tendency for media and communications researchers to operate with an overly broad and vague understanding of 'audience participation', applying it across the board to a myriad of different practices without reflexive consideration of their conceptualisation of the term and without detailed analysis of the limits to 'audience participation' in the practices analysed. 'Participation' is often reduced to, or conflated with, 'access', which is a question of the availability of media production technologies and of presence in a specific media practice such as an online chat forum, or to 'interaction' which represents the form of communication established between actors. Carpentier argues that both 'access' and 'interaction' are prerequisites for 'participation'; 'participation' is distinct from and *more* than 'access' and 'interaction' in that it involves the engagement of actors in decision-making processes in which 'power relationships [...] are, to an extent, egalitarian' (2011a: 31). It is, Carpentier argues, crucial to heed the qualification 'to an extent' since the political struggle over 'participation' centres on the *extent* of participation, with 'minimalist' understandings maintaining heavy power imbalances and confining citizen participation to 'access' and 'interaction' and 'maximalist' understandings arguing for the active participation of citizens in decision-making processes based on principles of 'participatory' democracy (Carpentier 2011a: 30–1). Endorsing this, we would like to add that another reason why it is important to stress that power relations can only ever be egalitarian 'to an extent' is that the taken-for-granted, positive nature of 'participation' may lead to a lack of attention to the operation of power imbalances and thus may construct a vision – from a Foucauldian perspective, an illusion – of participatory practices as power-free spaces for communication among equals. The vision may blind proponents to the workings of processes of exclusion as well as inclusion in 'participatory' forms of science and environment communication.

The book shows how approaches from within and across STS and environmental studies and media and communication studies – for example, actor-network theory, dialogic communication theory, discourse theory and analysis, and quantitative approaches involving an online experiment and survey – can provide insight into the communicative practices that construct, reproduce and obstruct the roles of citizens in forming views and acting in relation to social, political and ethical aspects of scientific and environmental developments. The chapters focus on various social and institutional settings, from citizen consultation forums to the media, and on diverse themes: interactions between researchers and citizens; formats and structures for public engagement in science and the environment; the mass mediation of scientific and environmental citizenship; ICTs and citizen participation; and citizen activism in relation to governmental policymaking about an environmental issue. Together, the chapters produce an in-depth, research-based analysis of how participation and citizenship are played out in the communication of science and environment across a wide terrain of fields of practice in a range of countries across Eastern, Northern and Western Europe and the US: Bulgaria, Denmark, Netherlands, Sweden, Finland and the US.

We have divided the book into two parts. Part I presents analyses of public participation in the mediation of science and the environment. Chapter 2 focuses on how 'citizens' are constructed and represented in media production practices. Chapter 3 explores how 'citizens' are constructed in media representations, while the remaining three chapters in this part look at how citizens themselves initiate practices in which they, in some way or another, *participate* in science or environment communication, partly or wholly through the use of online media. Part II explores public participation in formal public engagement exercises constructed and conducted by researchers or government officials as part of the dialogic turn in scientific and environmental governance.

In the first chapter of Part I, Chapter 2, Ursula Plesner theorises the construction of the 'citizen' in the production and communication of social scientific knowledge via the mass media in terms of an approach inspired by actor-network theory. Applying this approach, the chapter explores how citizens *participate* in social science communication in the sense that citizen voices *make a difference* for the production and communication of social scientific knowledge via the mass media, for instance through journalists' and researchers' co-constructions of citizens' needs and wants. Theoretically, the chapter argues for a conception of the mass mediation of science as consisting of dialogic moments, and thus questions the view of the mass mediation of science as a linear, top-down process. This argument is based on empirical studies of the production of specific media texts, consisting of interviews with journalists and scientists about their interactions in relation to these texts, as well as textual analyses. The chapter adds to the discussion of how citizens may participate in various stages of the production and communication of scientific knowledge by placing analytical attention *in between* studies of public engagement exercises (with the very deliberate and visible participation of citizens) and studies of media representations (with a concern with textual representations of citizen voices). Its contribution is to show how negotiations about citizens' concerns and abilities take place in informal settings behind the scenes of mass mediation and how those negotiations make a difference for both the production and the communication of science.

In Chapter 3, Annika Egan Sjölander and Anna Maria Jönsson focus on the construction of the public in news discourses on environmental risks in both traditional and online media. The chapter takes as its starting point the observation that there is wide recognition that, given the environmental risks we are facing, there is a pressing need for active public participation in environmental communication. The initiatives for involving the public vary greatly across practices and so do the conception(s) of 'the public'. The media are an actor in the public sphere and an arena for public discourse, shaping and influencing access and possibilities for participation. *How* the public is constructed and represented in environmental news is important in relation to principles of deliberative democracy and ideals of a public sphere. Drawing on theories of deliberation and the public sphere, a detailed empirical analysis is presented of different forms of 'participation' and roles for the public as citizens in cases of news coverage of climate change and the use of biofuels.

In Chapter 4, Pavel P. Antonov explores how journalists respond to a citizen-led campaign against the government's plans to reverse anti-smoking legislation in Bulgaria. Changes in the culture of journalism and the professional identities of journalists are traced to the embedding of a neo-liberal discourse in the everyday rationality of post-socialist journalism. Drawing upon Couldry's (2010) work on the loss of 'voice' and Phillips' work on 'dialogue' (Phillips 2011), the analysis shows how the new culture and identities are articulated in the course of the citizen-led campaign against the government's plans to liberalise the anti-smoking ban in Bulgaria. The analysis is based on data collected during 2009–2010 by means of participant observation of the campaign's press coverage and semi-structured interviews with journalists and decision-makers in two Bulgarian mainstream media newsrooms.

In Chapter 5, Hedwig te Molder addresses issues relating to science communication among online communities. Many practices of science communication by professional science communicators start from the assumption that the publics need or desire the communication offered. However, many communities are *already* talking science and technology, or at least discussing the fields to which these insights apply, often from a non-technology perspective. The chapter applies a discursive psychological perspective, focusing on the *social-interactional goals* performed by the arguments of discourse communities (cf. Potter 1996; te Molder and Potter 2005; Veen et al. 2011). This perspective is applied in analysis of online interactions among patients with celiac disease ('gluten intolerance'), who reject the pill that was promised to replace their lifelong gluten-free diet. The analysis shows that this 'rejection' was targeted not so much at the pill itself but at the experts' suggestion that the pill would fix everything. This suggestion was felt by patients to undermine the value of their present life and autonomy.

Chapter 6 by Ashley Andersen et al. is also about online interaction, in this case, online news posts about scientific issues. The chapter presents an account of a study that explores, by way of an online experiment and survey, how Internet users' passive observation of comments on online news posts influences their degree of support for science. Past research shows that those who are heavy users of the Internet are also very interested in science and technology. In the light of this research, they examine differences across different groups of online users in the effects of online comments on support for science. They do not find evidence that two characteristics of the comments themselves – heterogeneity and incivility – affect support for science. However, they do find that online users are more likely to support science. Furthermore, those who write blogs and read political blogs and comments attached to news stories or blog posts are more likely to support science when exposed to a heterogeneity of viewpoints in the blog comments.

In reading the studies presented in Part II, the reader should be able to trace similarities and differences across the different formal engagement practices analysed in the chapters and also across the different theories and methods applied in the analyses. In the first chapter in Part II, Chapter 7, Louise Phillips presents an empirical analysis of how principles of deliberative democracy are played out in communication processes in the deliberations of the citizen participants in a case of consensus-oriented public engagement. The case analysed is the citizen consultation on climate change in Copenhagen, which forms part of the global citizen consultation, World Wide Views on Global Warming. World Wide Views was organised by the Danish Board of Technology and took place in 38 countries including Denmark on 26 September 2009 in advance of the UN Climate Change Conference, Copenhagen, 7–18 December 2009. The analytical framework combines dialogic communication theory, building on the work of Bakhtin on multi-voicedness (Bakhtin 1981), and Chantal

Mouffe's post-structuralist critique of deliberative democracy's emphasis on the need for, and possibility of, reasoned political consensus. For Mouffe, the ideal underpinning deliberative democracy of 'consensus without exclusion' (Mouffe 2000: 48) is illusionary since consensus is always 'the expression of a hegemony and crystallization of power relations' (Mouffe 2000: 49). The chapter focuses both on the ways in which the deliberations open up for multiple citizens voices and for dialogue across those voices and on the ways in which they exclude voices and construct a unitary and singular national and global 'citizen voice' through the application of a procedure for rational argumentation based on principles of deliberative democracy. The chapter argues for the value of detailed empirical analysis as a foundation for reflexive recognition and discussion of the inexorable workings of dynamics of exclusion in consensus-oriented communication processes in participatory practices of public engagement with science and technology.

Anders Horsbøl and Inger Lassen focus in Chapter 8 on another case of public engagement in relation to climate change – an initiative of a Danish town council in which citizens take part in processes of public participation designed to achieve 100 per cent reliance on renewable energy in 2015. In those processes, local administrators position citizens as 'activists' in practices based on principles of participation and dialogue. The chapter analyses a series of meetings between citizens and representatives of the municipality from a discourse analytical perspective, treating the meetings as spaces for discursive negotiation and struggle. The analysis shows that the initiative is infused with tensions between top-down and bottom-up dynamics, and, on the basis of the analysis, obstacles are identified that may discourage citizen participation in environmental matters.

In Chapter 9, Maja Horst analyses a spatial installation that she designed in order to communicate social scientific research in line with principles of dialogue and participation underpinning public engagement in science and technology; the aim of the installation was to create a space for dialogue about science in relation to central social, cultural and ethical questions. The social scientific research communicated in the installation investigated the social, cultural and ethical aspects of stem cell research and was the work of a Danish group of social scientists. The installation was fabricated as an 80 m^2 'gaming board', in which visitors would pass through a number of different rooms, each contextualising stem cell research in a particular way. In each of these rooms, visitors would encounter different dilemmas and questions and be asked to engage by physically marking their preferences or answers. Theoretically, the installation was based on actor-network theory and the installation was designed to let visitors experience the basic axioms of this theoretical framework.

Chapter 10 by Pauliina Lehtonen and Jarkko Bamberg presents a collaborative research project with a citizen panel that was organised to find meaningful ways for citizens in a Finnish city to affect the development of their neighbourhood. The work of the panel aimed at developing participatory practices by utilising the potential of information and communication technology. In this process, the articulation of residents' local knowledge and the mediation between residents' local knowledge and the city council were viewed as crucial. The dialogical process with the panel helped the researchers to identify characteristics of interactive online spatial tools such as interactive maps and simulations which could support the articulation and translation of local knowledge into the domain of planning and administration. In the chapter, Lehtonen and Bamberg propose that online spatial tools have the potential to function as facilitators for the meaningful exchange of knowledge through three mechanisms of knowledge translation: by giving access to information from a perspective familiar to residents; by aiding the translation of the administration's technical-rational information through the use of illustrative visualisations; and by giving residents multimodal means of producing input for administrators and planners.

To conclude then, across its chapters, *Citizen Voices* is designed to provide *both* empirical insight into the extent to which and ways in which 'citizen voices' are articulated and heard in different cultural and institutional contexts *and* a range of theories and research methodologies that foreground the role of communication processes in the 'participatory' mode of governance. The chapters all highlight the implications of particular ways of conceiving and practising communication for citizens' possibilities for taking a stance and acting on social, political and ethical questions in relation to scientific and environmental developments and problems.

References

Arnstein, S. R., 'A Ladder of Citizen Participation'. *Journal of the American Institute of Planners*, 35:4 (1969), pp. 216–224.

Aubert, A. and Soler, M., 'Dialogism: The Dialogic Turn in the Social Sciences'. In J. Kincheloe and R. Horn (eds), *The Præger Handbook of Education and Psychology*. Westport, CT: Greenwood Press, 2006.

Bakhtin, M., *The Dialogic Imagination: Four Essays*. Ed. Michael Holquist. Trans. Caryl Emerson & Michael Holquist. Austin and London: University of Texas Press, 1981.

Benhabib, S., 'Deliberative Rationality and Models of Democratic Legitimacy'. *Constellations*, 1 (1994), pp. 25–53.

Blok, A., 'Experts on Public Trial: On Democratizing Expertise through a Danish Consensus Conference'. *Public Understanding of Science*, 162:2 (2007), pp. 163–182.

Carpentier, N., 'The Concept of Participation. If They Have Access and Interact, Do They Really Participate?' *Communication Management Quarterly*, 6:21 (2011a), pp. 13–36.

—— *Media and Participation: A Site of Ideological-Democratic Struggle*. Bristol: Intellect, 2011b.

Carpentier, N. and Dahlgren, P., 'Introduction: Interrogating Audiences –Theoretical Horizons of Participation'. *Communication Management Quarterly*, 6:21 (2011), pp. 7–12.

Corbett, J., *Communicating Nature: How We Create and Understand Environmental Messages*. Washington: Island Press, 2006.

Coenen, F. (ed.), *Public Participation and Better Environmental Decisions: The Promise and Limits of Participatory Processes for the Quality of Environmentally Related Decision-Making*. Berlin: Springer, 2010.

Couldry, N., *Why Voice Matters: Culture and Politics after Neoliberalism.* Thousand Oaks, CA: Sage, 2010.

Cox, R., *Environmental Communication and the Public Sphere.* London: Sage, 2006.

Dahlgren, P., 'Parameters of Online Participation: Conceptualising Civic Contingencies'. *Communication Management Quarterly,* 6:21 (2011), pp. 87–110.

Delgado, A., Kjølberg, K. and Wickson, F., 'Public Engagement Coming of Age: From Theory to Practice in STS Encounters with Nanotechnology'. *Public Understanding of Science,* pp. 1–20. Published online ahead of print, 11 May 2010.

Dietz, T. and Stern, P. C. (eds), *Public Participation in Environmental Assessment and Decision Making.* Washington: National Academies Press, 2008.

Dryzek, J. S., *Deliberative Democracy and Beyond – Liberals, Critics, Contestations.* Oxford, Oxford University Press, 2000.

Elam, M. and Bertilsson, M., 'Consuming, Engaging and Confronting Science: The Emerging Dimensions of Scientific Citizenship'. *European Journal of Social Theory,* 62:6 (2003), pp. 233–251.

Felt, U. and Fochler, M., 'Machineries for Making Publics: Inscribing and De-Scribing Publics in Public Engagement'. *Minerva,* 48:3 (2010), pp. 219–238.

Fischer, F., *Democracy and Expertise: Reorienting Policy Inquiry.* Oxford: Oxford University Press, 2009.

Gastil, J. J. and Levine, P. (eds), *The Deliberative Democracy Handbook: Strategies for Effective Civic Engagement in the 21st Century.* San Francisco: Jossey-Bass, 2005.

Gómez, A., Puigvert, L. and Flecha, R., 'Critical Communicative Methodology: Informing Real Social Transformation through Research'. *Qualitative Inquiry,* 17:3 (2011), pp. 235–245.

Goven, J., 'Deploying the Consensus Conference in New Zealand: Democracy and De-Problematization.' *Public Understanding of Science,* 12:4 (2003), pp. 423–440.

Habermas, J., *Between Facts and Norms: Contributions to a Discourse Theory of Law and Democracy.* Cambridge, MA: MIT Press, 1996.

Hansen, A., *Environment, Media and Communication.* London: Routledge, 2010.

Harrison, S. and Mort, M., 'Which Champions, Which People? Public and User Involvement in Health Care as a Technology of Legitimation'. *Social Policy & Administration,* 32:1 (1998), pp. 60–70.

Horst, M., 'In Search of Dialogue: Staging Science Communication in Consensus Conferences'. In D. Cheng, M. Claessens, T. Gascoigne, J. Metcalfe, B. Schiele and S. Shi (eds), *Communicating Science in Social Contexts: New Models, New Practices.* New York: Springer Publishing, 2008.

——— 'Caring for Discomfort: Science Communication Experiments between Diffusion, Dialogue and Emergence'. In L. Phillips, M. Kristiansen, M. Vehviläinen and E. Gunnarsson (eds), *Knowledge and Power in Collaborative Research: A Reflexive Approach.* London: Routledge, 2013.

Horst, M. and Irwin, A. , 'Nations at Ease with Radical Knowledge. On Consensus, Consensusing and False Consensusness'. *Social Studies of Science,* 40:1 (2010), pp. 105–126.

Irwin, A., 'Constructing the Scientific Citizen: Science and Democracy in the Biosciences'. *Public Understanding of Science,* 10:1 (2001), pp. 1–18.

—— 'The Politics of Talk: Coming to Terms with the "New" Scientific Governance'. *Social Studies of Science*, 36:2 (2006), pp. 199–230.

Irwin, A. and Michael, M., *Science, Social Theory and Public Knowledge*. Maidenhead: Open University Press, 2003.

Kerr, A., Cunningham-Burley, S. and Tutton, R., 'Shifting Subject Positions: Experts and Lay People in Public Dialogue'. *Social Studies of Science*, 37:3 (2007), pp. 385–411.

Kurath, M. and Gisler, P., 'Informing, Involving or Engaging? Science Communication, in the Ages of Atom-, Bio- and Nanotechnology'. *Public Understanding of Science*, 18:5 (2009), pp. 559–573.

Lester, L., *Media and Environment: Conflict, Politics and the News*. Cambridge: Polity, 2010.

Lewis, J., Wahl-Jorgensen, K. and Inthorn, S., 'Images of Citizenship on Television News: Constructing a Passive Public'. *Journalism Studies*, 5:2 (2004), pp. 153–164.

Michael, M., 'Publics Performing Publics: Of PiGs, PiPs and Politics'. *Public Understanding of Science*, 18:5 (2009), pp. 617–631.

Mol, A., 'Ontological Politics: A Word and Some Questions'. In J. Law and J. Hassard (eds), *Actor Network Theory and After*. Oxford: Blackwell Publishing/The Sociological Review, 1999/2005.

Mouffe, C., *The Democratic Paradox*. London and New York: Verso, 2000.

Phillips, L., *The Promise of Dialogue: The Dialogic Turn in the Production and Communication of Knowledge*. Amsterdam: John Benjamins Publishing, 2011.

Potter, J., *Representing Reality: Discourse, Rhetoric and Social construction*. Sage: London, 1996.

Renn, O., Webler, T. and Wiedemann, P. (eds), *Fairness and Competence in Citizen Participation: Evaluating Models for Environmental Discourse*. Boston: Kluwer, 1995.

Stirling, A., '"Opening up" and "closing down": Power, Participation and Pluralism in the Social Appraisal of Technology'. *Science, Technology and Human Values*, 33:2 (2008), pp. 262–294.

te Molder, H. and Potter, J. (eds.), *Conversation and Cognition*. Cambridge: Cambridge University Press, 2005.

Trench, B., 'Towards an Analytical Framework of Science Communication Models'. In D. Cheng, M. Claessens, T. Gascoigne, J. Metcalfe, B. Schiele and S. Shi (eds), *Communicating Science in Social Contexts: New Models, New Practices*. New York: Springer Publishing, 2008.

Veen, M., Gremmen, B., te Molder, H. and van Woerkum, C., 'Emergent Technologies Against the Background of Everyday Life: Discursive Psychology as a Technology Assessment Tool', *Public Understanding of Science*, 20:6 (2011), pp. 810–825.

Wilsdon, J. and Willis, R., *See-Through Science: Why Public Engagement Needs to Move Upstream*. London: Demos, 2004.

Whitmarsh, L., O'Neill, S. and Lorenzoni, I. (eds), *Engaging the Public with Climate Change: Behaviour Change and Communication*. London: Earthscan, 2010.

Wynne, B. 'Public Engagement as a Means of Restoring Public Trust in Science – Hitting the Notes but Missing the Music?' *Community Genetics*, 9:3 (2006), pp. 211–220.

PART I

Public Participation and Media

Chapter 2

When Citizens Matter in the Mass Mediation of Science: The Role of Imagined Audiences in Multidirectional Communication Processes

Ursula Plesner

This chapter examines how citizens *come to matter* when journalists and scientists interact to produce media texts with research-based content. It shows how conceptions of citizens make a difference for the production and communication of scientific knowledge, to a large extent through journalists' and scientists' constructions of citizens' needs and wants. Theoretically, the chapter argues for a conception of the mass mediation of science in terms of negotiations and dialogic moments, and thus questions the view of the mass mediation of science as a linear, top-down process. This argument builds on empirical studies of the production of specific media texts based on interviews with journalists and scientists about their interactions in relation to those texts, as well as textual analyses.

The so-called dialogic turn in communication studies has stirred an interest in forms of communication of research-based knowledge that do not rely on the mass media but – often in creative ways – integrate communication with publics or interest groups in various stages of the research process. From the perspective of dialogic communication theory, mass mediation is either ignored as an object of analysis (Pauly 2004) or (sometimes implicitly) constructed as a one-way, top-down process, without possibilities for feedback and not easily reconcilable with democratic ideals of inclusion, participation and dialogue. When we look to science communication studies or the field of research on Public Understanding of Science (PUS), the above described understanding of mass mediation is reproduced to some degree. The mass media tend to be conceptualised here as an institution mediating between science and the public, and citizens tend to be seen as receivers of information through the media. However, there is an emerging interest in both fields to reconceptualise the role and function of the mass media in relation to the communication of research-based knowledge. This chapter aims to contribute to an understanding of mass mediation as a set of multidirectional, relational processes where entities in networks acquire meaning in relation to one another. In this endeavour, the chapter adds to the part of the PUS research field that questions the strict division between science, the media and publics, and to the strand within science communication studies that questions the view of mass mediation as a one-way transmission from sender over medium to receiver. The foundation for such critiques was laid in the late 1970s in qualitative media studies with the introduction of the concept of the active audience and the burgeoning of audience studies with their focus on the active meaning-making taking place in reception processes. Also, discourse analytical approaches have theorised text/audience relations as complex, dialogical and multidirectional and theorised mass mediation as a kind of cultural circuit rather than a linear process (eg. Schrøder and Phillips 2007). However, I believe that a view of the mass media as a site for one-way communication still persists in the field of science communication studies, and this chapter shares audience studies' and discourse analytical media studies' ambition to challenge this view. To add to their contributions, this chapter offers a distinctive perspective, placing an emphasis on *practices* of negotiation and dialogue.

The approach to the mass mediation of science laid out here also implies a focus on how macro actors (Czarniawska and Hernes 2005) such as science, mass media and publics or citizens are brought into being through micro processes. In this chapter, special attention is paid to the ways in which citizens are invoked in mass mediation processes, and come to make a difference for how actors communicate and media texts turn out. Today, the mass mediation of science takes place in both traditional media like television, radio and newspapers, and on new platforms for interpersonal interaction like blogs and discussion fora – and all these converge so that there seems to be an abundance of entry points for participation and dialogue (Carpentier 2011). And of course, the most direct way to observe citizen voices in the mass media would be in letters to the editor, phone-in programmes, direct quotes of 'common people', polls, and new types of journalism such as citizen journalism, or on electronic communication platforms such as blogs and webpages. However, in this chapter, it will be argued that in the types of mass media traditionally seen as one-way communication channels such as newspapers or radio, a lot of negotiations take place in the course of production of a particular media text, and the inherently dialogic nature of language ensures that citizens actually matter for the mass communication of science.

Hence the focus of this chapter is not direct, dialogic communication between scientists and citizens, but how citizens are taken into account in media production processes. I believe that the ways in which citizens are taken into account by journalists and scientists in media production processes are important because they tend to be an overlooked part of citizens' influence on the circulation of academic knowledge. The theoretical claim is that we become sensitive to this when we consider the mass media sites for negotiation, and that this can be studied through a practice-based approach inspired by Actor-Network-Theory (ANT). The latter shares methodological principles with other qualitative approaches such as discourse analysis, but is not built on an idea of interconnectedness between text and ideology, and stays on a descriptive level rather than jumping to discussions of the ideological implications of a particular language use or other macro phenomena.

In the theory section below, I will indicate how the traditions of PUS and science communication have informed the theoretical position of this chapter, and position myself in relation to those fields. I then point to studies that have shifted their attention from studies of actual audiences to the performative effect of audience conceptions. This is followed by a methods section that accounts for an analytical strategy focusing on negotiations in mass mediation processes, inspired by ANT's dissolution of the micro/macro distinction (Latour 2005). In the analysis, three vignettes are presented. The first two demonstrate how reflections on, and understandings of, citizens or publics make a difference for the communication of science. The third illustrates how negotiations are central to the production of media texts, and thus counters the view of mass mediation as a one-way communication process. To conclude the chapter, I summarise the analyses and argue for the value of a theorisation of mass mediation processes in terms of the concept of negotiations.

Between public engagement and media representations of publics

The role of citizens or publics has been theorised and researched extensively within two different traditions, PUS and the branch of science communication studies that has emerged in the intersection between science and technology studies and media studies. In this section, I will outline how these two traditions have been concerned with citizens and publics, and what kinds of communication processes they have been interested in exploring. This creates a foundation for arguing that there is an important field of enquiry not covered by the research agendas of these traditions – namely, the communication processes where citizen concerns, needs or abilities emerge in the course of mass media production. I propose to integrate the concepts of negotiations and dialogic moments into a framework which can highlight crucial aspects of the diverse communication processes that precede the printing or airing of a mass media product.

Citizens and communication in the PUS tradition

PUS has been called a multidiscipline (Irwin and Michael 2003: 19) concerned with exploring and gauging the relationships between 'science' and the 'public'. The tradition is often described as consisting of three strands, each with different views of the role of science, the role of the public and the promise of science communication. Intrinsic to these different strands of PUS are different models of science communication – captured by the notions of dissemination/diffusion, dialogue/deliberation and conversation/negotiation. For discussions of these, see Michael (2002), Trench (2008) and Horst (2008). Horst points out how these are connected to the three strands of PUS: traditional PUS, critical PUS and network perspectives on science/public relations. The assumptions of PUS and communication studies have developed in a parallel manner. PUS was initially primarily concerned with the public's *understanding* of science, and communication was considered a technical issue of getting the message through, to remedy a deficit in understanding. Then a concern arose with the public's active participation in, and engagement with science (captured by the abbreviation PES, Public Engagement with Science), mirrored by the trend in communication studies to consider people active users rather than audiences and to take their needs into account. Both led to an interest in dialogic communication formats. At present, these conceptualisations are still in play, but are supplemented by the third strand of PUS – namely, network perspectives on science/public relations, which rest on a less hierarchical understanding of science/society and communicator/user relations and a focus on the circulation of knowledge and communication in networks (see Michael 2002; Plesner 2009). It is this third strand of research on the relationship between science and the public that informs the production and analysis of the empirical material in this chapter. It has inspired my attempt to view elements of mass mediation as interwoven with many other elements in complex networks, and to avoid an essentialising view of scientists, public and the mass media in which they are treated as distinct groups with fixed borders and particular characteristics.

In terms of empirical studies, PUS/PES has primarily produced insights into the workings of a wide variety of communication initiatives meant to address the supposed science/public divide, for instance consultations, debates and public events. It seems to have had little interest in exploring the mass mediation of science. This has been the domain of a branch of science communication studies specialising in mass mediation.

Citizens and communication in science communication studies

Before describing the branch of science communication studies concerned with mass mediation in more detail, I will sketch out how science communication scholars have dealt with more general questions relating to citizens and communication. Closely related to the traditional PUS, parts of the science communication field have investigated the public's knowledge of, and attitudes towards, science. Such studies include the so-called Eurobarometer surveys and other surveys measuring 'scientific literacy' (e.g. Claessens 2008; Miller 1998). A series of Danish reports on public attitudes towards and sources of knowledge about science also fall within this tradition (e.g. Albæk et al. 2002; Siune and Vinther 1998a, 1998b, 1998c). There is a large subfield concerned with institutional dialogue initiatives and similar areas of study, for instance exploring, and critically interrogating, the potential for direct dialogue between researchers and publics (e.g. Horst 2011; Phillips 2011).[1] Within this area, we find scholars occupied with the development and theorisation of dialogic communication initiatives, such as consensus conferences (e.g. Blok 2007; Horst 2008; Powell and Lee Kleinman 2008), science cafés (e.g. Riise 2008) and the like. Besides the first group of scholars, concerned with people's knowledge of science and ways in which to enhance this knowledge, and the second group of scholars, interested in initiatives to ensure the robustness of the knowledge production of academia through dialogue with the public, a number of science communication scholars are preoccupied with the role of the mass media in the communication of scientific knowledge. Some have analysed media representations of science (e.g. Allan 2002; Carvalho 2007; Maeseele and Schuurman 2008; Marks et al. 2007), while some are closer to journalism studies' concern with source relations and interactions between scientists and media or communication professionals (e.g. Dunwoody and Scott 1982). Others conceptualise the interplay between mass media and the production of science (e.g. Bucchi 1998; Hilgartner 1990; Brossard 2009). In particular, Bucchi (1998, 2008) has sought to bring science communication and mass mediation issues together, arguing for a rethinking of science communication models in order to better understand the functioning of today's mass media in relation to science. He draws a picture of two science communication traditions – one dominated by transfer metaphors (e.g. reception, flow, distortions and targets) and one characterised by an interest in dialogue. He argues, then, on the one hand, that our understanding of science communication may benefit from stepping out of the transfer metaphor to investigate the multiple interactions of specialist and popular discourse. On the other hand, this should not lead us to abandon more linear, top-down models of communication, since some kinds of science communication are best understood as such (Bucchi 2008: 66–68). But most importantly, Bucchi proposes a third view of science communication where the idea is that knowledge is in constant circulation and less in need of translation:

> the need has been invoked for another, more substantial shift to a model of knowledge co-production in which non-experts and their local knowledge can be conceived as neither an obstacle to be overcome by virtue of appropriate education initiatives (as in the deficit model), nor an additional element that simply enriches professionals' expertise (as in the critical-dialogical model), but rather as essential for the production of knowledge itself. Expert and lay knowledge are not produced independently in separate contexts to encounter each other later; rather, they result from common processes carried forward in 'hybrid forums' in which specialist and non-specialists can interact.
>
> (Bucchi 2008: 68)

According to Bucchi, such forums could be the mass media. Bucchi, then, belongs to a trend in science communication studies that sees mass media not only as sites where linguistic translations of science are made by communication professionals but as sites of negotiation. Logan (2001: 153) refers to a similar development in 'the interactive tradition', which has launched the idea that mass communication has become more of an informal conversation, and a shared and multidirectional experience. It is unclear precisely how, but Logan draws on scholars who talk about the empowerment of citizens that allows them to enter public arenas, and about lay participation in journalism.

What we see above is a simultaneous concern with more dialogic forms of science communication and a rising interest in reconsidering the conception of mass mediation of science as a linear communication process. But still, relatively little research and theorisation about the possible dialogical aspects of the mass mediation of science have been carried out.

Questioning mass mediation as a one-way communication process

In this chapter, I propose an approach to the empirical study and theorisation of mass mediation that revolves around the concepts of negotiation and dialogue, highlighting the moments in which two-way communication takes place and avoiding operating in terms of broad, general categories such as 'science', 'the media' or 'audiences'. As we shall see in the analysis below, specific actors' accounts of the practices and interaction going on around media production processes make it obvious that the entirety of the communication of science through mass media does not take place within the media text itself, and knowledge does not simply travel from researchers to media users. There are opportunities for negotiations of meaning before the technical production of the text, throughout the production, and after the production. To see this requires a practice-oriented, qualitative, inductive approach as well as a sensitivity to the discovery of dialogic moments.

Conversely, to hold onto an image of mass mediation as one-way communication, we would have to stubbornly hold onto the differences in scale between the individual and the monstrous media machinery, a difference in scale that

> arouses special concern. How does one encourage mutuality, active listening, and responsiveness among newspaper, magazine, radio, movie, and television audiences that range from the thousands to the tens of millions? Scholars have often judged such gatherings as incapable of producing dialogue ... the phrase *the media* still denotes much the same set of social practices as mass once did. When they talk about 'the media', most Americans mean massive, heavily capitalized, technologically sophisticated, professionally managed, star-driven systems of communication.
>
> (Pauly 2004: 244)

Pauly, who is a media theorist, offers inspiration as to how media representations can open up spaces for dialogue. I prefer to use his diagnosis of our common way of conceptualising 'the media' as an occasion to propose thinking differently about scale (Latour 1999: 258) in relation to the media. If we avoid thinking in terms of micro (the individual) and macro (the media machinery), we are able to see how mass mediation consists of a number of concrete interactions and manifestations. When we refrain from seeing 'the media' as a one-way, top-down communication apparatus, it is possible to see how communication processes linked to the production of media texts have consequences for individuals, and, by extension, for researchers' science communication contributions.

Now, with this approach to the mass mediation of science, we can begin to look at particular elements that make a difference for the production of particular science communication texts. According to the methodological approach of this chapter, these elements can be anything: the talk by the coffee machine, journalists' lists of sources, webpages of scientific journals or ideals about academic knowledge as a public good. We should try to rid ourselves of truisms such as the idea that the mass mediation of science is marked by journalists' sensationalist approaches or researchers' unwillingness to communicate in a clear and simple manner. In the following analysis, I highlight particular elements that make a difference for the production of a media text, namely explicit and implicit conceptions of citizens in the mass mediation of science. 'Citizens' emerged in the empirical material as an entity judged by actors to make a difference to their work, and this called for a closer investigation of how this entity had an impact on the mass mediation of research. The last part of this section is devoted to discussing similar theoretical approaches to the possible performative function of imagined audiences, that is other studies that have argued that *conceptions* of audiences do not only reside in actors' minds, but make an impact on actual work practices.

The performative function of imagined audiences

The public or the audience is portrayed in different ways in science communication studies. Either simply (maybe implicitly) as the raison-d'être of communication efforts, as actually existing users or receivers of information, or as imagined audiences. In the context of this chapter, the latter sense of the term is most relevant. Here, audiences are seen as constructions, and as an entity to which scientists, science communicators and journalists have to relate and adjust. In science communication studies, I have found surprisingly few remarks on the constructions of audiences on the basis of which journalists operate – apart from recurrent references to the audience as incapable of understanding or appreciating a wide range of topics or concepts (see Logan 2001: 142). One empirical study of imagined audiences argues that experts have models and theories of the competences of lay actors, and that this structures the interaction of experts and laypeople (Marenta et al. 2003: 151). The aim of the study is to analyse experts' conceptions of laypersons. These are captured by the concept of 'imagined lay persons' (ILPs). ILPs are functional constructs, and have no necessary resemblance with real laypeople. The point is that experts have no face-to-face interaction with the public that they might be interested in addressing. Lacking this kind of experience, they assemble laypersons (in their imagination) in different ways, so that it makes sense to communicate with them. Laypersons may be ascribed economic interests, political motives or epistemic competences, and this is integrated into the communication strategies of experts. Marenta et al. (2003: 159) show that experts grant laypeople a quite reduced amount of interests and capacities, because seeing them as more complex would make it too difficult to communicate with them. Another study has shown that in spite of the widespread recognition of the need for two-way communication and public engagement, scientists tend to conceive of the public as unreceptive and in need of pedagogical communication (Davies 2008: 430). Despite strands of literary studies and media studies theorising the impact of 'imagined audiences' or 'audiences invoked' on writing processes and textual products (Scheidt 2006; Ong 1975; Ede and Lunsford 1984), it seems that few science communication studies have been concerned with how images of the audience are performative. The present chapter is intended to contribute to filling this gap.

In the following analysis, I try to integrate the above insights. It is inspired by PUS' conception of science/public relations as a complex network, and it has an agenda similar to the branch of science communication concerned with communication processes between relevant actors in the mass mediation of science. Finally, it is in accordance with the consensus view within contemporary qualitative audience studies that mass mediation is a dialogic or multidirectional set of communication processes, rather than a one-way linear process. As I will delineate in the following methods section, this analysis is carried out in a concrete empirical study through a focus on negotiations, dialogic moments and the role of imagined audiences.

A case study of negotiations and dialogue in mass mediation

In this chapter, I present one particular case study stemming from a series of case studies that examined the production processes leading to different concrete media products dealing with aspects of social science (Plesner 2009). In this section, I will present an account of the research strategy underpinning the case study, the production and types of empirical material, and the analytical strategy applied to the material.

The research strategy was the same for all the cases, namely to 'follow the actors' (Latour 2005) involved in the production of a particular media product, to interview the people involved, and to analyse these interviews as well as the media products themselves. This was done in order to shed light on the negotiations that led to the final text, an ambition coming from the wish to explore the theoretical point that mass mediation need not be seen as a one-way communication process. Following the actors is a strategy with several implications that I cannot explore here – for instance the important implication that texts are treated as part of a network of meaning-making objects on a par with other objects (see Plesner 2009, 2011). This chapter is based on textual analyses, so the implication of 'following the actors' relevant to highlight here is the dissolution of micro/ macro distinctions. The dissolution of micro/macro distinctions sets the approach apart from, for instance, discourse analyses of the construction of meanings in production, text and reception, because when analysing texts, it does not look beyond specific concrete situations for ideological patterns or descriptions of context.

The entry point into the empirical material for this case began with an interview with the director of communication at a Danish university. I had heard him give a talk about the relations between experts and the public, and I knew that he was active in writing on and debating these issues. The director mentioned a couple of researchers, whom I contacted. From the interviews with these researchers, my attention was led to specific texts – and to another researcher, who, according to her colleague, had just been through the 'media machinery' and had a lot to tell about the interactions in and around the production of a radio programme. Tracing the negotiations that led to the radio programme and analysing both the accounts of its coming-into-being and the programme itself for dialogic moments became the point of departure for the present case. Besides an interview with the participating researcher, I interviewed the person producing the programme and the journalist hosting the broadcast debate. I thus talked to the main actors involved in the production of the radio debate with the exception of another researcher who participated in the radio debate but could not find the time to participate in my investigation. In the analysis, the voice of this researcher is thus weaker than those of the others, but his position and arguments stand out as powerful, not least because they are backed up by the status of natural science established in the radio programme. In addition to the interview material and the research-based texts, the analysis is based on a podcast of the radio debate and other texts pointed to by interviewees as important, such as the host's script for the debate (as well as his notes for the script manuscript) and other texts written by the researcher.

The radio programme was part of a series of four hour-long radio broadcasts on the theme of the brain, which ran on Denmark's Radio Channel 1 in Spring 2007. The programme in question here was titled 'The Brain Goes to School', and revolved around the idea of separating boys and girls in school, due to differences in their brain development. In the following, I will give an account of how the programme came into being. Elsewhere, I have described – in quite some detail – the negotiations and translations that took place in the process of developing the concept behind it, and I have discussed how knowledge was negotiated before, under and after the broadcast (Plesner 2009). The negotiations of meaning in the programme – and in the interviews – revolved around a controversy regarding the status of different kinds of research-based knowledge. I have analysed this controversy as an example of the multidirectional communication processes that take place in the course of a media production process and offer empirical evidence for the claim that negotiations and dialogues not only take place in the radio debate itself, but also before and after the radio broadcast. In this chapter, I focus primarily on the moments of negotiation and dialogue where citizens, public or imagined audiences influence the production process. The concepts of negotiation and dialogue are not used synonymously, but to point to different aspects of the relational dimension of mass mediation processes. Negotiation here refers to the collaborative assemblage of elements into a media product whereas dialogue points to both the inherently dialogic nature of language and the experience of mutual understanding and recognition.

When coding the empirical material, the analytical strategy was twofold. I have searched for negotiations over meaning regarding a social scientific argument, to capture dialogic moments, and I have searched for situations where citizens or audiences seem to make a difference for the shaping of social scientific arguments in the mass media. Again, the point of this strategy has been to highlight the relational, dialogic aspects of mass mediation, in order to reflect upon the mass media as something other than a channel for the one-way communication of science to the public. This obviously makes the analysis blind to all the instances where the mass media function as a one-way communication channel where uncontested scientific statements are reproduced or to the instances where journalists misrepresent science because of a lack of dialogue and negotiation. However, such phenomena have been documented extensively elsewhere (e.g. Brechman et al. 2009; Hartz and Chapell 1997; Kristiansen 2007; Evans 1995), and the following analysis should not be understood as a corrective to such observations about the workings of the mass media in the coverage of science, but as an additional type of story that widens our conception of the relationship between science, citizens and the mass media.

Analysis

The following analysis consists of three vignettes, which illustrate different aspects of negotiations and dialogues in the mass mediation of science. By using the term vignette, I indicate that they are meant to be short analytical descriptions, each providing a particular insight into an idea or setting. The two first revolve around how considerations about citizens or publics make a difference for the communication of science. The third unfolds how the mass mediation of science consists of many more multidirectional communication processes than the one-way communication model of mass mediation would suggest. It details how extensive journalistic research and negotiations feed into media products and how the communication processes throughout the production have profound impact on the participating researcher's experience of science communication and her field. It also indicates that the rationale for all this negotiation is a concern with democracy, expressed through the ambition of engaging citizens in debates about science.

Vignette 1: Dialogues with imagined others

Although numerous interactive formats and citizen journalism of course make it possible for journalists to be in direct contact with media users if they want to be receiver-oriented, these are neither the sole nor the most common ways of taking audiences into account. In relation to the questions of how it is possible to know what 'ordinary people' or 'media users' want and understand and which concepts journalists need to translate (and how), the radio host and journalist Simon talks about a dynamic process of negotiations between colleagues and about an extensive amount of analysis and media research describing target groups. A lot of feedback comes from focus groups and a lot of considerations about how to address particular audiences are distilled from such research and written into the format of a given medium or programme. In this way, discussions of media research as well as articulations of rhetorical techniques go into the establishment of 'routine' practices and 'professionalism'. Simon describes the practices of taking 'the other' into account with imagery such as setting out hooks and opening doors. And 'the other' is constantly present in his work as a horizon he has to navigate in relation to:

> It is really important that we make ourselves clear. Like translating loan-words, constantly being clear about what we are talking about and not shifting to insiders' language. We need to make sure that we turn to the audience and ask 'are you following us?'[2]

We see how these considerations are put to work in the first question/answer part of the radio programme. Here, it is clear how Simon constantly judges whether expert language is understandable or needs to be translated:

Simon (radio host): And Marie, there is a huge difference between boys' and girls' brains, and the children's ability to learn when they start school. That is why we have to teach boys and girls separately, according to the researcher Ann Elisabeth Knudsen. What do you think about that?

Marie (researcher): First, you need to pay attention to the leaps between the levels in Ann Elisabeth Knudsen's argumentation here. You see, we jump from a level which is a statistical entity, namely an average boy's and girl's frontal lobe, and so on.

Simon (radio host): She applies the same yardstick to all boys and the same yardstick to all girls?

Marie (researcher): Yes. And then we jump to another level, which is the class room, or anecdotes about the class room, which are performative of versions of girls and boys that we can recognize, but also very reductionist, I mean distorted in relation to what reality is also like.

Simon (radio host): That means she draws some stereotypical images of boys and girls. But why is it wrong to educate boys and girls separately if there is a difference between their brains?[3]

In this way, journalists engage in dialogic, interactive aspects of the communication of research. They can neither be seen as neutral transmitters of social scientific knowledge, nor should we consider them all-powerful agenda-setters, successful in achieving a discursive closure around the professional framings of their stories.

The point of this vignette is to illustrate how journalists' professional agenda is to a large extent governed by conceptions of the interests and abilities of citizens or the public. They are conscious about 'taking listeners or readers by the hand' and representing them, posing 'their' questions and imagining their needs for knowledge and explanation. This is what I term a constant *dialogue with imagined others*. It should be noted, though, that this is not about free imagination, although journalists may read evidence such as opinion polls rather freely, and make claims about citizens or public opinion that are 'impressionistic and involve a degree of poetic license' (Lewis et al. 2004: 157). But besides actually using polls, media research, interactive media formats, etc., journalists' judgements are also formed by the informal discussions they have at dinner tables, with family members, or places like the hairdresser's. It should not be forgotten that journalists lead lives as citizens and media users, among other citizens and media users, and these experiences shape their understandings of the wishes and needs of 'citizens'.

Vignette 2: When 'the other' enters language

Even if the above-described constant concern with what the media user might understand is common for journalists, consideration of the public's wants and needs is not restricted to journalists alone. Researchers too use different discursive repertoires in different situations. The researcher Marie who was positioned as a somewhat inaccessible researcher in the radio programme demonstrates, in other texts, an ability to communicate dialogically in the way she addresses different publics. Marie can, in fact, be used as an example of a researcher who works with a range of different communication formats which take different kinds of users into account. This is not a question about a deliberate choice of terminology but the capacity to use an appropriate language in different situations. In my interview with her, she pointed out how she had been engaged in different kinds of communication of research to a broader public. When we turn to some of these contributions (in this case a chapter in a non-academic anthology and an article for a teachers' journal), we see that her communication of knowledge employs various rhetorical strategies. In those texts, it becomes clear that academic (social scientific) language is not a fixed set of attributes or techniques to be applied by a researcher. In between the 'traditional', condensed, technical writing (characterised by abstract language, specialist terms, long words and sentences, nominalisations, categorisations, etc.) and the experimental writing inspired by post-structuralism and feminism (characterised by the inclusion of subjective experience, sentiments, dialogues, etc.), there is a whole range of possible rhetorical strategies. These can be applied differently, depending on the author's conception of the audience. In the anthology chapter, the researcher deconstructs a dominant 'cultural reading' of nature (in a BBC TV animal programme) by contrasting it with other possible interpretations of biological 'facts': the programme shows how male seahorses carry the eggs of the female seahorse, nurture them and give birth after several months. The BBC TV programme explains this in the following way: the male 'can be sure that he is the father of the off-breed. Such a guarantee for his fatherhood makes it attractive for the male to identify with the father role'. The researcher analyses the voice-over in the following way:

> So the male makes a strategic choice, to ensure the reproduction of his genes ... And while he is taking care of the off-spring, the female seahorse is not engaged in new adventures. No, she is seeking food and producing more eggs. And whether she is (aggressively) spreading her eggs to other males – and in fact spreading her genes in all directions – this is left out of the story.[4]

Much of the analysis is kept in such a polemical, ironic, conversational tone. These sections go together with more generalising, abstract and categorising passages such as the following:

[BBC's animal programmes] support and reproduce, rather than render complex or break with, the dominant account. A dominant account where special gender codes, that is, particular understandings of gender, gender differences and nature, circulate and are reproduced hand in hand with a Darwinist and natural scientific tradition for causal explanations and categorizations.[5]

According to the researcher, this way of communicating academic analyses to a non-academic audience is grounded in a feeling of obligation to feed into debates on gender among citizens, and is adjusted to take account of the non-academic background of interested citizens. The same is the case when the researcher communicates to a professional community, as we see in the second text. This article is written for a teachers' journal, and is rather short. It has no references, and there is not a lot of specialist jargon in it. The interest seems to be in producing a type of communication that does not compromise the researcher but is still comprehensible. It does this by using examples and visualisations and by involving the reader through the use of second person singular and first person plural:

If you cast your eye over a school class, you will probably notice that there are children of different 'kinds' …

If we consider this issue from the point of view of a position called poststructuralism, we realize that 'kind' is not something you are, but something you become, though a huge number of micro-processes and negotiations through which it is settled who belongs to a category and who does not.[6]

These passages demonstrate that 'academic language' is not a singular thing, even if it is often characterised by a lot of nominalisations, abstract concepts, passives and the like. Also, there is no necessary connection between being an academic and using academic language. If we adopt this de-essentialising view of the 'nature' of academic writing, it makes sense to reflect upon the factors influencing the actual texts produced by researchers. Here, I will argue that a decisive factor is the skilled consideration of 'the other'. Not skilled in the sense that social scientists can deliberately plan and account for such communication considerations, but in the sense that vague ideas about the public and its capacities and interests make a difference in a specific instance of science communication. This is also why it makes sense to look at communication as much more than a toolbox, which can be put to use to solve problems of deficit and understanding. Of course, the toolbox approach to communication (e.g. Gascoigne and Metcalfe 1997; Shortland and Gregory 1991; Steinke 1995; Vaughan and Buss 1998) offers valuable insights about different rhetorical styles – and the deliberate switching between them – but it says little of the capacity of the language user to produce texts that address different 'imagined others' (or 'target groups', or 'model readers') through a complex mixture of different rhetorical strategies, wordings and levels of abstraction.

The point of this vignette differs slightly from the first one because citizens or the public do not enter the communicative process through conscious reflection by central actors in the mass mediation of science, but as 'others' inherently present in communication. Here, the dialogic aspect of the mediation of science is less deliberate and more of an inbuilt property of language. From this point of view, mass media texts and public communication of science can be seen as inexorably occupied with citizen concerns and abilities. This resonates with the discourse analytical point that the social or political is produced, reproduced and transformed through everyday, discursive practices – and that through media texts, we may get an idea about social relations and power relations in society. In qualitative media studies, this interconnectedness has been conceptualised as a 'cultural circuit' in which institutional discourses, media discourses and citizens' discourses shape each other – and where the textual dimension is an integral part of the circuit (Phillips and Schrøder 2005: 276). The idea of the cultural circuit has been taken up in discourse analytical research in science communication studies. Here, it accounts for the interrelationship between text and context in relation to mass media reporting on climate change, demonstrating how broadsheet print media are responsive to scientific and social learning and in turn inform policymaking and individual action (Carvalho and Burgess 2005). Rather than reflecting on macro elements of this cultural circuit, my analysis has focused on how considerations of 'the other' enter it.

Vignette 3: Negotiations and their feedback on science

In the course of the production of the radio programme mentioned above, negotiations before, during and after the programme had an impact not only on the framing of themes and knowledge claims but also on the researcher's future choice of research themes. The researcher's experience of not having her social scientific points acknowledged as valid – in relation to natural scientific claims about the brain – may be best described as a pseudo-dialogue with both producer and debate opponent. About the preparation of the programme, she tells the following story:

> Well, a radio producer phoned me, and we talked for half an hour. It began over the mail, and then she phoned me. And she began telling me what the take on the programme would be. And she starts by saying 'Well, we know from brain research' … and, you know, 'brain research shows that …' and we talk for half an hour, and I try to disturb that one-dimensional understanding of brain research: 'you need to know that it is not so one-dimensional, what brain research says' … and try to lay out some of those arguments about … arguments that counter the 'truth' of [one of the expert voices of the pre-produced parts of the program]. And in fact I have the impression that we communicate, and that she takes in some of my arguments and moderates some of her statements. But also that she has adopted that discourse. I said that it was important for

me … or, I tried to challenge the idea behind the programme, that [the other researcher] represents brain research.[7]

The producer, on her part, had arrived at the idea behind the programme through journalistic research, which had provided her with a lot of very different input. To make it easier to construct a coherent programme, she had settled on the premise 'Are our schools built in accordance with our brains?' – and her built-in answer to this question, which underpinned her production choices, was in the negative:

[T]he more we know about brain research, the more this research progresses, the more we see that this is not the way we learn, at all. It has taken 150.000 years, or, we have had the same brain for 150.000 years, approximately. And what is it, for about 200 years that we have sent our children to school in the way we do it now? All considered, it does not work that well … this is not where we learn. And that is why I had to figure out, okay, this is my premise, and I also know that I need to have two guests in the studio, who have to disagree, fundamentally, a good debate has to come out of this, and this happens when they disagree.[8]

According to the actors' accounts, this position was established in the preparatory deliberations about the programmes. In editorial meetings, producers, host and editors had been talking about different scenarios, that is, which debates seemed possible to create. But these negotiations had to come to an end at an early stage: 'And then at a certain point, you draw a line, and this is what we'll work on from now on, then you just have to find two debaters willing to discuss this'.[9] The result of the editorial processes was that a quickly assembled mass of knowledge about the brain – which can be communicated from many possible angles – was translated into a single premise. In the presentation of the programme,[10] a range of categorical modalities indicate that we have to do with a field of scientific research – brain research – which offers a set of well-established truths. Statements such as 'Earlier we thought that … Today we know that …' and 'The brains of girls and boys develop differently' signal an accomplished, accepted knowledge, and this almost makes the question in the end of the section seem rhetorical: 'Maybe the time has come to separate the children in the classroom at least some of the time?'

This work process entailed that the debate part of the programme had to revolve around the above-described premise. Hence, in the preparation for the debate, the host talked to the participants, making extensive notes with their points and examples. When these notes were turned into a manuscript, a lot of nuances disappeared in order to formulate a clear-cut position. For instance, the psychiatrist who is one of the debaters came up with several arguments in the preparatory talk with the host for softening the sharp division between boys and girls: 'Of course we see girls who have the same profile as boys. … Girls who are extrovert and boys who are intellectual.'[11] Hence, in the host's preparatory notes, the psychiatrist does not have a clear-cut position as a gender essentialist. This part of the material which shows that the psychiatrist does not want to draw strict lines between boys and girls is *not* turned into questions to the opponent. Instead, the psychiatrist's position is phrased as his opponent's point of view and turned back against him in the following way:

[Question 1d]
By dividing the children into boys and girls, you force them into a stereotypical – and simplified – image of what gender is about. Individuals are much more different than indicated by the one-sided image drawn by brain researchers?[12]

The consequence of all this negotiation and translation work before the programme is a rather tight steering of the debate, aimed at creating two opposing sides. This is not easy to achieve for the host, but in the end the two debaters get into heated discussions and take up very antagonistic positions, and this leaves the researcher Marie with a bad feeling:

When the interview ended I had [an aftermath] with my opponent and the journalists. He continued discussing, but I told him I could not discuss with him because he intimidated me. And then I walked out. I got my stuff and I met the journalists, and I said I was sorry … I was annoyed with the fact that I had not been able to find my arguments, but I had been intimidated. But they could not understand that. They had obtained a great sound. A debate sound. They could not hear that he attacked my professionalism. They were just in the process of producing great debate sound.[13]

Hence, when we dig into the negotiations that take place around media productions with a scientific content, it is possible to see how specific interactions have consequences for specific individuals, and, by extension, for researchers' specific science communication contributions and experience of their field:

I become totally exasperated in those situations, because there is no learning taking place … I had gender research as an entry point for my PhD project, but I have toned down that dimension, in order not to run into the same stuff again. In that sense, my engagement has vanished. Because it feels like fighting against windmills, right? And because I could not see myself taking the same discussion again and again. And that is also why I have stayed out of debate land. But now we are considering writing a debate book for use in schools. A debate book, not a research project … It is exhausting when research is politicized in that way.[14]

While it might be inappropriate to talk about the dialogic aspect of mass mediation in relation to the quote above, because the researcher talks about a *lack* of mutual understanding, the incident can be interpreted as dialogic in a Bakhtinian sense, because it shows how expectations of the other are built into language. Also, the passage shows how the mass mediation of research can have a significant feedback function. While the researcher has the experience of not being able to engage in a 'real' dialogue, she is so disturbed by the experience that it works back on her choice of future research topic. It is generally acknowledged that mass mediation does influence the production of scientific knowledge, for instance by providing ideas and metaphors that are picked up by scientists (see Bucchi 2008: 63 for references to such studies). Lewenstein refers to studies that 'argue that media presentations are not merely part of the social context in which science exists but instead are the direct causes of some aspects of scientific work'. He remarks that such studies 'support a model of science communication more complex and interactive than the traditional, unidirectional model' (Lewenstein 1995: 357).[15] The type of influence of mass mediation I have been discussing above is less productive but, nevertheless, this example of feedback in mass mediation can be seen as additional evidence of the two-way communication between 'science' and 'the media'.

Also, all the negotiations and translations analysed above can be seen as driven by a concern with democracy, expressed through the ambition of engaging citizens in debates over science. The host acknowledged that the debate had been an unpleasant experience for the researcher, and that the programme had favoured particular claims of natural scientists. However, he had a clear agenda of interrogating these claims from a more political angle, not because he believed journalists and debaters have the right to enter the domain of scientific argumentation, but 'because we are political, emotional, thinking human beings'.[16] So there is a political dimension in the appreciation and search for conflict, namely the effort to engage people. According to the host, the debate form is very dynamic in the sense that it allows for the treatment of a complex topic. When this format is used, listeners do not need to possess prior knowledge of the topic, and the aim is not to inform. The aim is to engage, and if people get some information as well, this is fine, in his view. In that sense, the journalist's appreciation of this particular radio format overshadows the ambition of communicating science. Science is positioned as something for citizens to engage in, not just 'something for experts to argue about'. The host also makes it clear that the goal of producing radio dealing with science is not to dig for 'the truth' about a given issue, but to popularise, to identify issues that are easy to relate to, and to not be afraid of *discussing* science[17]:

> …rather than saying, here we have some experts speaking, then we accept that and make notes in our little notebook, so that we can be tested in the statements of the brain researchers, rather than this, we wanted to discuss some ethical and societal consequences of what the brain researchers were telling us.[18]

This final vignette has explored the multidirectionality of the communication processes of a media production process in order to demonstrate the specific ways in which negotiations allow media stories of science to take a number of different directions. This challenges the assumption, still underpinning much work in science communication studies, that the mass mediation of science is a one-directional communication process with a scientist in the position of sender, the journalist in the position of translator, the text as a neutral medium, and the citizen at the other end of the line as a receiver.

Here, I have not mentioned how – in the hour-long broadcast – several citizens (more specifically, teachers and school children) were asked for everyday stories about gender in the class room, as well as their opinions about a partial separation of boys and girls in the school. Instead, I have focused on an overlooked impact of citizens on the mass mediation of science, namely the democratic ideal of engaging people though various journalistic techniques. As these techniques can be confused with manipulative simplification of science justified with reference to an all-pervasive media logic (Plesner 2011), I think this is an important point to highlight. When journalists are criticised for not taking seriously their role as the watch dogs of democracy, we should acknowledge less obvious instances of their taking citizens into consideration.

Conclusion

The empirical interest in this chapter has been what we may call the communicative space between science, media and citizens, where citizens are neither actual people engaging with science nor represented textually in the mass media. Instead they appear as imagined others to relate to in a wide range of negotiations in mass media production processes.

The concepts of negotiation, dialogue and multidirectionality have been used to highlight how communication is never a unidirectional transmission process but always marked either by negotiations with actual communication partners or by implicit considerations of 'the other'. This Bakhtinian point about 'the other's presence in language is in accordance with studies of mass mediation that have argued for the significance of 'imagined audiences' (Brake 2009; Marwick and Boyd 2011; Peterson 2003). The analysis has illustrated how such considerations of the other influence the production of mass media texts. It has exemplified how journalists constantly rephrase statements with an imagined audience in mind and how researchers adjust to their audiences in specific instances of communicating knowledge. It has also shed light on instances where actors experience feedback, which has consequences for their practices. The analysis thus showed how researchers are not necessarily cut off from dialogue, interaction and feedback. Concrete encounters with individuals and texts seem to have impact on the particular researcher's activities; they are constitutive of new texts, they work upon the mood of the researcher, upon the inclination to engage further in communication to the public, and even upon the researcher's wish to continue doing research with a gender perspective.

The analytical concern with multidirectionality overlaps with other qualitative approaches to the mass media, which are now widespread in media studies, but not as widespread in science communication studies. While these other qualitative approaches stress the complexity of meaning-making at all stages in the media production process and the idea of the multidirectionality of communication processes, my approach offers a distinctive lens for analysing the specific nature of that multidirectionality based on the dissolution of micro/macro distinctions. In media analyses, this implies, for instance, that the media is not seen as a macro actor governed by a particular logic and that texts are analysed for their performativity in particular situations, not as expressions of ideologies or power relations.

The empirical story above can be seen as having implications for the robustness of social scientific knowledge in various ways. On one level, the processes described can be said to devalue social science by generating an audience-driven, populist research agenda. But on another level, such instances of feedback ensure that research is marked by the interaction with non-researchers, and thus it can be said to be developed with an inbuilt relevance. The same is the case for the production of media texts. Not only researchers, but also journalists experience the relational or dialogic aspects of communication of research in the mass media. They are met with discursive contestations of their framings, and their media products are evaluated informally, discussed publicly, and have consequences for journalists' credibility. All in all, we may conclude that the mass mediation of social science does not leave the parties involved untouched.

The chapter has added to discussions of how citizens may participate in various stages of the production and communication of scientific knowledge by placing analytical attention *in between* studies of public engagement exercises (with the deliberate and visible participation of citizens) and studies of media representations (with a concern with textual representations of citizen voices). Its contribution is to provide insight into the particular ways in which communication processes around the mass mediation of science are dialogic and multidirectional, and to show how this dialogic, multidirectional nature allows for negotiations about citizens' concerns and abilities to take place in informal settings behind the scenes of mass mediation. It has pointed to instances where this both makes a difference for the communication of science and affects the production of science.

While we have seen studies of the mass mediation of social scientific knowledge that attempt to avoid giving primacy to either the production, the text or the consumption of mass mediation (e.g. Deacon, Fenton and Bryman 1999), we still need to develop research strategies in relation to mass media research which do not lead us to work with conveniently delineated groups of senders, mediums and receivers where researchers are seen as the origin of the communication process. The claim of this chapter is that we can do this through a focus on negotiations and feedback. This orientation demands a strategy of changing scale in the approach to mass mediation, away from conceiving of it as macro-level phenomena to looking at interactions in concrete relationships. When actors describe how they go about finding sources, putting together radio programmes, interacting with colleagues or making themselves available to journalists, the analysis of such mundane practices, interactions and negotiations makes the idea of a top-down flow untenable. Instead, an image of mass mediation as more relational and dialogic emerges. A future task of mass media studies with such a focus could be to explore a variety of multidirectional communication processes in mass mediation and cultivate the concepts aimed at describing them (see Black 2008), so that we become attuned to the workings of dialogue, debates, discussions, deliberations and negotiations.

References

Albæk, E., Christiansen, P. M. and Togeby, L., *Eksperter i medierne. dagspressens brug af forskere 1961–2001*. Aarhus: Institut for Statskundskab, Århus Universitet, 2002.

Allan, S., *Media, Risk and Science*. Buckingham: Open University Press, 2002.

Black, L. W., 'Deliberation, Storytelling, and Dialogic Moments'. *Communication Theory*, 18:1 (2008), pp. 93–116.

Blok, A., 'Experts on Public Trial: On Democratizing Expertise through a Danish Consensus Conference'. *Public Understanding of Science*, 16:2 (2007), pp. 163–182.

Brake, D. R., 'As if Nobody's Reading?: The Imagined Audience and Sociotechnical Biases in Personal Blogging Practice in the UK'. Ph.D., London School of Economics, 2009.

Brechman, J., Lee, C. J. and Cappella, J. N., 'Lost in Translation? A Comparison of Cancer-Genetics Reporting in the Press Release and Its Subsequent Coverage in the Press'. *Science Communication*, 30:4 (2009), pp. 453–474.

Brossard, D., 'Media, Scientific Journals and Science Communication: Examining the Construction of Scientific Controversies'. *Public Understanding of Science*, 18:3 (2009), pp. 258–274.

Bucchi, M., *Science and the Media: Alternative Routes in Scientific Communication*. London: Routledge, 1998.

———— 'Of Deficits, Deviations and Dialogues – Theories of Public Communication of Science'. In M. Bucchi and B. Trench (eds), *Handbook of Public Communication of Science and Technology*. London: Routledge, 2008.

Callon, M., 'The Role of Lay People in the Production and Dissemination of Scientific Knowledge'. *Science, Technology & Society*, 4:1 (1999), pp. 81–94.

Carpentier, N., 'Contextualising Author-Audience Convergences'. *Cultural Studies*, 25:4–5 (2011), pp. 517–533.

Carvalho, A., 'Ideological Cultures and Media Discourses on Scientific Knowledge: Re-reading News on Climate Change'. *Public Understanding of Science*, 16:2 (2007), pp. 223–243.

Carvalho, A. and Burgess, J., 'Cultural Circuits of Climate Change in UK Broadsheet Newspapers, 1985–2003'. *Risk Analysis*, 25:6 (2005), pp. 1457–1469.

Claessens, M., 'European Trends in Science Communication'. In D. Cheng, M. Claessens, J. Metcalfe, B. Schiele and S. Shi (eds), *Communicating Science in Social Contexts – New Models, New Practices*. Springer Science, 2008.

Czarniawska, B. and Hernes, T., 'Constructing Macro Actors according to ANT'. In B. Czarniawska and T. Hernes (eds), *Actor-Network Theory and Organizing*. Malmö /Copenhagen: Liber/CBS, 2005.

Davies, S. R., 'Constructing Communication: Talking to Scientists about Talking to the Public'. *Science Communication*, 29:4 (2008), pp. 413–434.

Deacon, D., Fenton, N. and Bryman, A., 'From Inception to Reception: The Natural History of a News Item'. *Media Culture and Society*, 21:1 (1999), pp. 5–31.

Dunwoody, S. and Scott, B. T., 'Scientists as Mass-Media Sources'. *Journalism Quarterly*, 59:1 (1982), pp. 52–59.

Ede, L. and Lunsford, A., 'Audience Addressed/Audience Invoked: The Role of Audience in Composition Theory and Pedagogy'. *College Composition and Communication*, 35:2 (1984), pp. 155–171.

Evans, W., 'The Mundane and the Arcane – Prestige Media Coverage of Social and Natural-Science'. *Journalism & Mass Communication Quarterly*, 72:1 (1995), pp. 168–177.

Gascoigne, T. and Metcalfe, J., 'Incentives and Impediments to Scientists Communicating through the Media'. *Science Communication*, 18:3 (1997), pp. 265–282.

Hartz, J. and Chappell, R., *Worlds Apart: How the Distance between Science and Journalism Threatens America's Future*. Nashville: First Amendment Center, 1997.

Hilgartner, S., 'The Dominant View of Popularization: Conceptual Problems, Political Uses'. *Social Studies of Science*, 20:3 (1990), pp. 519–539.

Horst, M., 'In Search of Dialogue: Staging Science Communication in Consensus Conferences'. In D. Cheng, M. Claessens, J. Metcalfe, B. Schiele and S. Shi (eds), *Communicating Science in Social Contexts: New Models, New Practices*. Springer Science, 2008.

——— 'Taking Our Own Medicine – On an Experiment in Science Communication'. *Science and Engineering Ethics*, 17:4 (2011), pp. 801–815.

Irwin, A. and Michael, M., *Science, Social Theory and Public Knowledge*. Maidenhead: Open University Press, 2003.

Kristiansen, B., 'Forskningsbaseret viden i massemedierne – et bidrag til demokratiet? En analyse af PISA 2003 i den trykte dagspresse'. Ph.D. thesis, Roskilde University, 2007.

Latour, B., 'Give Me a Laboratory and I Will Raise the World'. In M. Biagioli (ed.), *The Science Studies Reader*. New York: Routledge, 1999.

——— *Reassembling the Social – an Introduction to Actor-Network-Theory*. Oxford: Oxford University Press, 2005.

Lewenstein, B. V., 'Science and the Media'. In S. Jasanoff, G. E. Markle, J. C. Petersen and T. Pinch (eds), *Handbook of Science and Technology*. Thousand Oaks: Sage, 1995.

Lewis, J., Wahl-Jorgensen, K. and Inthorn, S., 'Images of Citizenship on Television News: Constructing a Passive Public'. *Journalism Studies*, 5:2 (2004), pp. 153–164.

Logan, R. A., 'Science Mass Communication – Its Conceptual History'. *Science Communication*, 23:2 (2001), pp. 135–163.

Maeseele, P. A. and Schuurman, D., 'Biotechnology and the Popular Press in Northern Belgium: A Case Study of Hegemonic Media Discourses and the Interpretive Struggle'. *Science Communication*, 29:4 (2008), pp. 435–471.

Marenta, A., Guggenheim, M., Gisler, P. and Pohl, C., 'The Reality of Experts and the Imagined Lay Person'. *Acta Sociologica*, 46:2 (2003), pp. 150–165.

Marks, L. A., Kalaitzandonakes, N., Wilkins, L. and Zakharova, L., 'Mass Media Framing of Biotechnology News'. *Public Understanding of Science*, 16:2 (2007), pp. 183–203.

Marwick, A. E. and Boyd, D., 'I Tweet Honestly, I Tweet Passionately: Twitter Users, Context Collapse, and the Imagined Audience'. *New Media & Society*, 13:1 (2011), pp. 114–133.

Michael, M., 'Comprehension, Apprehension, Prehension: Heterogeneity and the Public Understanding of Science'. *Science, Technology and Human Values*, 27:3 (2002), pp. 357–378.

Miller, J., 'The Measurement of Scientific Literacy'. *Public Understanding of Science*, 7:3 (1998), pp. 1–21.

Ong, W., 'The Writer's Audience is Always a Fiction'. *PMLA*, 90:1 (1975), pp. 9–21.

Pauly, J. J., 'Media Studies and the Dialogue of Democracy'. In R. Anderson, L. A. Baxter and K. N. Cissna (eds), *Dialogue – Theorizing Difference in Communication Studies*. Thousand Oaks: Sage, 2004.

Peterson, M. A., *Anthropology and Mass Communication, Media and Myth in the New Millennium*. Oxford: Berghahn Books, 2003.

Phillips, L. J., *The Promise of Dialogue: The Dialogic Turn in the Production and Communication of Knowledge*. Amsterdam: John Benjamins Publishing, 2011.

Phillips, L. and Schrøder, K. C., 'Diskursanalytisk tekstanalyse'. In M. Järvinen and N. Mik-Meyer (eds), *Kvalitative metoder i et interaktionistisk perspektiv*. Copenhagen: Hans Reizels Forlag, 2005.

Plesner, U., 'Disassembling the Mass Mediation of Research – A Study of the Construction of Texts, Relations and Positions in the Communication of Social Science'. Ph.D. thesis, Roskilde University, 2009.

Plesner, U., 'Studying Sideways – Displacing the Problem of Power in Research Interviews with Sociologists and Journalists'. *Qualitative Inquiry*, 17:6 (2011), pp. 471–482.

Powell, M. and Lee Kleinman, D., 'Building Citizen Capacities for Participation in Nanotechnology Decision-making: The Democratic Virtues of the Consensus Conference Model'. *Public Understanding of Science*, 17:3 (2008), pp. 329–348.

Riise, J. 'Bringing Science to the Public'. In D. Cheng, M. Claessens, J. Metcalfe, B. Schiele and S. Shi (eds), *Communicating Science in Social Contexts: New Models, New Practices*. Springer Science, 2008.

Sanden, M.C.A van der and Maijman, Frans J., 'Dialogue guides awareness and understanding of science: An essay on different goals of dialogue leading to different science communication approaches'. *Public Understanding of Science*, 17:1 (2008), pp. 89–103.

Scheidt, L. A., 'Adolescent Diary Weblogs and the Unseen Audience'. In D. Buckingham and R. Willett (eds), *Digital Generations, Children, Young People, and New Media*. Mahwah, NJ: Lawrence Erlbaum, 2006.

Schrøder, K. C. and Phillips, L., 'Complexifying Media Power: A Study of the Interplay between Media and Audience Discourses on Politics'. *Media, Culture & Society*, 29:6 (2007), pp. 890–915.

Shortland, M. and Gregory, J., *Communicating Science: A Handbook*. New York: Longman, 1991.

Siune, K. and Vinther, T., *Folk og forskning. danskerne om forskningspolitik*, No. 5, Århus, Analyseinstitut for Forskning, 1998a.

—— *Folk og forskning. danskernes kilder til viden om forskning*, No. 4, Århus, Analyseinstitut for Forskning, 1998b.

—— *Folk og forskning. danskernes opfattelse af forskning*, No. 1, Århus, Analyseinstitut for Forskning, 1998c.

Steinke, J., 'Reaching Readers – Assessing Readers' Impressions of Science News'. *Science Communication*, 16:4 (1995), pp. 432–453.

Trench, B., 'Towards an Analytical Framework of Science Communication Models'. In D. Cheng, M. Claessens, J. Metcalfe, B. Schiele and S. Shi (eds), *Communicating Science in Social Contexts: New Models, New Practices*. Springer Science, 2008.

Vaughan, R. J. and Buss, T. F., *Communicating Social Science Research to Policy Makers*. London: Sage, 1998.

Notes

1 See also Sanden and Maijman (2008).

2 Interview with radio host, 23.08.07, lines 613–617.

3 Podcast 35.11–36.00.

4 Anthology chapter on gender and sexual normativity in animal programmes, p. 101.

5 Anthology chapter on gender and sexual normativity in animal programmes, p. 97.

6 Article in a teacher's magazine on 'gender hostages in the class room'.

7 Interview with researcher, 13.04.07, lines 70–80.

8 Interview with radio producer, 14.08.07, lines 151–159.

9 Interview radio producer, 14.08.07, lines 434–435.

10 On www.dr.dk/P1/p1-temaer/Hjernerejsen/Udsendelser/AndenHjernerejse [Accessed on 4 December 2007].

11 The radio host's notes.

12 The radio host's manuscript for the debate.

13 Interview with researcher, 13.04.07, lines 253–259.

14 Interview with researcher, 13.04.07, lines 397–422.

15 This is different from STS discussions of how knowledge can be understood as co-produced in a process where laypeople are not only listened to in relation to technoscientific developments but actively engage in building up a body of knowledge of something that concerns them (e.g. Callon 1999).

16 Interview with radio host, 23.08.07, lines 329–333.

17 Interview with radio host, 23.08.07, lines 38–44.

18 Interview with radio host, 23.08.07, lines 26–29.

Chapter 3

Contested Ethanol Dreams – Public Participation in Environmental News

Annika Egan Sjölander and Anna Maria Jönsson

We live in a society heavily preoccupied with the handling of environmental and technological risks (cf. Beck 1992). Politics and policymaking in relation to environmental risk have been transformed by societal changes such as globalisation and deregulation (Castells 2008). These transformations involve a form of *governance* in which different actors at different levels participate. Among policymakers and social scientists, there is an increasing adherence to the view that, for societies to be able to deal with global risks, there is a need for governance based on trans-national decision-making and the participation of stakeholders and citizens. This form of governance is sometimes described as 'good governance' (cf. Whiteside 2006). 'Good governance' can also be defined as 'reflective'. It favours transparency and supports the participation of different stakeholders and the public. As a normative model, it shares several characteristics with ideas of a deliberative democracy and the public sphere ideal (Habermas 1962). Many practices of interactive or participatory governance are based directly on models of deliberative democracy (cf. Gastil and Levine 2005) and in these models participation is generally understood as communication (cf. Carpentier 2011). Governance involves citizens and stakeholders in network-like constellations (Felt and Fochler 2010), and 'dialogue' is the underpinning communication model (Phillips, Carvalho and Doyle, Chapter 1, this volume). Here, dialogue refers to horizontal two-way communication and some level of agency is a prerequisite for participation in such dialogue. The participatory paradigm is linked to the idea of 'civic science' where the public/citizen is considered as a kind of alternative expertise and seen as a crucial part of the science–policy relationship (cf. Bäckstrand 2003).

However 'the public' is framed, its role is crucial for the handling of emerging challenges such as climate change and other complex risks still lying ahead of us. It is a starting point for this chapter that citizens' voices – representatives of 'the public' or laypeople – should be heard in the public discourse on environmental issues, and since media is a major arena for this discourse and important in framing risks, the public/citizens should be able to participate in the mediated public sphere.

Despite agreement on the importance of public participation in decision-making procedures and debates about environmental issues, the initiatives for involving the public vary greatly and so do the conceptions of 'the public'. The notion of the public in relation to media-centred late-modern societies and its struggles with environmental problems is still an underdeveloped research area that requires more attention. We start from the premise that public participation in environmental governance is a fundamental part of governing environmental risks, and that the media could work as one vital arena for public participation. Participation includes at least some level of agency and is often equated with concepts like involvement and engagement. In relation to this, mediated participation can be seen as either indirect, involving the public, for example, in terms of representation (journalists speaking of the public opinion, etc.), or direct, engaging the public through interaction and co-production (e.g. in readers comments, letters-to-the-editor, etc.). In this chapter, we discuss conceptions of the public and analyse (mediated) roles for the public/citizens in relation to climate change and the use of biofuels and, in particular, the debate in Sweden about ethanol for transport. The Swedish way of promoting the use of ethanol stands out in comparison to other countries – due to close cooperation between science/policy/industry plus the public's activity and involvement in discussions about the fuel – which makes it interesting to study.

The aim of this chapter is to identify and analyse conceptions of 'the public' in Swedish environmental news about ethanol in print news media and online, and to explore its implications in terms of public participation in environmental communication and governance. First of all, we focus on representation and roles and how 'the public' is framed, looking at different conceptions of the public in news media. Second, we address the issue of different forms and levels of public/citizen participation and discuss the meanings and implications of different mediated conceptions of the public. We also discuss how citizenship and public participation are performed and affected by different contexts for news production.

Against the backdrop of theories on environmental governance and deliberation, we take on the normative perspective that the governing of environmental risks requires an inclusive policymaking process, and that this also means inclusive media. As for theory, we draw on two major strands in research in Science and Technology Studies (STS): (1) the 'participatory turn debate', and (2) the conceptualisation of publics and combine these with theories on media, citizenship and participation. Together, these perspectives help us identify different forms of mediated public participation.

First, we present our theoretical framework, focusing on environmental governance and the participatory turn and linking this to the role of the public and citizenship in relation to print and online news media. After a brief overview of previous research in public representations and participation in news media, we turn to our case study of biofuels for transport, analysing different conceptions of the public in the Swedish ethanol debate, as well as different forms of public engagement and levels of participation in the news media. Finally, we summarise our findings and discuss their wider implications regarding mediated participation and the role of 'the public' in the environmental news discourse.

Theoretical framework

Environmental governance, communication and the participatory turn

Participation by stakeholders and the public is an important ingredient in governance, according to governance theory. As discussed above, the very concept of governance refers to a form of political decision-making that involves 'new' actors, levels and arenas compared to the traditional government model (cf. Pierre and Peters 2000), and is often claimed to be well-suited for handling environmental problems (Kern et al. 2008). Models of governance involve the participation of a wide constituency of social actors in decision-making networks rather than hierarchical top-down relations between government and others. Deliberation is ideally based on full information and the representation of different relevant points of views, and this requires equal opportunities for people to participate in this process (Nip 2006: 215). Interaction between people is also one important part of the creation of a community, as well as of deliberation (Nip 2006: 215). Community is a mental construct that can refer to a particular space, as well as a sense of belonging (cf. Anderson 1983).

In the field of governance theory the 'participatory/deliberative turn' is hailed as an improved mode of governing societies and reaching collectively binding decisions. Political discussions should involve those affected by the decisions. Participation is also a key ingredient in some concepts of citizenship (cf. Isin and Turner 2002) and most certainly so in the concept of environmental citizenship (following the tradition of environmental governance and citizenship, cf. Bäckstrand et al. 2010; Durant et al. 2004; Lemos and Agrawal 2006; Saunier et al. 2007).

In the field of media and communication studies there is also a vast body of literature on different forms of (mediated) citizenship and participation. We do not strive to give a full presentation of this research, but present some of the ideas, concepts and findings with particular relevance for our study. Participation is a broad concept, characterised by an 'omnipresence' in media studies and attached to diverse, shifting, and often rather vague meanings (cf. Carpentier and Dahlgren 2011). In this field of research, participation is often linked to ideas of democracy and different kinds of political participation are in focus. This 'participatory turn' is motivated by increased distrust in political institutions. The trend of widespread distrust of major institutions in society, such as politics and science, has led to an increased will to involve the public. However, there are critical voices in relation to the ways in which participation is generally used in media studies. Carpentier (2011) is one of those who raise concerns. He suggests that we should differentiate between access, interaction and participation, with participation distinguishing itself through its close link to issues of power. Carpentier and others are also critical of the fact that participation is often seen as beneficial by default.

Although recognising many of the definitions and broad uses of participation and how these vary depending on democracy models etc., we define participation ourselves in rather broad terms. We include aspects of access, representation and interaction (defined by Carpentier (2011) as structurally different from participation) and consider participation as a continuum with different levels and forms of engagement. Our starting point is the normative assumption that 'good' environmental governance includes public participation. We wish to study the role of the media in this context. Mediated participation is thus seen as a form of political participation, and participation as a prerequisite for deliberation. Our perspective on participation is connected to the 'maximalist' model (Carpentier 2011: 25) and resembles the 'strong democracy' model (cf. Bäckstrand 2003: 33) where democracy is seen as a combination of representation and participation, and where attempts are made to maximise participation and to equalise power relations. Public participation is important, but who is this 'public' and what does 'participation' entail?

In order to discuss different roles for the public, Rosen (1997: 17) makes a distinction between 'citizen' as opposed to 'consumer' and 'client' (cf. Lewis et al. 2005). To position people as citizens means, for example, to treat them as potential participants in public affairs, to address them as potential decision-makers and learners, and as a deliberative body – a public with issues to discuss (Rosen 1997: 17). Common conceptions of the public such as 'public interest' and 'public opinion' are also used for political purposes. As Felt and Fochler (2010: 223) argue, it is crucial 'to understand what rhetorical constructs of publics (in general or particular) are accepted in a given setting, and for what cultural or social reasons'. In their research, Felt and Fochler (2010: 220) study 'how public engagement settings as political machineries frame or pre-scribe particular kinds of roles and identities for the participating publics in relation to "the public at large"', as well as how participants themselves perform being 'publics' (cf. Michael 2009). In a similar way, we wish to analyse how news settings online and offline can frame and 'pre-scribe' different roles for the public and how participants perform and define themselves as publics, in the debate on environmental issues, and more particularly in the Swedish news media discourse on biofuels for transport.

The concept of 'good' governance, promoting transparency, deliberation and participation, is frequently understood as an ideal model for democracy, and shares many ideas with earlier public sphere theories (cf. Habermas 1962; Fraser 1990). It is argued that public participation makes decisions more legitimate, robust and easier to implement, and much attention has been directed towards the role of deliberative activities and processes for public participation such as public information, public hearings, conferences and advisory groups (see e.g. Hagendijk and Irwin 2006; Lidskog et al. 2010; Brake and Weitkamp 2009). The main objectives of these activities have generally been to communicate information about decisions to be taken, as well as to hear about public opinion *before* making any final decisions. Two-way symmetric communication is necessary to make such a process 'successful' (Janse and Konijnendijk 2007: 24). These processes are also a matter of power. Participants generally have a greater influence over how issues are framed than those who do not, for example, in news production. To be represented in the news media discourse could be about taking part in the discussion or at least the ability to express your voice (directly or indirectly).

Governance theory generally frames the public as *concerned* publics, meaning those affected by decisions, what Beck (1992: 61) describes as 'the voices of the side-effects'. This is different from the concept of the public predominantly used in theories on the public sphere that draw on models of deliberative democracy (Dahlgren 2005; Fraser 1990; Habermas 1962). Models of deliberative democracy refer to citizens in general and the notion of the public interest.

However, the literature criticising this participatory turn has grown, pointing out that public participation is often too tightly framed by policymakers and organisers and does not mean any real shift of power (see, Irwin 2001; Lezaun and Soneryd 2007; Michael 2009).

Researchers on the public/science/policy interface have also highlighted problems with participatory processes relating to the issue of whom 'the public' actually represents and the type of people interested in participating (Janse and Konijnendijk 2007: 25). Dahlgren (2006: 276) has also pointed out limitations in relation to models of deliberative democracy. He questions what kind of talk actually counts as deliberation and the use of rationality as an ideal. Dahlgren also refers to the view that in most political discussions people do not actually deliberate but merely repeat what they have heard from different professional opinion makers. He also puts forward the claim that there are other relevant forms of civic agency. We will, however, in this chapter focus on the deliberative ideal and how it relates to mediated participation.

Governance, as well as the public sphere, are complex theoretical concepts that are both descriptive and normative. A public sphere can be defined as communicative spaces for deliberation on public matters, and, this space is *mediated* to a large extent in contemporary societies (Dahlgren 1995, 2006). The (mass) media and journalism can therefore be understood as a form of deliberative arena. According to Felt and Fochler (2010: 229), there is also a connection between mediated public discourse and different kinds of participatory events, since mediated discourses are important for the framing of the issues to be addressed: 'Public debates (or lack of debate) about the issues discussed in the engagement exercises are a further crucial factor for the construction of mini-publics'. The problems and possibilities identified in relation to the democratising potential of public engagement activities such as consensus conferences and citizen forums seem to be much the same in relation to 'mediated' public participation in news media.

The so-called political crisis, referring to low and declining voter turnouts etc., has also led to discussions about public engagement and participation in traditional politics, including the meaning of citizenship and the role of the public (cf. Lewis et al. 2004, 2005; Blumler and Gurevitch 1995). One important explanation for this decline is the lack of a common arena for discussions among citizens (cf. Lewis et al. 2004).

The main points we draw on from theories on governance and the participatory turn are that public participation in various forms is a fundamental part of environmental decision-making and that there are different ways of defining the public. We draw on this knowledge in order to analyse mediated public representation and participation and to discuss the possible implications of those in environmental communication/science governance. The relation between news media, citizenship and participation will be further discussed in the next section.

Public participation in the news

In media and communication research, the role of citizens or the public is generally discussed in terms of representation and participation. The ways in which journalists frame their stories and reports of the world are also understood to affect citizen participation and engagement (cf. Lewis et al. 2004). In their study of how public opinion and citizenship are represented in television news in the United Kingdom and the United States, Lewis et al. (2004) conclude that citizens in their study mainly are framed as passive observers who express emotions, and that these representations offer no room for citizens' expression of political opinions or solutions to problems and at best can be seen as commentators (not advocates). They identified five main ways or categories, each with different levels of engagement and involvement, through which citizens were represented and participated in the news: (1) as references to public opinion polls or surveys; (2) as inferences about public opinion (without reference to polling data); (3) as vox pops (when ordinary citizens appear in the news); (4) as demonstrators/protesters; and (5) as 'some people say', which is a reference to a section of public opinion (Lewis et al. 2004: 156).

The idea that the public/citizens can play different roles in, and for, journalism is also expressed in journalistic models that focus on an extended audience–journalist interaction in the actual news production phase. 'Public journalism' is an example of a movement that started in the United States about two decades ago and that can be considered a predecessor for citizen involvement in news over and above more traditional kinds of activity such as writing letters-to-the-editor. Initially, public journalism involved citizens *before* the news production actually started; more recent forms, like 'interactive journalism', 'civic journalism' or 'citizen journalism', also involve the public in the actual production process. This kind of journalism entails user-generated content and often takes place in an online media environment. The democratic potential of these online media and the content produced by the 'public' has been widely discussed, focusing among other things on the issue of participation (cf. Dahlgren 2005, 2011; Gripsrud 2009; Day and Schuler 2004; Trenz 2009; Thurman 2008; Thurman and Hermida 2008, Örnebring 2008). Dahlgren, for example, analyses political participation with a special focus on the online media environment, focusing on how 'various forms of media may function in a positive or negative manner in regard to citizens' political involvement in democracy' (Dahlgren 2011: 87). This work is also relevant in our analysis of conceptions of the public in different kinds of news media. According to Mythen (2010), citizen journalism has a great potential for public engagement in media debates about risk since it allows for a greater plurality of voices and alternative agendas to be expressed. However, there are limits like distortion and unequal access to economic and cultural resources.

As noted above, a lot of media research on citizenship focuses on public representation and participation in news media. A conclusion that is often made is that the news media articulate an elitist discourse (cf. Shoemaker and Reese 1996) and this seems to embrace the field of environmental news. According to Cox (2006) spokespersons from government and the industry dominate the environmental news discourse, while views of 'ordinary' citizens or 'side-effects' (cf. Beck 1992) are much rarer. The public source here is mainly a reactive voice used to illustrate an issue, in contrast to elite sources, and therefore with no real influence on the framing of a subject. However, some research has shown an increase in the representation of citizen voices over time. For instance, in an analysis of environmental news in British television, Cottle (2009) found that citizens were more frequently cited than scientific experts and government sources. Those voices of the public were, at the same time, mainly used to personalise the subject and to provide a 'human interest' perspective. It is hard therefore to view such types of interviews as part of a deliberative process, and by that we mean when members of the public are included on equal terms in collective decision-making and there is an open discussion and exchange of arguments going on (cf. Bäckstrand et al. 2010; Dahlgren 2006). Framing studies also show that appearance in news is closely related to the degree of influence over how a problem, its causes and solutions are framed (cf. Entman 1993). That is also why scholars continue to scrutinise and problematise the relatively poor representation of women in the news, a gendered pattern repeated in everything from science reporting (Chimba and Kitzinger 2010) to local news (Ross 2007).

Previous research has also shown that different kinds of media frame the role of citizens and 'the public' differently. The tabloid media, for example, tend to make more room for the citizens and give the public a more active role (Jönsson and Örnebring 2011; Hansen 2010). The dominance of elite sources over public and citizen voices in news media reflects a widespread news value and has been thoroughly discussed in news sociology research (cf. Shoemaker and Reese 1996). Lack of citizens' representation has also been understood, especially during the 1970s and 1980s, as linked to ideological discourses and discussed in terms of power and hegemony (Hall et al. 1978).

Having presented our theoretical framework and previous research on public participation and citizen roles in the news media, we will now turn to our empirical analysis. Here we focus on different framings and conceptions of the public in traditional and online news about biofuels for transport, using a case study approach. We will discuss examples of the specific ways in which citizens have participated in the ethanol debate, including which opportunities to do so different types of (mass) media have enabled.

Cases and analytical strategies

The use of fossil fuels is a global environmental problem that has risen to the top of the political agenda because of climate change and the urge to reduce carbon footprints.[1] Scientists, politicians, environmentalists, industry and business leaders, and journalists alike, have all shared concerns regarding carbon dioxide emissions. Similar worries have been identified in citizens' perspectives on climate change (Berglez and Olausson 2010). The biofuel ethanol (E85) has been widely promoted to motorists as a green alternative to fossil fuels and as an answer to 'Peak Oil', particularly in Sweden (Börjesson et al. 2008: 15; Christensen 2005). For about a decade, key policymakers and institutions from local to (inter)national levels have supported its use and have invested significant sums in research and development (R&D) activities to realise plans for industrial domestic production of 'second generation' ethanol (based on forest products). These decisions have been partly driven by a wish to decrease the country's dependency on imported oil. After years of rapid growth due to a number of political decisions favouring its use, Swedish ethanol consumption dropped in 2009. The governance of ethanol involves a tax exemption on renewable fuels since 2004, the implementation of a 'Pump Law' in 2006 requiring petrol stations of a certain size to provide at least one renewable fuel, free parking and exemption from congestion charges, plus a premium of 10 000 SEK (€ 1000) supplied by the state for every purchase of a new 'green' car (Swedish Energy Agency 2011: 13; Börjesson et al. 2008: 15).

Counterarguments pointing out problems associated with the production, distribution and use of ethanol have also been raised. These sceptical voices have gained more prominence in the Swedish ethanol debate in recent years. Today, biogas seems to be a more popular choice among 'green' consumers. Renowned motor journalists writing for national newspapers are among the opinion leaders that have been taking a clear stand against the use of ethanol instead of petrol or diesel (Egan Sjölander, forthcoming).[2] Scientists have also been divided in pro and con groups regarding this 'fuel of the future' (Eklöf 2011).

The polarised discourse regarding the benefits and flaws of this renewable fuel has not only involved decision-makers from different sectors, it has also engaged the wider public. Citizens have debated the issue on numerous occasions in both traditional and online media, writing letters-to-the editor, blog posts etc. We would argue that such debate has taken place to a relatively large extent, given the widespread decline in interest among the population in western democracies when it comes to public affairs and party politics (cf. Blumler and Gurevitch 1995; Lewis et al. 2005; Dahlgren 2011). Although the ethanol issue is complex, for many people it is probably more concrete compared to the vast and abstract problem of climate change. Therefore it is easier for a citizen to relate to and form an opinion about (cf. Sjölander 1998). To some it may come as no surprise that the fuel debate has engaged a wider public. Private motorists have been the main target for the national ethanol 'campaign', and car users have had to make up their minds about converting their existing vehicles from petrol or diesel or buying a new 'green' car.

As mentioned above, the Swedish promotion of the use of ethanol stands out in comparison to other countries. The governance of the issue has been sold by leading policymakers as an example of the nation's environment-friendly profile, that is, as a role model for others to emulate. The close cooperation between science/policy/industry regarding this biofuel, and the public's activity and involvement make it interesting to study. In this chapter we analyse ways in which citizens have participated in the ethanol debate. We also look into what opportunities for participation the different types of (mass) media have offered citizens. We have interpreted people that post comments online as members of the public unless it is evident that they are politicians or experts working in the field. Public participation is, as described above, defined in relatively broad terms to include both activity online and/or representation in the environmental news discourse. We have not distinguished between different forms of participation or levels of engagement, as Dahlgren (2011) suggests, with the exception of participants posting only one comment online compared to those who interact and take part in a more extensive dialogue with other readers.

Our empirical analysis is based on a study of two different types of events chosen from the Swedish media discourse on ethanol that attracted a lot of interest. We have chosen these cases since they articulate a discourse about which there has been public engagement, and, at the same time, they differ in relevant ways and thus provide us with a diverse empirical material on mediated public participation in environmental communication relating to ethanol. Our first case is a local media debate with global dimensions generated by investigative journalism, while the second case is staged primarily on the national scene and represents another journalistic genre, namely that of science/environmental reporting. The cases include print and online news media, as well as different types of outlets (broadsheet, tabloid and local press), and journalistic genres. Our main research questions are as follows:

(1) What different conceptions of 'the public' (including how the public position themselves, and how the public is framed by journalists) are applied in these cases and what are the main roles ascribed to the public/citizen in these events? How is 'the public' addressed and how is its perspectives represented and by whom?
(2) Does the public/citizen engage with the issue and what do they get to talk about? What type of public participation is performed and by whom?
(3) Can differences between traditional and online news media, and different journalistic genres be identified regarding public participation?

The Ethanol Dream

Our first case is based on an ambitious series of investigative journalism published in three regional liberal newspapers (*Norra Västerbotten*, *Västerbottens-Kuriren* and *Örnsköldsviks Allehanda*) in the summer of 2009.[3] The analysis builds on a content analysis of themes and arguments in the 114 printed newspaper articles including three letters-to-the-editor, and interviews with all 11 journalists and editors-in-chief involved in the production. Readers' comments posted on the newpapers' websites in relation to the series (about 150 in total) have also been analysed.

'The Ethanol Dream' series was a unique cooperation between different newsrooms in what has been labelled the 'BioFuel Region'. This densely forested northern part of the country plays a special role since a lot of R&D activities concerning the development of so-called second-generation ethanol, based on cellulose, are concentrated here. The hopes of developing and producing a new 'green oil' based on forest products and on an industrial scale have led local governments in three counties to invest significant amounts of money (1,4 billion SEK or € 1,4 million) in a locally based international company that produces and distributes ethanol (SEKAB).

The journalists working with 'The Ethanol Dream' set out to collectively scrutinise decisions taken by their respective local politicians to financially support this private business. They also tried to track down what had happened with the previous investments of 'taxpayers' money' in the company and who was responsible. Even if investigative journalism is relatively rare, scrutiny of (local) politics is routine work for reporters (Ekström et al. 2006). The initiative to start this investigation came from the editors-in-chief and all three were personally involved in the work. Together they introduced the series on the front pages:

> Today, the newspapers Örnsköldsviks Allehanda, Norra Västerbotten and Västerbottens-Kuriren start the common series 'The Ethanol Dream'. We have cooperated between newsrooms in order to raise a number of fundamental questions to the ones responsible, and in order to deliver the responses to you readers: How could the dream of the fuel of the future result in risking over one million of taxpayers' money? When did it go wrong and why? And who is responsible?
>
> (NV 2009 06 12; VK 2009 06 12 ÖA 2009 06 12, *our translation*)

The readers are addressed directly in the series (with 'you') and right from the start the public, as 'taxpayers', learn that they even risk having to end up paying for the whole ethanol adventure. They are in Beck's (1992) term a 'concerned public' but in a very general sense. At the same time, the local papers promise to exercise their democratic 'watchdog' function of people in power and to hold the responsible ones accountable. In this instance, the political role of citizens as voters is present. However, the public is primarily described as taxpayers in the series with the journalists acting on their behalf (as guardians of the money). Even if the public's interest motivates the whole series, no layperson or 'ordinary people' are heard in it apart from the first day's long feature article with two female SEKAB workers who risk losing their jobs and a short vox pop in one of the papers. The public is addressed in different, mainly indirect, ways, but on the whole has a very passive role in the series. This pattern echoes results from Lewis et al.'s (2004, 2005) research on how the public are constructed in television news in the United States and the United Kingdom. When asked about this absence of citizen voices in the series, one of the interviewed experienced reporters explained that 'I think I know what the public opinion is'. He also stressed that many, many readers get their say on the newspaper's website anyway. Right from the beginning, a channel for the readers to participate in the newsrooms was opened up in the form of a dedicated common e-mail address, asking the public for hints and tips about the SEKAB 'affair'. However, there were no visible signs in the news reports that the online user-generated content had been taken into account or drawn on. At the same time several of the interviewed journalists said that the series was generally well received by the readers. Some thought that the public's response had been surprisingly weak given the 'huge sum of money involved and as few as three letters-to-the-editor were received and published in the printed newspapers. Those authors praised the media's initiative to investigate, but one criticised the naming of SEKAB's CEO as 'Ethanol Jesus' (VK 2009 06 24). Another classified the investigation as incomplete since it lacked a review of ethanol from environmental and energy perspectives (NV 2009 07 13). The project leader for 'The Ethanol Dream' published a response in the same edition and emphasised that their aim was never to question the use of ethanol as such, only the money roll from the municipality-owned energy companies. Another of the journalists claimed that they decided early on not to discuss pro and cons regarding this fuel since the issue was so contentious, at least unless they could reveal the real truth about it. He also thought that that story had already been told and therefore was not relevant, even if of great public interest for motorists. These newsroom choices are part of the explanation why common positions in the commentators' field among the public, such as 'energy consumer' and 'motorist', were not reflected in the print media.

Looking only at the print newspapers, one can easily get the impression that the story about the fuel of the future did not attract much public interest at all. However, studying the web versions of the series reveals quite another picture. Online, more than 150 different comments were posted in relation to the series and the majority of them showed a high degree of engagement from the readers. As noted above, journalists did not appear to draw on these comments in their news reports, and very little was mentioned about the online discussion during the interviews with the journalists. One of the reporters mentioned lack of time as the main explanation for why he did not often follow up on this type of net-based response and debate. All this taken together suggests that public participation was of low priority for the professionals' work.

A dialogue between members of the public was also established in the commentator field and they reacted to each other's inputs, not least regarding how environmentally friendly ethanol is. A handful of readers reacted strongly to the claim by Chricke, who wrote 'that ethanol is a good alternative to oil' and that it is positive that 'our politicians dared to invest in SEKAB' and a new and environment-friendly technique in order to save 'the whole of Mother Earth' since the market do not (readers' online comments, Chricke ÖA 2009 06 12). The author labels himself 'green' and is happy if his tax is used to finance green techniques. Another participant with the name 'Realist' contests these viewpoints by referring to problems with the deforestation of the rainforest, causing carbon dioxide emissions and resulting in extinction of species. The author also refers to 'the theft of land from people that need it for food in order to produce fuel for Swedes' (Reader's comments, Realist ÖA 2009 06 12). Similar arguments against the use of ethanol have been heard at both the national and the global level in (mass) media as well as in expert and political debates.

Also several of the critical participants spoke from a position of taxpayers. About a third of all citizen comments expressed different kinds of distrust with the involved actors and institutions. Governing local politicians were the main target for the public's frustration, but SEKAB's leaders and the media itself were also clearly hit by the critique. An illustrative example of these viewpoints was expressed by a writer who called him/herself 'Sceptic':

[T]he whole affair turned out like this when the promises of a Swedish ethanol production contained ALL arguments that our politicians wanted to hear – everything from employment in rural areas, environmentally friendly, to a break with our oil dependency etcetera. EVERYTHING that sounds good. No wonder that they jumped on the train without any critical thoughts and common sense like 'If anything sounds too good to be true it always is'. And then when the reports about ethanol production in competition with food production in the Third World and increased food prices for the poor came, the politicians and others pulled out very quickly. 'Gö-ö-ö-öh ... did not think about that ...'. Politicians and the media are steered by political correctness more than anything else, and the slightest risk of being perceived as exploiters of poor people pricked the air of the dream like a balloon.

(Reader's comment on the VK website 2009 06 16)

Despite the global dimension of the issue, the discussion about 'The Ethanol Dream' was mainly kept within a local frame in the commentators' field, just like the use of sources by the professional journalists. As far as we could tell, very few, if any, of the criticised 'people in power' took part in the online debate. Even if it is likely that some of the reader's comments would have been sent in as letters-to-the-editor if the opportunity to publish online did not exist, we can clearly identify a difference regarding public participation between print and online news media, for example, when it comes to the number of people actually taking part in the debate. It was much harder to find other differences in these deliberations, for example, regarding forms or levels of engagement among the public, when comparing different newspapers and websites to each other.

The Wibe report

The second case that we have chosen represents a different kind of news story and unfolds around the publication of a research report. Like 'The Ethanol Dream', it sparked significant public debate among professionals and citizens alike. As mentioned, the event primarily unfolds on the national scene starting with the publication of the research review *The Carbon Dioxide Effect of Ethanol*, written by the late Professor Sören Wibe (2010). We have studied the print and online coverage including the public debate following the launch of the report in national and local media.[4]

The Wibe report was commissioned by the Government's Expert Group of Environmental Studies and the aim was to present state of the art research regarding the carbon dioxide effect of ethanol and its impact on food prices (Wibe 2010: 9). Growing expert controversies regarding these issues, in themselves a characteristic of the risk society (Beck 1992), formed the background to the study. In the press release, the Expert Group together with Wibe (2010) stressed the importance of this knowledge (for policy) since not only Sweden 'have ambitious and costly programmes to replace fossil fuels with bioethanol'. The author of the report was a professor in forest economics, as well as a relatively well-known politician in Sweden. Wibe had been a member for many years of both the Swedish and the European parliament (representing the Social Democratic party). At the time however, Wibe was the leader of a small EU-critical party called Junilistan. Although he was commissioned to undertake the review in his role as a professor/expert, public perception was also influenced by his other prominent role as politician. For instance, one of the critical readers rhetorically asks: 'Is Wibe not a climate sceptic? And when does a party leader speak in favour of anything else then [sic] his party?' (Signature Cykla mera, SvD website 2010 01 19). The frequently blurred boundaries between science and politics in media-centred late modern societies are illustrated in this case (Beck 1992; Cottle 2009).

The growing importance of news management is also apparent (Enbom 2009). For instance, Wibe and the Expert Group used a media strategy in order to expose the research results widely and to take part in the ethanol debate. Measured by the sheer amount of coverage in traditional and online (news) media, their attempt to reach out was relatively successful. Over forty Swedish newspapers covered the story the very day the report was published and Wibe was interviewed in both radio and television broadcasts. The polemic tone and 'unexpected' main message that ethanol does not decrease emissions of carbon dioxide helped since they matched central news values such as conflict and unexpectedness (Government's Expert Group and Wibe 2010; Schudson 1982).[5]

The very same day as the report was made public and a press seminar for journalists was held, Wibe published a debate article online in the second biggest broadsheet (the independent conservative newspaper *Svenska Dagbladet* with a daily circulation of 192,100 in 2010) where he strongly argued against the use of ethanol.[6] The main conclusion in his report, 'Ethanol worse for the environment than petrol', constituted the headline. The author stressed that not only the environment, but also the economy and the world's poor, would benefit from a complete stop to all support for ethanol. Referring to studies published in *Science* and reports by international organisations such as FAO, OECD and the World Bank, Wibe claimed that the current ethanol programmes, primarily in the United States and the European Union, unintentionally also lead to more carbon dioxide emissions globally. Wibe argued that ethanol production led to a parallel increase in demand for new land to be used for fuel, food or feedstock. Shortly after the article was published online, the major news agency in Sweden (Tidningarnas Telegrambyrå, TT) transformed it into a news story and distributed it to newsrooms nationwide. The vast majority of the media coverage is based on this TT article. Wibe's opinion piece was printed in *Svenska Dagbladet* the day after (SvD 2010 01 20).

Wibe's viewpoints were disputed in the same newspaper a couple of days after by the chairperson for the Swedish Association of Green Motorists (SvD 2010 01 22). The NGO placed emphasis on Wibe's political affiliation and accused him of being 'extremely negative' and not modern enough. Wibe in turn replied to Green Motorists accusing them, and the environmental movement in general, of dogmatism and of ignoring facts and politicising research (SvD 2010 02 02). Another group of researchers also wrote a critical response, stating that Wibe's conclusion lacked scientific grounds and that the research review was insufficient (*Sydsvenska Dagbladet* 2010 01 26). None of these authors discussed the issue from citizens' perspectives. One could say that the public view on the matter was absent from the printed press.

However, a lively online debate at several newspapers' websites about the good and bad sides of ethanol took place among the public, alongside the professionals' responses in the printed press.[7] This is where and when 'the public' enters the scene in the studied case since citizen perspectives are not addressed directly by Wibe (or the others). The first day as many as 187 readers' comments (260 in total), plus links to 16 different bloggers (32 in total), were posted on the SvD website discussing Wibe's point of view. Only one of the commentators mentions a professional affiliation in his/her self-presentation (Mattias Goldmann from Green Motorists). This activity from readers is no exception when it comes to discussions about the use of (bio)fuels, as we have pointed out above. The ethanol debate seems to engage a relatively large, primarily male, part of the public. This points to the important question of who gets to represent the public (at large). As in this particular instance on SvD's website, only two out of the 55 participants are female. In Aftonbladet's web comments, 93 per cent are men. The majority of the professional stakeholders that debate the use of biofuels in public, (motor) journalists included, are also men (Egan Sjölander 2010). This gendered pattern follows stereotypes regarding science and technology, cars included, that link them to masculinity which in turn can have a negative impact in terms of public participation, especially for female citizens (Chimba and Kitzinger 2010; Ross 2007; Sjölander 2001). Studies of online comments in general in Sweden show that about 5 per cent of the public make comments on news articles at least once a week and more frequently among young people. However, in contrast to our results, there seems to be little difference between men and women (Bergström 2008).

The content analysis reveals that the most frequent theme in these comments are different forms of critique towards ethanol. About 40 per cent of the comments next to Wibe's article are sceptical to its use, in comparison to between 10 and 15 per cent of the participants defending the ethanol programme. The most appreciated contribution (shown in the number of 'like' clicks) among Aftonbladet's readership is signed Congaman and he stresses, like several others, that they were right all along:

> Cars are my big interest. I and people like me have been arguing for years that ethanol is bad for the environment, but we have constantly been beaten up by tree huggers that accuse us of being idiots. The information was there for anyone that searched for some knowledge. But politicians and tree huggers were, as usual, not interested at all in basing their decisions on knowledge. Instead they used tax money to subsidise dirty ethanol and overtax the clean diesel. Who is responsible for all the thousands of consumers that politicians and tree huggers alike fooled into buying an ethanol car?
>
> (Reader's comment, Congaman on the AB website, 2010 01 19)

Congaman highlights here that people who can be understood as 'the public' – in their roles as motorists and fuel consumers and articulated as 'I and people like me', 'we', 'anyone' and 'thousands of consumers', but excluding tree huggers and politicians – have been a central part in the governance of climate change since ethanol-driven cars have been promoted as the solution. Another example of the public constructing themselves as motorists is an author signing him/herself as 'Ethanol', who demands comprehensive information from public sources regarding how environment-friendly ethanol is in comparison with petrol/diesel, and where it comes from. Further, (s)he argues that 'we choose ethanol today since it currently is the best option compared to petrol. As soon as other better biofuels exist we will transfer to them instead' (Reader's comments, Ethanol SvD 2010 01 19).

Another dominant theme in these texts is distrust of established institutions, including lack of legitimacy for decision-makers. The public articulate, in various forms, sharp critique of politicians, environmentalists and researchers alike. Government and the Green Party are the target for most of this critique. One of the commentators in the local press called Lars writes that

> The worst is that the environmental lobby with Maud [*Olofsson, then leader for the Centre Party, our addition*] and Maria [*Wetterstrand, then leader for the Green Party*] in the front will dismiss this report as complete nonsense. They cannot deal with facts, even if they think they are wise. What do you think will happen if the Green Party gets their way and phases out nuclear power?

The SEKAB affair is another example of this theme of distrust that is brought up. In these articulations, 'the public' is constructed in opposition to, or at least as different from, these criticised groups even if the word 'citizen' hardly gets mentioned in these discussions. Further, embedded in this critique is also the viewpoint that 'the public' is affected by others' decisions. Seen from a dialogic perspective, quite a large proportion of the comments are responses to previous participants. We have identified 70 such comments out of 187 when looking at the SvD comments. Quite a few also contain references to scientific sources and other mass media, such as public service television (SVT) and the UK *Guardian*. We struggle to see any differences regarding public performances between different media types, apart from a stronger connection to the local in the web comments in the regional press. It is clear, however, in these two cases that it is the citizens themselves that introduce the public's perspectives when deliberating about ethanol. Citizen views on the matter were seen as irrelevant in the journalists' work with 'The Ethanol Dream', and the public hardly even gets mentioned in the journalists' coverage and debate following the release of the Wibe report. Without the possibility to comment online, citizen voices would have been almost absent from the debate.

Deliberation and distrust – ways to look forward

The main aim of this chapter has been to identify and analyse different conceptions of 'the public' in environmental news in print and online media. We started off from the premise that public participation in mediated communication can be seen as a fundamental part of governing environmental risks. Using a case study approach focusing on biofuels for transport as a way of tackling climate change, and in particular the contemporary Swedish debate regarding ethanol, we analysed how citizenship and public participation are performed and shaped by different contexts for news production.

Based on this analysis, as expected, one of our main conclusions is that there are differences between print news and online news in terms of public participation, especially when it comes to the sheer number of people taking part in the debate. Differences regarding the level of engagement between different newspapers or journalistic genres are, however, much harder to find, perhaps due to the size of the empirical study. We can see, however, that dialogue between members of the public is often established in the commentator field in online media. Interestingly enough, no journalists took part in these online discussions. Instead it is mainly the citizens themselves that put forward the public's perspectives when deliberating about ethanol.

In traditional news, the public are generally addressed as an anonymous collective, as in references to 'the public opinion'. Such references are often powerful in our society and since these types of interpretations are made by so many stakeholders, it is important to reflect upon the power to represent public opinion (cf. Myers 2004). In 'The Ethanol Dream' case, the journalists themselves claimed to know public opinion and the investigative reporting was undertaken on behalf of the public as taxpayers. However, citizen perspectives on the matter were not considered important to write about in the series. In the second case as well, there are few references to 'the public' or citizens' perspectives, if any at all in the printed press.

Studies before this one have shown that mediated discourse is an elite discourse to a large extent, allowing experts/scientists and other officials to take most of the mediated space. The relatively marginalised role of the citizens is also confirmed in our cases, even if there are opportunities for public deliberation and citizen involvement in the online news media that we have studied. At a very general level, it can be stated that the new media environment and the interactive character of the online media actually can strengthen deliberative processes, as well as promote more inclusive decision-making processes in the area of environmental risk governance and form a springboard for the mobilisation of 'publics' in grassroots activism. Traditional forms of deliberation have mainly taken place at a national level and there are several obstacles to deliberation on global environmental issues (cf. Bäckstrand 2003). The media and perhaps especially online media could play a crucial role in this context.

Another major observation that can be made from our analysis of the ethanol debate is that participation is related to issues of (dis)trust in many ways. On the one hand, frustration can spark public engagement, for example, in online media. On the other hand, repeated critique, for example, of established forms and institutions for decisions-making can reinforce distrust among citizens and in turn undermine possibilities for further participation in elections.

According to Nip (2006: 9) and Anderson (1983) the interactive element of the deliberation online that took place in the studied cases regarding this biofuel can also help to create a sense of belonging and community among the citizens. However, there are a number of challenges and limitations to this mediated deliberation. The public is mainly placed in a reactive position in the news discourse, and female opinion-leaders and citizens play a marginalised role. Besides, many online features are actually not used to their full deliberative potential since the public only on occasions take an active part in the production process, and also 'the public' does not include everyone. This points to a fundamental challenge in relation to the democratic and deliberative potential of online media, and that is the '95/5-problem', suggesting that only a small fraction of the public actually do engage in these processes. In our cases, there was, as highlighted, a clear predominance of men who took part. As Mythen (2010: 53) states, 'The real test for citizen journalism lies in the extent to which it is able to give a voice to the excluded and disenfranchised'. The ability to participate is unevenly spread and the question arises as to what should be done about the 'non-line communities' and differences in financial resources, education and technological skills (cf. Nip 2006: 224; Mythen 2010: 53). Ideally, deliberation is based on full information and the representation of different relevant points of views. Further, it requires equal opportunities for people to participate in this process, which is also hard to achieve.

'The public' are, in our cases, mainly conceptualised as taxpayers and motorists/consumers, both by the professionals in the press and by themselves online. This can be seen as a restriction in relation to traditional ideas of what citizenship means. According to Rosen (1997: 17), to position people as citizens means to treat them as potential participants and decision-makers in public affairs, and as a deliberative body. However, in media studies today there is a growing acceptance of a wider understanding of citizenship embracing consumption and hybrids of citizen-consumers, and breaking with the view of citizen and consumer as antithetical roles (cf. Cohen 2003; West 2006). Still, it seems plausible that a consumer frame indicates a possible ideological stance that could very well be different from the frame focusing on the public as citizens. In the environmental discourse this could be important in the constant tension between economic and environmental or social sustainability.

Journalists frame the public in different ways and assign different roles to them. They also decide who gets to represent the public (opinion). Framing is also a way for the media to enact their role in implementing and performing symbolic politics (cf. Entman and Rojecki 1993). In line with Habermas's critique of 'representative participation', Goven (2006) argues that the reduction of citizenry from the most fundamental part of democracy to a 'mini-public' (Goodin and Dryzek 2006), parallel to and with the same value as any other stakeholder, might end up in a 'symbolic de-valuation' of the role of the public in governance processes. This suggests that increased involvement of the public is a deliberative illusion, which actually decreases public influence. Further, constructions of 'the public' as an entity could easily suppress the plurality of heterogeneous voices of 'multiple' publics. The public is not an entity representing one particular interest or a unitary whole. This is, however, how the media in general tend to frame the public.

So then, what does all of this mean? What can be said about the role of 'the public' in environmental news discourse(s)? We believe that in order to come to terms with the environmental problems of our time, there is, following 'good governance' ideals, a need to involve different stakeholders at multiple levels (cf. Dahlgren 2011). We also argue that it is crucial to increase the involvement of citizens in such processes. Here, the media play a two-fold role; on the one hand they are a tool for raising awareness (agenda-setting) about environmental problems and creating common agendas to be acted upon, and on the other hand, the media could also work as arenas for public deliberation. Online media and different forms of citizen journalism have increased these possibilities, but it is still important to analyse whether or not this will increase or decrease citizen involvement and influence in political processes in the end. For one thing, to appear in the news does not equal influence over the agenda, and voices in the news are not necessarily 'primary definers' or in possession of any power to define problems (cf. Hall et al. 1978). Also, a too strong focus on mediated participation in mainstream media runs the risk of ignoring more radical forms of participation (cf. Carpentier and Dahlgren 2011) including the public(s) who choose not to take part in this mainstream discourse, but rather use and produce alternative media as well as participate elsewhere.

There is a clear political economy and a linear mode of public participation in news media (cf. Felt and Fochler 2010). Seen at a global level, the distribution of mediated participation probably will follow the same pattern as the (uneven) distribution of risks (cf. Beck 1992), thus increasing the global inequalities in risk management.

References

Aftonbladet (2010), Experter: Etanol ökar utsläppen. (Experts: Ethanol increase emissions). www.aftonbladet.se [Accessed on 20 January 2010].

Anderson, B., *Imagined Communities.* London: Verso, 1983.

Beck, U., *Risk Society.* London: Sage, 1992.

Berglez, P. and Olausson, U., 'The "Climate Threat" as Ideology: Interrelations between Citizen and Media Discourses'. Paper presented at the conference 'Communicating Climate Change II – Global Goes Regional', Hamburg: University of Hamburg, Germany, 2010.

Bergström, A., 'The Reluctant Audience: Online Participation in the Swedish Journalistic Context'. *Westminster Papers in Communication and Culture*, 5:2 (2008), pp. 60–80.

Brake, M. L. and Weitkamp, E., *Introducing Science Communication: A Practical Guide.* Basingstoke: Palgrave Macmillian, 2009.

Blumler, J.G. and Gurevitch, M., *The Crisis of Public Communication.* London and New York: Routledge, 1995.

Bäckstrand, K., 'Civic Science for Sustainability: Reframing the Role of Experts, Policy-Makers and Citizens in Environmental Governance'. *Global Environmental Politics*, 3:4 (2003), pp. 24–41.

Bäckstrand, K., Khan, J., Kronsell, A. and Lövbrand, E. (eds), *Environmental Politics and Deliberative Democracy: Examining the Promise of New Modes of Governance.* Cheltenham/ Northampton MA: Edward Elgar, 2010.

Börjesson P., Ericsson K., de Lucia, L., Nilsson L. J. and Öhman, M., *Hållbara drivmedel – finns de?* Rapport 66, Lund, Miljö- och Energisystem, Lunds Universitet, 2008.

Castells, M., 'The New Public Sphere: Global Civil Society, Communica Global Governance'. *The ANNALS of the American Academy of Political an* 616:1 (2008), pp. 78–93.

Carpentier, N. and Dahlgren, P., 'Introduction: Interrogation Audiences – Theoretical of Participation'. *Communication Management Quarterly*, 6:21 (2011), pp. 7–12.

Carpentier, N., 'The Concept of Participation'. *Communication Management Quarterly*, 6:2 (2011), pp. 13–36.

Chimba, M. and Kitzinger, J., 'Bimbon or Boffin? Women in Science: An Analysis of Media Representations and How Female Scientists Negotiate Cultural Contradictions'. *Public Understanding of Science*, 19:5 (2010), pp. 609–624.

Christensen, L., *Formering för samhandling: Framväxten av Biofuel Region*. Visanu 7, Stockholm: Vinnova, 2005.

Cohen, L., *A Consumers' Republic: The Politics of Mass Communication in Postwar America*. New York: Vintage, 2003.

Cottle, S., *Global Risk Reporting: Journalism in the Global Age*. Maidenhead: Open University Press, 2009.

Cox, R., *Environmental Communication and the Public Sphere*. Thousand Oaks: Sage, 2006.

Dahlgren, P., *Television and the Public Sphere*. London: Sage, 1995.

Dahlgren, P., 'The Internet, Public Spheres, and Political Communication: Dispersion and Deliberation'. *Political Communication*, 22:2 (2005), pp. 147–162.

Dahlgren, P., 'Doing Citizenship: The Cultural Origins of Civic Agency in the Public Sphere'. *European Journal of Cultural Studies*, 9:3 (2006), pp. 267–286.

Dahlgren, P., 'Parameters of Online Participation: Conceptualising Civic Contingencies'. *Communication Management Quarterly*, 6:21 (2011), pp. 87–110.

Day, P. and Schuler, D., 'Community Practice: *An Alternative Vision of the Network Society*'. In *Community Practice in the Network Society: Local Action/Global Interaction*. London: Routledge, 2004, pp. 3–20.

Durant, R., Fiorino, D. and O'Leary, R. (eds), *Environmental Governance Reconsidered: Challenges, Choices, and Opportunities*. Cambridge/London: MIT Press, 2004.

Egan Sjölander, A., '"The Ethanol Dream" Scrutinised – Local News as Investigative Journalism'. Paper presented at the *International Association for Mass Communication Research* world congress 'Communication and Citizenship', July, Braga: IAMCR, 2010.

––––––– *Mediala etanoldiskurser. En studie av hur den svenska nationella och regionala/lokala pressen hanterat etanolfrågan från 2005–2010*. Forthcoming.

Enbom, J., *Facket i det medialiserade samhället. En studie av LO:s och medlemsförbundens tillämpning av news management*. Medier och kommunikation Nr 13. Umeå, Institutionen för kultur- och medievetenskaper, Umeå universitet, 2009.

Entman, R. M., 'Framing: Toward Clarification of a Fractured Paradigm'. *Journal of Communication*, 43:4 (1993), pp. 51–58.

Entman, R. M. and Rojecki, A., 'Freezing Out the Public: Elite and Media Framing of the U.S. Anti-Nuclear Movement'. *Political Communication*, 10:2 (1993), pp. 155–173.

Eklöf, J., 'Success Story or Cautionary Tale? Swedish Ethanol in Co-existing Science-Policy Frameworks'. *Science and Public Policy*, 38:10 (2011), pp. 795–806.

1, L., 'Journalism and Local Politics. A Study of Scrutiny
ialism'. *Journalism Studies*, 7:2 (2006), pp. 292–311.

or Making Publics: Inscribing and De-scribing Publics in
(2010), pp. 219–238.

here: A Contribution to the Critique of Actually Existing
6 (1990), pp. 56–80.

eliberative Democracy Handbook Strategies for Effective Civic
San Francisco: Jossey-Bass, 2005.

'Deliberative Impacts: The Macro-Political Uptake of Mini-
:2 (2006), pp. 219–244.

Goven, ,.. .ce, and Biotechnology: Acknowledging the Context of the Conversation'. *Inc ... Assessment Journal*, 6:2 (2006), pp. 99–116.

Government's Expert Group of Environmental Studies and Sören Wibe (2010), Press release/ Pressmeddelande 'Etanolen minskar inte koldioxidutsläppen' (Ethanol does not reduce CO2-emissions). www.ems.expertgrupp.se [Accessed on 20 January 2010].

Gripsrud, J., 'Digitising the Public Sphere: Two Key Issues'. *Javnost – the Public*, 16:1 (2009), pp. 5–16.

Habermas, J., *The Structural Transformation of the Public Sphere*. Cambridge, MA: MIT Press, 1962/1989.

Hagendijk, R. and Irwin, A., 'Public Deliberation and Governance: Engaging with Science and Technology in Contemporary Europe'. *Minerva*, 44 (2006), pp. 167–184.

Hall, S., Critcher, C., Jefferson, T., Clarke, J. and Roberts, B., *Policing the Crisis: Mugging, the State, and Law and Order*. London: Macmillan, 1978.

Hansen, A., *Environment, Media and Communication*. Milton Park: Routledge, 2010.

Irwin, A., 'Constructing the Scientific Citizen: Science and Democracy in the Biosciences'. *Public Understanding of Science*, 10:1 (2001), pp. 1–18.

Isin, E. F. and Turner, B. S., *Handbook of Citizen Studies*. London: Sage, 2002.

Janse, G. and Konijnendijk, C. C., 'Communication between Science, Policy and Citizens in Public Participation in Urban Forestry – Experiences from the Neighbourwoods Project'. *Urban Forestry and Urban Greening*, 6 (2007), pp. 23–40.

Jönsson, A. M. and Örnebring, H., 'User-Generated Content and the News: Empowerment of Citizens or Interactive Illusion?' *Journalism Practice*, 5:2 (2011), pp. 127–144.

Kern, K., Joas, M. and Jahn, D., 'Governing a Common Sea: Comparative Patterns for Sustainable Development'. In M. Joas, D. Jahn and K. Kern (eds), *Governing a Common Sea: Environmental Policies in the Baltic Sea Region*. London: Earthscan, 2008.

Lemos, M. C. and Agrawal, A. 'Environmental Governance'. *Annual Review of Environmental Resources*, 31 (2006), pp. 297–325.

Lewis, J., Wahl Jorgensen, K. and Inthorn, S., 'Images of Citizenship on Television News: Constructing a Passive Public'. *Journalism Studies*, 5:2 (2004), pp. 153–164.

_____ *Citizens or Consumers? What the Media Tell Us about Political Participation*. Maidenhead: Open University Press, 2005.

Lezaun, J. and Soneryd, L., 'Consulting Citizens: Technologies of Elicitation and the Mobility of Publics'. *Public Understanding of Science*, 16:3 (2007), pp. 279–297.

Lidskog, R., Soneryd, L. and Uggla, Y., *Transboundary Risk Governance*. London: Earthscan, 2010.

Michael, M., 'Publics Performing Publics: Of PiGs, PiPs and Politics'. *Public Understanding of Science*, 18:5 (2009), pp. 617–631.

Mythen, G., 'Reframing Risk? Citizen Journalism and the Transformation of News'. *Journal of Risk Research*, 12:1 (2010), pp. 45–58.

Myers, G., *Matters of Opinion: Talking about Public Issues*. Cambridge: Cambridge University Press, 2004.

Nip, J. Y. M., 'Exploring the Second Phase of Public Journalism'. *Journalism Studies*, 7:2 (2006), pp. 212–236.

Pierre, J. and Peters, G. B., *Governance, Politics and the State*. London: Macmillan, 2000.

Reader's comments, Chricke ÖA's website (2009), www.allehanda.se [Accessed on 1 September 2009].

Reader's comment, Congaman AB's website (2010), www.aftonbladet.se [Accessed on 1 February 2010].

Reader's comments, Cykla mera, SvD's website (2010), www.svd.se [Accessed on 1 February 2010].

Reader's comments, Ethanol SvD's website (2010), www.svd.se [Accessed on 20 January 2010].

Reader's comments, Realist ÖA's website (2009), www.allehanda.se [Accessed on 1 September 2009].

Reader's comments, Skeptisk VK's website (2009), www.vk.se [Accessed on 1 September 2009].

Rosen, J., 'Public Journalism as a Democratic Art'. In *Public Journalism: Theory and Practice – Lessons from Experience*. Dayton, OH: Kettering Foundation, 1997, pp. 3–24.

Ross, K., 'The Journalist, the Housewife, the Citizen and the Press: Women and Men as Sources in Local News Narratives'. *Journalism*, 8:4 (2007), pp. 449–473.

Saunier, R. E. and Meganck, R. A., *Dictionary and Introduction to Global Environmental Governance*. London: Earthscan, 2007.

Schudson, M., 'The Politics of Narrative Form: The Emergence of News Conventions in Print and Television'. *Daedalus*, III (1982), pp. 97–112.

Shoemaker, P. and Reese, S., *Mediating the Message: Theories of Influences on Mass Media Content*. White Plains: Longman, 1996.

Sjölander, A., 'Opinionsbildningen – en kärnfråga. En studie av TV-nyheternas rapportering från förstudierna i Storuman och Malå kommun'. In R. Lidskog (ed.), *Kommunerna och kärnavfallet. Svensk kärnavfallspolitik på 1990-talet*, pp. 181–210. Stockholm: Carlssons, 1998.

————— 'En könad kärnfråga'. In B. Lundgren and L. Martinsson (eds), *Bestämma, benämna, betvivla. Kulturvetenskapliga perspektiv på kön, sexualitet och politik*.Lund: Studentlitteratur, 2001, pp. 105–128.

Svenska Dagbladet (2010), 'Etanol större miljöbov än bensin' (Ethanol worse for the environment than petrol). By Sören Wibe. www.svd.se [Accessed on 20 January 2010].

Swedish Energy Agency/Statens energimyndighet, *Transportsektorns energianvändning2010*, ES 2011:05, Eskilstuna, Swedish Energy Agency, 2011.

The Swedish Association of Green Motorists/Gröna bilister. http://www.gronabilister.se/ [Accessed on 1 February 2010].

Thurman, N., 'Forums for Citizen Journalists? Adoption of User Generated Content Initiatives by Online News Media'. *New Media and Society*, 10:1 (2008), pp. 139–157.

Thurman, N. and Hermida, A., 'A Clash of Cultures: The Integration of User-Generated Content within Professional Journalistic Frameworks at British Newspaper Websites'. *Journalism Practice*, 2:3 (2008), pp. 343–356.

Trenz, H. J., 'Digital Media and the Return of the Representative Public Sphere'. *Javnost: The Public*, 16:1 (2009), pp. 33–46.

West, E., 'Mediating Citizenship through the Lens of Consumerism: Frames in the American Medicare Reform Debates of 2003–2004'. *Social Semiotics*, 16:2 (2006), pp. 243–261.

Whiteside, K. H., *Precautionary Politics: Principle and Practice in Confronting Environmental Risk*. Cambridge, MA: The MIT Press, 2006.

Wibe, S., *Etanolens koldioxideffekter - en översikt av forskningsläget, Rapport till Expertgruppen för miljöstudier, 2010:1*, Stockholm: Regeringskansliet, Finansdepartementet, 2010.

Örnebring, H., 'The Consumer as Producer – of What? User-Generated Tabloid Content in The Sun (UK) and Aftonbladet (Sweden)'. *Journalism Studies*, 9:5 (2008), pp. 771–785.

Mass media and unpublished sources

Norra Västerbotten

NV (2009 06 12) 'Vad gick fel?' (What went wrong?). Published in Norra Västerbotten 12 June 2009.

NV (2009 07 13) 'Ofullständig granskning av Sekabaffären' (Non-complete investigation about the Sekab affair). By En miljömupp. Published in Norra Västerbotten 13 July 2009.

NV (2009 07 13) 'Svar direkt:' (Direct response). By Bertholof Brännström, journalist på VK och projektledare för Sekabgranskningen. Published in Norra Västerbotten 13 July 2009.

Svenska Dagbladet

SvD (2010 01 20) 'Etanol storre miljöbov än bensin' (Ethanol worse for the environment than petrol). By Sören Wibe. Published in Svenska Dagbladet 20 January 2010.

SvD (2010 01 22) 'Replik: Etanol är mycket bättre för miljön än bensin' (Reply: Ethanol much better for the environment than petrol). By Jakob Lagercrantz. Published in Svenska Dagbladet 22 January 2010.

SvD (2010 02 02) Miljörörelsen mot sin intellektuella undergång (The Green's towards intellectual destruction). By Sören Wibe. Published in Svenska Dagbladet 2 February 2010.

Sydsvenska Dagbladet

Sydsvenska Dagbladet (2010 01 26) 'Fel om etanolens klimatpåverkan' (Wrongs about the environmental impact of ethanol). By Pål Börjesson, Lars J Nilsson and Göran Berndes. Published in Sydsvenska Dagbladet 26 January 2010.

Västerbottens-Kuriren

VK (2009 06 12) 'Tungt bokslut för Sekab' (Very bad result for Sekab). Published in Västerbottens-Kuriren 12 June 2009.

VK (2009 06 24) 'Intressant om Sekab – men oseriöst av VK' (Interesting about Sekab – but not serious of VK). By Bäst att tänka efter före! Published in Västerbottens-Kuriren 24 June 2009.

Örnsköldsviks Allehanda
ÖA (2009 06 12) 'Sekabs förlust i fjol. 328 miljoner kronor' (Sekab's loss last year.328 million crones). Published in Örnsköldsviks Allehanda 12 June 2009.

Unpublished sources

Recordings and transcripts from 11 interviews in 2010 with journalists and editors-in-chief from VK, ÖA and NV working with 'The Ethanol Dream' series.

Notes

1   The production of ethanol has increased significantly in recent years particularly in the US (using corn) and Brazil (from sugarcane) (Börjesson et al. 2008: 16). The 'Peak Oil' concept refers to the idea that the world has a finite reserve of oil and that it is running out rapidly.

2   The role of the (mass) media in contemporary efforts to introduce bioethanol as motor fuel in Sweden is the subject of a study by Annika Egan Sjölander and part of 'The Fuel of the Future: A Research Programme on the Science, Technology and Selling of Biofuels in Sweden' financed by The Swedish Research Council for Environment, Agricultural Sciences and Spatial Planning (Formas). Some findings from this project are presented here.

3   *Norra Västerbotten, Västerbottens-Kuriren and Örnsköldsviks Allehanda* are all well established and the dominant papers in their respective town/region. ÖA has a circulation of 17,000 and was established in 1894. NV, with a circulation of 24,000, celebrated its hundredth birthday in 2010 and VK, founded in 1910, prints 31,000 copies six days a week. For a comprehensive analysis of 'The Ethanol Dream'-series, see Egan Sjölander (2010).

4   The newspapers that we have focused on are the national broadsheet *Svenska Dagbladet* and the national tabloid *Aftonbladet*, plus *Västerbottens-Kuriren*, which is the leading local newspaper where Sören Wibe lived. All the newspapers published an article about the results of the report in their online editions the first day, which in turn generated a number of comments from the readers. We have studied this public participation and classified, for example, what subjects were discussed, the amount of dialogue between commentators and what gender/age the commentators were (if presented).

5   The headline in *Aftonbladet*'s online version rephrased it to be even more 'dramatic': 'Experts: Ethanol Increases Emissions' (AB/TT). Available: http://www.aftonbladet.se/ nyheter/article12093930.ab [Accessed on 19 January 2010].

6   SvD online. Available: http://www.svd.se/opinion/brannpunkt/etanol-storre-miljobov-an-bensin_4111731.svd [Accessed on 19 October 2010].

7   Most of the debate naturally took place at *Svenska Dagbladet*'s website, but comments were also published at other newspapers sites such as the one of *Aftonbladet, Dagens Nyheter, Göteborgs-Posten and Sydsvenska Dagbladet.*

Chapter 4

Citizen Action and Post-Socialist Journalism: The Responses of Journalists to a Citizen Campaign against Government Policy towards Smoking

Pavel P. Antonov

reviously unorganised citizens campaigned in Bulgaria's capital, Sofia, during Spring 2010 against the intention of members of parliament (MPs) from the ruling majority to cancel a complete ban on tobacco smoking. The ban had been part of the country's Health Act since 2009 and had been scheduled to enter into force on 1 June, 2010. In the almost complete absence of effective public participation mechanisms, the mass media offered a channel for citizens' arguments in favour of the ban to reach those in power and potentially influence their decisions. Journalists working in mainstream media newsrooms served as gatekeepers of this channel, their professional and personal judgements often determining the amount and quality of media coverage of the public campaign. Since journalists' judgements underpin the extent to which and ways in which the media represent citizen voices, understanding the justifications and circumstances that lead to journalists' judgements is important as part of an analysis of the ways in which citizens' voices on a serious environmental health issue are heard and acted upon by government in a post-socialist society. Based on the perspective of a journalism practitioner equipped with a set of social research methods, this chapter offers an account of journalists' engagement with citizens' demands for participation in the shaping and enforcement of anti-smoking legislation, an environmental and health issue of collective interest.

This chapter draws on a wider project that explores the impact of the spread of a particular discourse – the discourse of professionalism – on the everyday practice of post-socialist journalism. Designed as doctoral research in the field of geography at the Open University in the UK, the project aims to assess the specific tensions and interactions that appear within post-socialist journalism practice around issues of collective relevance like climate and environmental change. Building upon the analytical framework and empirical material of this wider project, the chapter focuses on the specifics of journalists' engagement with a collective social movement demanding participation in government decision-making about tobacco control.

The aim of the chapter is to enhance our understanding of journalists' responses to citizens' aspirations for effective participation in governmental decision-making about issues of collective social, environmental and health importance. In order to do so, the chapter empirically examines how journalists perceive and define their own professional and personal roles and obligations in a spontaneous civic campaign, aimed at preventing a planned decision of the government in post-socialist Bulgaria to liberalise tobacco control policies. The campaign group and the campaign itself was titled 'BezDim' ('Smoke-Free') and I took part in it myself as an active member. Journalists' practices of engagement with citizen campaigning in relation to government anti-smoking policy is a highly relevant topic for analysis from the perspective of public participation in science communication. It is important because policymaking about smoking generates broad public debate and requires collective action to facilitate effective public participation in government decision-making. Through the empirical study, the chapter contributes to the present volume's exploration of practices of articulating, marginalising and silencing citizen voices in different social, political and media contexts.

I will begin by introducing my analytical framework and the choice of Bulgaria as the empirical context. I will then discuss the concepts of 'dialogue' and 'voice' in the context of public participation in tobacco control legislation and the role played here by journalists in mainstream mass media. Further, I will delve into some notions of professionalism in journalism, which have been empirically tested in the course of my field study. After describing the specifics of the chosen public participation case and the methods and implementation of this research, I will present the chapter's main findings and conclusions.

Analytical framework

In order to analyse how journalists perceive and define their own professional and personal roles and obligations in a spontaneous civic campaign about environmental health, the chapter builds a theoretical framework based on perspectives developed across the social sciences including political science and media and communication studies. It draws on two perspectives to link public participation to the practice and identity development of journalists: the dialogic turn in communication, science and technology studies, conceptualised lately by Phillips (2011); and Nick Couldry's (2010) conception of 'voice' as a process of social empowerment.

Public participation as dialogue and voice

In a report, launched in August 2011, the World Health Organisation (WHO) confirmed that the involvement and cooperation of citizens, consumers and patients have become essential for good health-related governance and decision-making (WHO-Europe 2011). By suggesting that it is getting increasingly difficult for governments to make good health and environment-related policy decisions without engaging with publics, the UN's health policy body seems to side with a scholarly view that prioritises the normative democratic aspects of public participation (e.g. Coenen 2009; Fischer 2009). Here, governance is viewed as a field in which government and other societal actors collaborate in communication processes designed to lead to collectively binding decisions (Felt and Fochler 2010). The spread of this form of governance can be understood as part of a dialogic turn in which communication is conceived not as a one-way flow of knowledge but as a dialogue among participants where knowledge is co-produced collaboratively (Phillips 2011; Smith 2005). Among the different stakeholders whose voices are expected to be articulated in the dialogic process of public participation, journalists are of particular relevance as gatekeepers in relation to the presence in mainstream mass media of the collective voices of the public. In comparison, the access of authorities and political decision-makers to mass media coverage is traditionally institutionalised through the system of beats and government press offices, while the interests of the business sectors are increasingly well protected as well (Bennett 2002).

The seemingly underprivileged position of collective and public voices in the process of 'dialogue', as far as mass media are concerned, invites further conceptualisation of 'voice' as a collective value that goes beyond the views or voices of particular groups and enables greater diversity and social cooperation (Couldry 2010). Voice in this sense is a process that is closely linked to pluralism, diversity and liberal democracy – and to the process of 'dialogue' – as opposed to a dominant market and economy-related neo-liberal discourse, which heavily circumscribes collective participation in participatory forms of democratic activity. Public participation offers a fascinating meeting point of the two concepts, which provides an extra dimension to each of them: a stronger sense of participation, understood as interactivity, interdependence and reflexivity in the process of 'voice'; and emancipated prominence of collective public voices in relation to the ones of other stakeholders, such as government or business, in the process of 'dialogue'. From the perspective of public participation, it is important, then, to analyse the extent to which journalists open up for dialogue, and tolerate 'voice' in general, and the articulation of civic voices in mainstream media pages and news broadcasts in particular.

Understanding professional journalism

To understand the professional judgements and actions of journalists that enable or disable 'dialogue' and 'voice', a closer look at the notion of journalistic professionalism is required. The normative principle underpinning the journalism profession within the terms of the 'Fourth Estate' theory of democracy is that the free press should act as the watchdog, guardian or voice of citizens (McQuail 2005). But the social and democratic responsibility function of journalism has always been counterpoised by the persistent demand of media owners that it should reflect and serve their interests (Carr-Saunders and Wilson 1933, quoted by Albridge and Evetts 2003; McQuail 2005). An Anglo-American model of journalism pervades contemporary western media systems which is dominated by market ideas and commercialism (Hallin and Mancini 2004).

Over time, a discourse of professionalism in journalism has been constructed and utilised by managers in news organisations, by journalists themselves and by the public as well (Aldridge and Evetts 2003). Employing mechanisms of occupational socialisation and identity formation within the professional community, this discourse introduces effective self-discipline and control of journalists' working practice (Fournier 1999). This is how it works: first, the parameters of what should be considered professionally acceptable are set and imposed on journalists both by means of training and education and by in-house organisational controls; then journalists impose these parameters on each other as part of professional socialisation, and struggle to comply with them in order to maintain their professional self-identity. The discourse of professionalism is linked to the spread of market and economic values as part of a neo-liberal discourse across social fields including the mass media and journalism (Couldry 2010; Harvey 2005; Bourdieu 1998). Its consequences include, among others, the entrenching of individualism and increased denial of collective and social values by journalists (Aldridge and Evetts 2003).

The post-socialist context

What makes the post-socialist media landscape of Bulgaria an appropriate empirical context for the purpose of this chapter? The choice of Bulgaria can be seen as a response to Downing's (2008) call for expanding the knowledge of journalism practices in relatively less studied regions. Moreover, the choice is justified by the view that, as part of the post-socialist region of Central and Eastern Europe (CEE), Bulgaria belongs to a pilot testing ground for the neo-liberal doctrine (Smith and Rochovská 2007).With its own pre-1990 traditions of journalism weakened and lacking the safeguards and traditions of western journalism that relate to its democratic and social functions, Bulgaria – as part of CEE – has offered little resistance to the market- and economy-dominated model of journalism that advances from the West. On this background, it offers a suitable empirical field for examining journalists' engagement with collective environmental and health causes in relation to issues of democracy and public participation.

Campaigning for a smoking ban – the BezDim case description

The case description below presents an account of the events, developments and actions that led to the postponement of the smoking ban in closed public spaces in Bulgaria, focusing on the aspirations of a spontaneous collective movement to participate in a pending governmental decision on the ban's cancellation. This description builds upon research field notes, some relevant scholarly sources and news reports from the broadcast media and the press that could be accessed online.

A total ban on smoking in closed public spaces had been adopted by Bulgaria's Parliament in 2009, as part of a new Health Act scheduled to come in effect from 1 June 2010. A new parliamentary majority cancelled the ban in May 2010 and replaced it with a partial ban. Driven by ruling majority MPs with reported vested interests in the tobacco trade (Mediapool 2010), the ban's cancellation has been backed by the government of Gerb, the centre-right political party founded and led by Prime Minister Boyko Borisov (Konstantinov 2010; Yordanova and Simeonova 2010).

The ban's cancellation reflected inherent political and ethnic tensions relating to Bulgaria's outdated tobacco farming industry and state-owned monopolist Bulgartabac. Tobacco growing and processing in Bulgaria is concentrated largely in areas inhabited by Muslims, a minority that had experienced government oppression and forced expulsion during the 1980s. As a result, its participation in Bulgaria's post-1989 pluralist democratic system has been channelled predominantly through a single political party – Движение за права и свободи (Movement for Rights and Freedoms, MRF), whose leadership is concentrated around Ahmed Dogan (Anagnostou 2005; Todorova 1998; Creed 1995).

The announced intention of ruling majority MPs to propose the cancellation of the smoking ban by the parliament triggered a massive outcry in the social media during February–May 2010. Several Facebook groups in support of the ban gathered over 5,000 followers. On the morning of 19 February 2010, a small group of protesters appeared at the gates of Bulgaria's Parliament and arranged the burning of cigarettes alongside the staircase.[1] The protest was titled 'Smoke for the MPs' and was meant to symbolise citizen resistance to the non-transparent way in which tobacco industry lobbyists were attempting to cancel the smoking ban.

In spite of the small number of participants – about a dozen – the action attracted media coverage, which linked it to the much greater number of critical voices online (BTV 2010). This gave impetus and much desired legitimacy to the offline protesters, so they soon grew in number and range of ideas. They formed an online steering group under the name България без дим (Smoke-Free Bulgaria) and launched a website at www.bezdim.org. The name, BezDim – or Smoke-Free –was established as the generic title of the group and the campaign.

The ban's opponents issued a plethora of messages that were circulated by mass media before, during and after the ban's cancellation (Zhelev 2010; Ivanov and Tonchev 2010; Tsenkova 2010; Simeonova and Yordanova 2010). The key ones were structured around:

- the potential harm on the hospitality and tourism industry by a total ban on smoking in closed public places;
- the alleged impossibility of enforcing a total ban by the Bulgarian state;
- the view of the smoking ban as a violation of smokers' human rights and individual freedoms; and
- the view of smoking as an integral part of Bulgarians' culture and traditions.

Chief communicators among the ban's opponents included MPs from the ruling majority, Prime Minster Borisov himself, hospitality industry representatives and opinion leaders from the entertainment sector (Simeonova and Yordanova 2010). A few clusters of citizens favouring the cancellation of the ban emerged, primarily online, but in spite of the comparatively large number of smokers in Bulgaria, their activities were comparatively insignificant.

The composition of the BezDim group of campaigners was quite different, although BezDim has not been the typical activist group or NGO. Apart from me, few of the core group members had had any substantial experience with social movements or non-profit fundraising. While people of various social backgrounds participated in the BezDim street demonstrations, the majority of the core group members had higher education and stable incomes above the average. Group members were from a wide range of professional backgrounds and many had the ability to decide on their time which gave the campaign vitality. The campaign also received financial backing from voluntary donations.[2] Few celebrities and popular opinion leaders took part in the campaign's events, and the participation of well-known political figures in the group was deliberately discouraged for fear of politicising, and hence weakening, the group's position.

Facebook and e-mail have been the primary communication environments of the initiative. Its access to the mainstream media was far from easy. The BezDim initiative therefore had to be proactive and creative in securing traditional mass media channels to communicate its messages so that they could reach and influence the political decision-makers. In an attempt to boost its outreach and capacity, BezDim sought contact with existing NGOs and other civil society actors. As a result, in April 2010 the Smoke-Free Life Coalition was formed as an informal entity that was open to existing groups, NGOs and any other organisations sharing two goals: to have the total smoking ban reinstated; and to ensure the enforcement of tobacco control legislation in Bulgaria (Coalition 2010). The primary strengths of BezDim remained rooted in its non-hierarchical, very open profile which encouraged – with the help of the Internet – the unlimited participation of any individual members of the public who wanted to voice support for the smoking ban and prevent political decision-makers from cancelling it. This profile has remained unchanged throughout the period of research.

The communication messages of the group were shaped by ongoing discussions, mostly online, among members and followers of the initiative. As a campaign that had emerged in response to intended policy decisions, BezDim has had to constantly reflect upon, and respond to, the messages of the opponents of the ban. A deliberate, proactive attempt was made by the BezDim members to reframe the public and media debate with an emphasis on:

- revealing the role of the tobacco industry and trade (including illegal) as the true beneficiaries of the smoking ban's cancellation;
- portraying the ban's reversal as a backward policy move that contradicts the country's commitments to the EU and the WHO;
- portraying the complete smoking ban as an achievement and a step towards improving the wellbeing and lifestyle of Bulgarians; and
- highlighting the health and social arguments in favour of a complete smoking ban, particularly with regard to young people and children.

(Coalition 2010; BezDim and Coalition 2010)

Most of the initiative's actions between March and May 2010 were designed to communicate these messages.[3] Pro-ban campaigners rallied in great numbers on the streets of Sofia, challenged Borisov to a public health-jogging session held in one of the capital's parks, marched backwards in front of the parliament to show that a reversal of the ban was a backward step, and even sneaked into the parliament to demonstrate on the gallery during the first reading of the Health Act's amendments. The creativity and level of participation of these actions earned them press coverage and positioned the smoking ban high on the public agenda – much to the surprise of its opponents.

Such prominence made it possible for the campaigners to voice their messages and challenge the arguments of the ban's opponents. There was a heated public debate and almost equal media attention to both camps. Under these conditions, the smoking ban was finally cancelled by the parliament on 28 April 2010, following a last creative protest rally outside the houses of parliament (Iliev 2010). Its slogan 'A smoke-free cup of coffee for the MPs' was designed to challenge the existing stereotype that smoking is culturally unavoidable in Bulgaria which had been heavily exploited by the smoking ban's opponents.

Research methods

I have applied a mixed social research methodology (e.g. Pryke et al. 2003) in order to collect the data for analysis of journalists' professional understandings and choices that prevent, restrict or enable public participation. Qualitative ethnographic research techniques have been used in order to explore journalists' practices, understandings and choices (see e.g. Hammersley and Atkinson 2007; Machin 2002; Whyte 1991). Participant observation has proved suitable for collecting complex, intricate and often personal data, as required in this case. It has been applied in a range of engagement contexts that shape a journalist's professional identity.

The analysis presented in this chapter is based on field notes, documents, media publications, event descriptions and semi-structured interviews which have been processed with the help of qualitative data processing software.[4]

As a fellow journalist and former colleague, I have been able to negotiate access to, and perform participant observation in, two newsrooms. At the same time, in my personal capacity as a non-smoker, I have joined the core group of active citizens and have been a key member of the campaign against the reversal of the smoking ban in Bulgaria.

I have handled this triple identity – of journalist, campaigner and researcher – with utmost care. I have carefully assessed my own level of involvement, in order to minimize the risks of influencing the field that I am aiming to research. At the same time, open access to both the camps of journalists and campaigners has provided me with a precious possibility to observe and be part of interactions – formal and informal – between journalists and the collective social movement around tobacco smoking. These interactions included joint planning and events coordination, reporting, interviewing and other professional practices, as well as chatting over coffee, dinner and the internet. Observing the boundaries between professional and personal engagement to a collective cause, and studying the ways in which journalists define these boundaries have become key aspects of my research. Journalists' professional engagement with editors, fellow-journalists, administrators, human resource and sales executives, as well as media owners and management, has been observed primarily in the newsroom environment. Interaction with protesters, politicians, press officers, experts and other stakeholders to the collective issue of tobacco smoking has taken place mainly in public venues — the parliament, streets and squares where civic activities have happened. Finally, personal encounters of journalists with their friends and colleagues have been useful for observing the boundaries of professionalism as perceived and defined by journalists themselves.

Research results: Voices, participation and science communication

In this section I present the main research results. The results focus on citizens' attempts to get their voices heard and engage in dialogue with decision-makers and also on the responses of journalists to the civic campaign against the lifting of the anti-smoking ban. Here, I focus on journalists' own accounts of the professional limitations, norms and practical arrangements that underpin their actions and decisions in relation to the campaign.

Dialogue refused

Campaigning in favour of a complete smoking ban, the citizen campaign group BezDin simultaneously explored different avenues in order to further participation in political decision-making. As noted above, the Internet and social networks like Facebook provided outlets for their voice. But although the use of Internet in the campaign deserves further scholarly attention, I will now focus on two other methods used to secure the influence of the citizen campaign on government policymaking: formal public participation formats and media coverage. The aim is to analyse journalists' decisions and actions in the light of the broader picture of public dialogue on tobacco control legislation in Bulgaria.

In line with EU law and international policy instruments like the UNECE (1998) Aarhus Convention, Bulgarian legislation includes various formal public participation mechanisms. These mechanisms have encountered ineffectiveness (Taylor 2010; O' Brien 2009) and public participation practices in relation to the lifting of the complete smoking ban in Bulgaria in 2010 seem to offer further proof of this. The documented developments in the case reveal the general reluctance of political decision-makers to engage in effective dialogue with the representatives of the public. This has been apparent even in the few situations in which public participation is prescribed by procedural or legal requirement such as in the case of hearings on the draft amendments of the Health Act by parliamentary committees.

There have been no documented attempts by authorities to engage in any sort of citizen consultation or other kind of formal public participation exercise in relation to the intended lifting of the smoking ban. While groups who supported the proposed legislative change, for example a Restaurant Owners' Association and certain existing anti-tobacco NGOs, have reportedly participated in the Parliament's Health Committee hearings (Committee 2010), no such opportunity has been available to BezDim members who lack the authority needed to gain access to such venues. Citizens campaigning in support of the smoking ban have had to rely on formally registered NGOs and journalists to obtain information about the content of the hearings.

The BezDim campaigners have placed higher hopes on the mass media in their pursuit of dialogue with political decision-makers. From February until May 2010, when the ban was eventually cancelled by the parliament, the BezDim group purposefully and proactively sought to attract journalists' participation, support and attention.[5] Over this period the BezDim campaign made use of any participation opportunities offered by mass media and undertook activities that produced substantial news coverage. I shall offer a brief overview of these activities below.

After the first spontaneous flash mob action in front of the parliament on 19 February 2010, described earlier, the campaign members held their first rally across the capital on 21 March 2010, where creative placards were successfully used to visualise the campaigners' messages on the media pages and screens (Kojuharov 2010). Further, the campaign launched two public happenings: a collective jogging for health and a 'backward march' in front of the parliament, each designed to illustrate a specific key message of the campaign. The former happening was meant to communicate in a positive and appealing way the benefits from the full smoking ban in terms of healthy lifestyle. Notably, it was designed as a venue for engaging with political decision-makers, and the campaigners sent a public invitation to Prime Minister Borisov, known for his passion for football, to come and run with them. A day later, after neither Borisov nor any other representative of the government appeared at the jogging action, hundreds of campaigners marched backwards in front of the parliament to illustrate their key message that a withdrawal of the smoking ban would be a retreat of the government from the EU's shared policy direction in the field of smoking prevention.

Each of the above-mentioned events enjoyed substantial media coverage and attracted journalists' interest and engagement, and sometimes opposition. But the doors of state institutions and the ears of political leaders stayed closed for the protesters and their arguments. On a number of documented occasions, political decision-makers, including Prime Minister Borisov, have purposefully sought to avoid any direct debate or discussion with the BezDim campaigners. In a media interview Borisov refused the jogging invitation. Later, he personally prevented the participation of citizens supporting the smoking ban in a live television talk show in which he took part.[6] BezDim campaign members were actually in front of the television building already when an editorial team member informed them that Borisov had made their absence a condition for his own participation. On his way out from the television studios the campaigners attempted to communicate to the prime minister through a megaphone while his motorcade slowed down and stopped for a few seconds in front of them so that he could observe them through the darkened window of his armoured sports utility vehicle. Apart from raising obvious questions regarding the editorial independence of Bulgarian media, this episode reiterates the resistance of political decision-makers to any form of dialogue with the BezDim campaign.

The denial of dialogue by authorities was partially broken after an emblematic event had taken place: a demonstration within the parliament by a small group of BezDim protesters at the time of the first plenary hearing on the ban's cancellation. Carefully prepared and executed, the action succeeded in postponing the vote until a later date (Novinite.com 2010). Powerful images of citizens holding hands on the Parliament's gallery with non-smoking signs on their chests were picked by most news broadcasts on that day, and thus reinforced their voice. Remarkably, within a day after that demonstration and its widespread coverage by mass media, the Chairwoman of Parliament Tsetska Tsatcheva initiated a direct meeting in her office with representatives of BezDim and the coalition of NGOs to which BezDim were linked. The meeting was an isolated opportunity for the BezDim campaigners to engage in direct dialogue with top level decision-makers, in this case Tsatcheva and the ruling majority's fraction leader Lachesar Ivanov (Tsantsarova 2010).

The above suggests that Bulgaria's 'political machinery', in Felt and Fochler's (2010: 3) terms, is not well equipped to accommodate citizens' voices and has prevented effective dialogue from happening in the case analysed. My analysis now concentrates on the 'media machinery', if I could borrow the term, and how it enabled dialogue, with a focus on journalists' understandings, decisions and actions in relation to the citizen campaign on the lifting of the anti-smoking ban.

Journalists among campaigners

Here I draw on the theorisation in my analytical framework of journalistic professionalism as a discourse that enhances control and self-discipline, generally in favour of the media owners' interests (Aldridge and Evetts 2003). There are normative aspects of professional journalism that stress its social responsibility functions and the 'Fourth Estate' theory. Most of these aspects have been incorporated into the Code of Journalistic Ecthics of the Bulgarian Media(Council 2004) signed by over ninety mass media organisations. In my analysis, I examine journalists' own judgements as to the level of engagement with the citizen campaign that is appropriate given the norms of journalistic professionalism.

It is important to emphasise that many journalists participating in the research have not necessarily kept the BezDim campaign in mind when discussing their views of professionalism and professional norms with me and each other. While I give priority to empirical material directly related to the BezDim campaign for the purpose of this chapter, some data with no direct relevance to smoking has also been used where appropriate – namely, descriptions of newsroom practices and editorial formats that are applied universally and journalists' accounts on aspects related to professional and personal engagements with collective or individual causes.

One direct form of engagement has been the participation of individual journalists in the campaign's planning and activities, documented in the course of my field research. One of the flash mob protesters at the parliament's gates on 19 February 2010 held an editorial position at a mainstream newsroom[7] and the editor of an online medical portal joined the BezDim core planning group within the weeks that followed.[8] News reporters and other editorial staff from various newsrooms have offered access to sources, photos and other forms of assistance in the course of the campaign.[9]

I have observed these journalists' actions and sought to understand their motives and their judgements of professional norms with regard to their personal involvement with the campaign. In some of these cases the journalists have been very careful to keep their support and involvement with the campaign separate from their daily professional duties. At least one research participant's account has provided evidence that pressure had been applied on her by the proprietor of a specialised web journal to limit her involvement in the campaign.[10] The reported reasons for the pressure included concerns about the potential loss of working time and what she has described as editorial 'jealousy', caused by her writing and submissions to the campaign's website.

In other cases the journalists have been quite relaxed and open with their news desks about their involvement with the BezDim initiative. In one instance, mentioned above, a news reporter had tipped the campaigners about a forthcoming visit of Prime Minister Borisov to a live talk show in her television studio.[11] Notably in this case she had taken the initiative herself and coordinated it with the producers and hosts of the show who apparently found it a professionally sound idea to bring the campaign citizens into the studio. Borisov's firm refusal to engage in any dialogue with the campaigning citizens caught all of them by surprise and forced them to change their minds.

A remarkable line of action has been taken by *Capital*, a business weekly newspaper considered among the few 'quality' media outlets (Tabakova 2007: 317), with its editorial policy of commitment to journalism standards promoted by Reuters and other western economic media outlets (Roudnikova 2008). In February 2010 *Capital* launched its own campaign in favour of the smoking ban (*Capital* 2010), while a senior editorial team member was closely involved with the BezDim initiative in his personal capacity. *Capital* and its sister daily newspaper *Dnevnik* reported systematically on all the developments around the cancellation of the smoking ban. They also ran several features, interviews and other articles, offering in-depth analysis of the political and scientific debate around the smoking ban, systematically concluding that the arguments for its weakening and liberalisation were economically unsound. In addition, a 'Causes' section has been designed on the newspaper's website, and an editorial team member has been assigned to maintain the website and provide it with content. 'The complete smoking ban should remain' has been one of the first of *Capital*'s online causes, which remains active online to date (*Capital* 2010). A letter was printed on behalf of the editorial team and distributed to all MPs prior to the first plenary reading of the proposed cancellation of the smoking ban.

Capital's institutional stand in favour of the smoking ban has not been isolated. Another media outlet, national television broadcaster BTV, a subsidiary of News Corporation (Ibroscheva and Raicheva-Stover 2007) has indicated support for the BezDim campaign. Unlike *Capital*, however, BTV's interest in institutional involvement has originated from the marketing and management rather than the editorial team and has not been as prominent.

Impartiality, objectivity, neutrality, as opposed to bias and taking sides, have been among the concepts of primary interest throughout my field work, triggered by debates on their place in the changing normative framework of journalism (McQuail 2005; Bennett 1996). This is why, while observing and documenting journalists' individual takes on the BezDim campaign, I have carefully investigated for any sense of institutional pressure on them to either suppress or support it. This would have provided solid argument in favour of the hypothesis that the profile of contemporary post-socialist journalism in Bulgaria is moving gradually to serve commercial and corporate ownership purposes such as possible advertising revenues from the tobacco industry. The former would have triggered a difficult comparison between the merits of journalists' independence and the norms of balance on the one hand and, on the other hand, for them to serve society's interests in the light of the 'Fourth Estate' theory.

While many of the journalist participants in my research spoke of pressure from media owners filtering through editorial decision-making into their individual work, no direct evidence of institutional pressure on journalists in relation to their involvement with the BezDim campaign has been collected. Similarly, there are no indications that pressure has been applied on journalists in the opposite direction – to support the campaign. On one witnessed occasion, journalists at an editorial meeting have openly discussed the decision of their editors to publish a lengthy article about the motivation of campaigning citizens.[12] I shall offer a brief extract from my field notes of this case to illustrate the tensions in, and style of, debate:

'The text on smoking is very good. Good style. Lively style', a woman said, who was standing in the back. Several confirming exclamations followed. And then a slim young man spoke up loud: 'Why did we run it?' There was a moment of silence. 'Because something's happening that matters', [deputy editor] Nicola replied. 'When? Is this news?' the slim one persisted. 'Well well, but you are a smoker, aren't you?' someone laughed from the opposite side of the room. 'It is not about the debate around the [smoking] ban, it is about this people telling the story of how they got together', Nicola said. 'No, no, it is below our level', the smoker continued, 'and it is too personal to be [in the] Society [section]'. 'It is specific and about real people', Nicola argued. 'And it is not heavy', another voice added approvingly.

Field notes G054 from April 2010

The described episode demonstrates that journalists rely on their own personal criteria of professionalism in order to justify or question editorial decisions. But it also shows that group dynamics, peer pressure and shared understandings of what is acceptable and what is not for the decisions made in the newsroom are influential in shaping the decisions and actions of individual journalists with regard to enabling collective social voices and public participation.

Smokers among journalists

Regardless of institutional and group pressures, individual journalists' opinions on issues of collective social importance represent another important factor to consider when analysing their professional attitudes and actions. As seen in the episode described above, in the specific case of the BezDim campaign in Bulgaria, these opinions have often been influenced by journalist's personal status as smokers or non-smokers. While no statistics on research participants' smoking habits is available, I have tried to investigate the potential link between smoking and journalists' professional judgement in some of the interviews related to the BezDim case.

Like most other active members of the BezDim initiative, the journalists who have more directly supported it have been either non-smokers or former smokers. Yet, this has never surfaced in the internal discussions as a leading motive for their involvement. The BezDim campaign seems to have appealed to its participants predominantly with its commitment to responsible governance, the rule of law and functioning democracy whereby the public's interest is guaranteed.

On the opposite side, there have been a few incidents in which smokers within the journalist community have acted purposefully to weaken the BezDim campaign. On one such occasion, a cameraman from a national television channel openly confronted the flash-mob protesters at the parliament's gates on 19 February 2010. He was part of a group of photojournalists, accredited to the parliament to cover a different event. When asked to invite his colleagues to photograph the flash mob, he refused, quoting his status as a smoker as the reason. Further, he explained that he did not believe that smoking is a top priority problem.

Probably the most informative incident of a similar kind took place on 21 April 2010, when a group of citizens successfully staged a brief protest action with the parliament. The action had been carefully designed to secure a photo opportunity for the press at the time when the proposed legal amendments were being discussed in the plenary meeting.[13] In order to successfully implement the plan, the BezDim protesters had to obtain individual access to the visitors' gallery and keep a low profile until the start of the plenary discussion when they simultaneously stood up and revealed non-smoking signs to the photographers and the MPs.

This kind of action is not permitted in the parliament's rules of procedure, so it had to be organised and implemented surreptitiously, while at the same time the press had to be notified to expect it. A reporter for a national daily newspaper confronted the activists while they were still waiting in front of the parliament's gates. When informed discretely about the forthcoming action, she responded loudly that she was fed up with their 'circus' and that their 'trick should not work this time'. She then went on to warn the security guards at parliament about the imminent action. In spite of this, the demonstration was successful (Novinite.com 2010), with all the cameras recording it, including the one held by the smoker cameraman mentioned earlier. While fellow campaigners demonstrated in the gallery, a journalist cooperating with the campaign delivered a brief statement to the press outlining the purpose of the protest and the BezDim initiative. In a remarkable move, several journalists then turned on their colleague who had tried to tip the security and accused her of a lack of professionalism. No such accusations were made against the campaign-friendly reporter by fellow journalists.

The episodes just described, as well as a number of journalists' interviews, confirm the importance of peer-pressure in establishing a shared understanding of what is professionally acceptable and what is not. Such an observation suggests that the ability of journalists to self-regulate and impose common professional standards on each other may be crucial when they make judgements about whether or not a citizen campaign on a collective environmental, social or health issue deserves media coverage.

Professionalism in the spotlight

Journalists who have taken an active stand in support of, or against, the BezDim campaign have in fact been a minority. The majority have simply reported on the campaign or otherwise acted upon the topic of the intended cancellation of the smoking ban based on their professional instincts, judgements and editorial routines. One of them, a smoker, has commented on her reporting of the 'backward march' on 11 April 2010. Followed by a cameraman, she stayed with the demonstrators until the end of the event. Her news report, aired by a satellite news television channel, seemed very detailed and sympathetic to the BezDim cause. However, the journalist denied any sympathy for their cause. On the contrary, she explained, as a smoker she personally opposed the idea of a complete smoking ban in public. The event had been assigned to her as a reporter on duty. In her view, staying longer than the competitor television news crews helped her obtain more diverse footage. She explained:

> The others [did not have] the passing [of the march] near the Russian church where there was a wedding, and the slogans changed from 'We want to breathe!' to 'Bitter! Bitter!' This is something I included in my report but the others did not have it, did they?
>
> Interview A0096 – 97 – 98 from April 2010

The reporter maintained that her report did not carry any bias in favour of or against the aim of the protest – the maintenance of the complete smoking ban. She had simply done her job which she defined as purely informative, excluding any possibility of judging whether anyone's cause was right or wrong. Her description seems to draw on a set of professional norms revolving around objectivity, neutrality and bias which have implications for the quality of reporting (Bennett 1996; Boykoff and Boykoff 2004, 2007).

A somewhat different view regarding objectivity has been offered by a senior editor at a Bulgarian press news desk:

> I don't quite believe in independent, objective journalism in which one dispassionately reviews all sides, and does not make any judgements. I believe more in the kind of journalism that fights for causes.
>
> Interview C0107-08 from May 2010

In spite of what appears as a sharp contrast of opinions, both respondents seemed to agree on one point – that standing up for a cause that one personally supports or believes in is beneficial for quality journalism. Variations of this standpoint have been shared by the majority of journalists who participated in my research. The formulation above is instrumental in posing relevant questions regarding the selection of 'causes' and the grounds for journalists' 'judgements'.

While most journalist participants in this research seemed to agree on the need to engage with issues that matter for them personally, fewer were at ease with the idea of joining or otherwise supporting collective action. When asked about the types of causes they would engage with, several respondents mentioned charitable and other causes that would benefit certain disadvantaged groups or individuals. Such causes could be global or very local. They would vary from collecting donations for the victims of the earthquake in Haiti to helping to improve the conditions in orphanages or homes for disadvantaged children across Bulgaria.

Apart from intensely covering such causes of interest in their daily reporting or editorial work, journalists have spoken of other types of action they were prepared to carry out, or had already carried out. These included initiating charitable collections – with the endorsement of the media employer; personal visits and contacts with victims' families; and arranging meetings to personally lobby state officials or other decision-makers to take a desired action.

In contrast, journalists seemed much less likely to act in similar ways on socially important issues involving collective citizen action other than charity donations or signing petitions. In addition to the focus on tobacco smoking and the postponement of the total ban which could be seen as a Bulgarian issue in the context of EU-wide policy developments, the present research has also sought comparison with public and media communication on global issues of climate change or very local problems of nature protection (Boykoff 2011, 2007; Carvalho 2007; Jacques 2008; Jacques et al. 2008; Oreskes and Conway 2010).

Getting journalists to justify their decision to apply or suspend norms such as objectivity and neutrality has turned out to be almost impossible in a number of examples. Indicatively, minutes after suggesting that objectivity had been her most important norm while reporting from the BezDim protest rally, the same respondent offered a passionate defence of her personal and professional struggle to help an emigrant family obtain citizenship status for their children. Here is how she justified her choices to act beyond the norms of objectivity, neutrality and bias, in direct reference to the 'Fourth Estate' theory:

> This is my decision, you know, my personal decision. Most journalists I know do not do this. The norm is that you should release your little report, send the news on air, and move on. Sorry. I do not think this is right. ... To me the utmost expression of professionalism is to chase [decision-makers] until the end, to change the laws. Because this is [my] job, isn't it? The meaning of journalism is to be some sort of a regulator of what is happening, of the other 'estates'. To search, to investigate, to spot what is not right.
>
> Interview A0096 – 97 – 98 from April 2010

Such a viewpoint reflects the formulations of the Code of Journalistic Ethics of the Bulgarian Media (Council 2004). After listing the groups of norms which ethical journalists and mass media are expected to abide by, in four sections, the code contains a fifth one, titled 'Public interest'. It grants exemption from all norms listed previously if it can be proved beyond doubt that the public interest has been served. The code then goes on to specify three strictly limited definitions of public interest, of which one is 'protecting health, safety and security'.

Most of my interviews and participant observations of editorial practice reveal a rather gloomy picture of contemporary Bulgarian journalism. This picture includes growing disillusionment among journalists with respect to their chances of affecting significant social and political changes and of critically investigating and suggesting solutions to social problems. Instead, many of them have complained about increasing pressure to deliver a product that can be sold on the market by the media company – in line with the market principles of the neo-liberal discourse.

These trends have been visible in the newsroom environment as well. Market-related terms have advanced in the newsrooms' technical vocabulary, especially in television. Editors and editors-in-chief have been observed to share more of their responsibilities with producers and chief producers. Frequent staff changes, the circulation of journalists from one newsroom to another, a persistent work overload and lack of time for quality work, and loss of motivation have been frequently observed and discussed.

A head of the news has been observed delivering direct instructions by the owner of the media channel to the journalists, and has appealed to their loyalty to 'the one who pays our salaries'. To give another example, a media co-owner has spoken of the need to 'demolish at least the top row of the wall between editorial and sales'. All these developments in journalists' working practices have confirmed the relevance of Aldridge and Evetts' (2003) concept of professionalisation as a discourse that paves the way for the tighter control and self-control of journalists' loyalty to the interests of media owners. They have suggested a parallel between the reality of contemporary Bulgarian journalism and the state of affairs described by Pierre Bourdieu (1998: 17) as the 'structural corruption' of journalism operating through mechanisms such as market competition.

Conclusion

The chapter has outlined key results of my study of a citizen campaign against governmental policymaking and journalists' reactions to that campaign. A central aim has been to enhance our understanding of journalists' individual and professional judgements that have consequences for the ability of citizens to participate in decision-making about issues of collective importance. To achieve this, the chapter has applied an analytical framework in which effective public participation has been conceptualised in terms of dialogue and voice.

The case of the BezDim public campaign against the intended lifting of a full smoking ban in Bulgaria revealed significant reluctance among political decision-makers to acknowledge and engage with the voices of citizens. By comparison, the mass media have been more welcoming to the participation of citizens and the communication of the messages of citizen campaigners. Some in the mass media, such as *Capital* weekly and BTV, have even sought to embrace support for the ban on smoking institutionally but no institutional pressure on journalists to serve the campaign has been documented. Similarly, there is no direct evidence that journalists have been institutionally encouraged to promote tobacco industry interests, although many research participants have spoken of mounting pressure on contemporary Bulgarian journalists to serve the commercial and other interests of media owners in their work.

Individual journalists have taken part in the campaign's planning or have otherwise supported it in their personal and professional capacities. At the same time, there were several instances in which journalists on duty openly confronted the campaign members and questioned their goals and messages, justifying this in terms of their own smoking habits. Both types of cases demonstrate the importance of journalists' personal motivations and opinions in interpreting the professional limitations that determine whether and the extent to which they are prepared to open up for the voices of citizens' collective campaign. In addition, newsroom dynamics as well as research participant interviews have brought to light the importance of peer-pressure and group decisions in relation to judgements as to what is professionally acceptable and what is not.

The participation of journalists in the collective planning and implementation of BezDim actions has been conceptualised as a practical manifestation of journalists' commitment to the social and democratic responsibility functions of their profession, laid out clearly in the Bulgarian code of media ethics. At the same time, isolated acts of smokers among journalists aiming to undermine the campaign have been deemed unprofessional by their peers. According to my analysis, the discourse of professionalism underpinned journalists' actions regarding collective campaigns on environmental and health causes. Drawing on norms within the discourse such as balance, objectivity and neutrality, many journalists who participated in the research have agreed upon the need for them to act professionally in relation to social causes that they personally care about.

A dividing line emerged in the definition of the kinds of causes that journalists felt free to engage with. Many journalists were sceptical, and even openly negative, about the possibility of engaging with collective citizen actions in relation to government smoking policy. This may be a response to external pressure to deliver commercially viable products or an expression of their own ambition to meet a set of changing professionalism criteria. Under all circumstances, their reluctance to engage with collective citizen action suggests that there are similarities between the processes changing contemporary post-socialist journalism practices in Bulgaria and the general trends observed in the West involving the advance of market and economic priorities in the journalistic field, as described by Bourdieu (1998).

References

Aldridge, M. and Evetts, J., 'Rethinking the Concept of Professionalism: The Case of Journalism'. *British Journal of Sociology*, 54:4 (2003), pp. 547–564.

Anagnostou, D., 'Nationalist Legacies and European Trajectories: Post-Communist Liberalization and Turkish Minority Politics in Bulgaria'. *Southeast European and Black Sea Studies*, 5:1 (2005), pp. 89–111.

Antonov, P., 'Да бъдеш там. Без дим: Как обикновените непушачи станаха активни граждани, въпреки помощта на интернет' [To Be There. Smoke-free: How ordinary non-smokers became active citizens inspite of the Internet's help] [Online], in *Capital*, Sofia, Economedia (2010). Available: http://www.capital.bg/politika_i_ikonomika/obshtestvo/2010/04/16/888168_da_budesh_tam_bez_dim/ [Accessed on 29 December 2011].

Bennett, W. L., 'An Introduction to Journalism Norms and Representation of Politics'. *Political Communication*, 13 (1996), pp. 373–384.

——— *News : The Politics of Illusion*, fifth edition. New York: Longman, 2002.

BezDim and Coalition, 'Предизвикателство:до Г-н Бойко Борисов, Министър-председател на Република България' [A Challenge to Mr. Boyko Borisov, Prime Minister of the Republic of Bulgaria] [Online], in Sofia, Smoke-free Bulgaria Citizens' Initiative Coalition for Life Without Tobacco Smoke (2010). Available: http://bezdim.org/wp-content/uploads/2010/04/2010apr6_predizvikatelstvo.pdf [Accessed on 30 December 2011].

Bourdieu, P., *On Television*. New York: The New Press, 1998.

Boykoff, M. T., *Who Speaks for the Climate?: Making Sense of Media Reporting on Climate Change*. Cambridge, New York: Cambridge University Press, 2011.

Boykoff, M. T. and Boykoff, J., 'Balance as Bias: Global Warming and the US Prestige Press'. *Global Environmental Change*, 15:2 (2004), pp. 125–136.

Boykoff, M. T. and Boykoff, J. M., 'Climate Change and Journalistic Norms: A Case Study of US Mass-Media Coverage'. *Geoforum*, 38:6 (2007), pp. 1190–1204.

Boykoff, T. M., 'From Convergence to Contention: United States Mass Media Representations of Anthropogenic Climate Change Science'. *Transactions of the Institute of British Geographers*, 32:4 (2007), pp. 477–489.

BTV, 'Расте недоволството срещу облекчаване на режима за пушене' [Growing dissatisfaction against the liberalisation of the smoking regime] [Online], in *bWeb*, BTV News (2010). Available: http://www.btv.bg//story/154920-Raste_nedovolstvoto_sreshtu_oblekchavane_na_rejima_za_pushene.html [Accessed on 29 December 2011].

Capital, 'Да остане пълната забрана за пушене на обществени места' [Let the complete smoking ban in public stay]' [Online], in *Interactive / Causes,* Sofia, Economedia (2010). Available: http://www.capital.bg/interaktiv/kauzi/870898_da_ostane_pulnata_zabrana_za_pushene_na_obshtestveni/ [Accessed on 4 January 2012].

Carr-Saunders, A. M. S. and Wilson, P. A., *The Professions.* Oxford: Clarendon Press, 1933.

Carvalho, A., 'Ideological Cultures and Media Discourses on Scientific Knowledge: Re-reading News on Climate Change'. *Public Understanding of Science*, 16 (2007), pp. 223–243.

Coalition, 'Становище [Statement]' [Online], in Sofia, Coalition for Life Without Tobacco Smoke (2010). Available: http://bezdim.org/wp-content/uploads/2010/04/STANOVISHTE_JivotBezDim_07.04.pdf [Accessed on 29 December 2011].

Coenen, F. H. J. M., *Public Participation and Better Environmental Decisions: The Promise and Limits of Participatory Processes for the Quality of Environmentally Related Decision-Making.* Dordrecht, London: Springer, 2009.

Committee, Health, 'Доклад за първо гласуване. Относно: Законопроект за изменение и допълнение на Закона за здравето, № 054-01-12, внесен от н.п. Иван Иванов и група народни представители на 18 февруари 2010 г' [First voting report. Regarding: draft law for the change and ammendmend of the Health Act, № 054-01-12, introduced by H.E. Ivan Ivanov and a group of people's representatives on February 18, 2010] [Online], in Sofia, Forty First People's Assembly of the Republic of Bulgaria (2010). Available: http://www.parliament.bg/pub/cW/233doklad_ZZ_tutunopushene.doc [Accessed on 29 December 2011].

Couldry, N., *Why Voice Matters: Culture and Politics after Neoliberalism*, first edition. Thousand Oaks, CA: Sage Publications, 2010.

Council, E., 'Етичен кодекс на българските медии' [Code of Journalistic Ethics of the Bulgarian Media]. in National Council for Journalistic Ethics (ed.), Sofia, 2004.

Creed, G. W., 'The Politics of Agriculture: Identity and Socialist Sentiment in Bulgaria'. *Slavic Review*, 54:4 (1995), pp. 843–868.

Downing, J., 'Social Movement Theories and Alternative Media: An Evolution and Critique'. *Communication, Culture & Critique*, 1 (2008), pp. 40–50.

Felt, U. and Fochler, M., 'Machineries for Making Publics. Inscribing and De-scribing Publics in Public Engagement'. Vienna, Department of Social Studies of Science, University of Vienna. Accepted for publication in Minerva, 2010.

Fischer, F., *Democracy and Expertise: Reorienting Policy Inquiry.* Oxford: Oxford University Press, 2009.

Fournier, V., 'The Appeal to "Professionalism" as a Disciplinary Mechanism'. *The Sociological Review*, 47:2 (1999), pp. 280–307.

Hallin, D. C. and Mancini, P., *Comparing Media Systems: Three Models of Media and Politics.* Cambridge: Cambridge University Press, 2004.

Hammersley, M. and Atkinson, P., *Ethnography: Principles in Practice.* Milton Park, Abingdon, Oxon, New York: Routledge, 2007.

Harvey, D., *A Brief History of Neoliberalism.* Oxford: Oxford University Press, 2005.

Ibroscheva, E. and Raicheva-Stover, M., 'First Green is Always Gold: An Examination of the First Private Television Channel in Bulgaria'. In I. A. Blankson and P. D. Murphy (eds), *Negotiating Democracy: Media Transformations in Emerging Democracies.* Albany: State University of New York Press, 2007, pp. 219–237.

Iliev, N., 'Bulgarian MPs Vote to Ease Limitations on Smoking in Public Places' [Online], in *The Sofia Echo*, Sofia, Economedia (2010). Available: http://sofiaecho.com/2010/04/28/893632_bulgarian-mps-vote-to-ease-limitations-on-smoking-in-public-places [Accessed on 30 December 2011].

Ivanov, V. and Tonchev, T., '"Цигарена" коалиция омекотява забраната за пушене. Емил Димитров, депутат от ГЕРБ: Иначе правим 3 млн. престъпници' ["Cigarette" coalition softens the smoking ban. Emil Dimitrov, GERB MP: We make criminals out of 3 mln people otherwise]. [Online], in *24 Hours*, Sofia, WAZ Media Group Bulgaria (2010). Available: http://www.24chasa.bg/Article.asp?ArticleId=368478 [Accessed on 10 December 2011].

Jacques, P., 'Ecology, Distribution, and Identity in the World Politics of Environmental Scepticism'. *Capitalism, Nature, Socialism*, 19:3 (2008), pp. 8–28.

Jacques, P. J., Dunlap, R. E. and Freeman, M., 'The Organisation of Denial: Conservative Think Tanks and Environmental Scepticism'. *Environmental Politics*, 17:3 (2008), pp. 349–385.

Kojuharov, G., 'Фотогалерия: Шествие против тютюнопушенето на обществени места' [Photogallery: March against tobacco smoking in public] [Online], in *Dnevnik*, Sofia, Economedia (2010). Available: http://www.dnevnik.bg/photos/2010/03/21/876430_fotogaleriia_shestvie_protiv_tjutjunopusheneto_na/ [Accessed on 30 December 2011].

Konstantinov, P., 'Bulgaria's Ruling Party Ready to Qualify Ban on Public Smoking' [Online], in The Sofia Echo, Sofia, Economedia (2010). Available: http://sofiaecho.com/2010/02/18/860514_bulgarias-ruling-party-ready-to-qualify-ban-on-public-smoking [Accessed on 30 December 2011].

Machin, D., *Ethnographic Research for Media Studies.* London: Arnold, 2002.

McQuail, D., *McQuail's Mass Communication Theory*, fifth edition. London: Sage Publications, 2005.

Mediapool, 'Рехав протест срещу запазване на публичното пушене' [Scarce protest against maintenance of public smoking] [Online], in Mediapool, Sofia, Mediapool (2010). Available: http://www.mediapool.bg/рехав-протест-срещу-запазване-на-публичното-пушене-news163275.html [Accessed on 30 December 2011].

Novinite.com, 'Bulgarian NGO Thrown Out of Parliament over Smoking Law Protest' [Online], in Novinite.com, Sofia, Sofia News Agency (2010). Available: http://www.novinite.com/view_news.php?id=115309 [Accessed on 29 December 2011].

O' Brien, T., 'A Long, Brown Shadow? The Impact of Non-Democratic Legacies on the Environment in Portugal and Bulgaria'. *Perspectives on European Politics & Society*, 10:3 (2009), pp. 308–325.

Oreskes, N. and Conway, E. M., *Merchants of Doubt: How a Handful of Scientists Obscured the Truth on Issues from Tobacco Smoke to Global Warming*, first US edition. New York: Bloomsbury, 2010.

Phillips, L., *The Promise of Dialogue: The Dialogic Turn in the Production and Communication of Knowledge*. Amsterdam, Philadelphia: John Benjamins, 2011.

Pryke, M., Rose, G. and Whatmore, S., *Using Social Theory: Thinking Through Research*. London: Sage Publications, 2003.

Roudnikova, I. (ed.), *K15: Невидимата история на вестник 'Капитал' [K15: The Invisible Story of the Capital Newspaper]*. Sofia: Iconomedia, 2008.

Simeonova, D. and Yordanova, L., '(Не)пълна забрана на пушенето – рунд парламентарен: ГЕРБ обмислят забрана на цигарите в заведенията за хранене [(In)Complete Smoking Ban – Parliamentary Round: GERB consder banning cigarettes in the restaurants' [Online], in *Capital*, Sofia, Economedia (2010). Available: http://www.capital.bg/politika_i_ikonomika/ obshtestvo/2010/04/14/887278_nepulna_zabrana_na_pusheneto_-_rund_parlamentaren/# [Accessed on 29 December 2011].

Smith, A. and Rochovská, A., 'Domesticating Neo-Liberalism: Everyday Lives and the Geographies of Post-Socialist Transformations'. *Geoforum*, 38 (2007), pp. 1163–1178.

Smith, J., 'Dangerous News: Media Decision Making about Climate Change Risk'. *Risk Analysis*, 25:6 (2005), pp. 1471–1482.

Tabakova, V., 'The Bulgarian Media Landscape'. In G. Terzis (ed.), *European Media Governance: National and Regional Dimensions*. Bristol, Chicago: Intellect Books, 2007, pp. 315–326.

Taylor, M., 'Citizen Participation and Civic Activism in Comparative Perspective'. *Journal of Civil Society*, 6:2 (2010), p. 145.

Todorova, M., 'Idnentity (trans)formations among Bulgarian Muslims'. In B. Crawford and R. D. Lipschutz (eds), *The Myth of 'Ethnic Conflict': Politics, Economics, and 'Cultural' Violence*. Berkeley: University of California, 1998, pp. 472–511.

Tsantsarova, M., 'Цецка Цачева: Среща' [Tsetska Tsatcheva: Meeting] [Online], in *Calendar Evening News*, Sofia, Nova TV (2010). Available: http://bezdim.org/media/ [Accessed on 29 December 2011].

Tsenkova, I., 'Контрареволюцията на пушачите: Защо не трябва да се смекчава забраната за пушене в заведения' [Smokers' Counterrevolution: Why the ban on smoking in pubs should not be softened] [Online], in Capital, Sofia, Economedia (2010). Available: http:// www.capital.bg/politika_i_ikonomika/obshtestvo/2010/02/26/865364_kontrarevoljuciiata_ na_pushachite/ [Accessed on 29 December 2011].

UNECE, Convention on Access to Justice, Public Participation in Decision-Making and Access to Justice in Environmental Matters, Aarhus, Denmark, United Nations Economic Commission for Europe, 1998.

WHO-Europe, 'Governance for Health in the 21st Century: A Study Conducted for the WHO Regional Office for Europe', Baku, World Health Organisation Regional Office for Europe, 2011.

Whyte, W. F., *Participatory Action Research*. Newbury Park, CA: Sage Publications, 1991.

Yordanova, L. and Simeonova, D., 'Туризъм за пушачи? Според член на здравната комисия британски граждани избират да живеят в България заради либералния решим на пушене' [Tourism for smokers? According to a Health Committee member British citizens chose to live in Bulgaria because of the liberal smoking regime] [Online], in *Capital*, Sofia, Economedia (2010). Available: http://www.capital.bg/politika_i_ikonomika/obshtestvo/2010/05/13/900036_turizum_za_pushachi/ [Accessed on 30 December 2011].

Zhelev, V., 'Cross-Party Alliance Waters Down Smoking Ban in Bulgaria' [Online], in Novinite.com, Sofia, Sofia News Agency (2010). Available: http://www.novinite.com/view_news.php?id=113616 [Accessed on 30 December 2011].

Notes

1   Source: Field notes H0001 from 19 February 2010.
2   The communication practices of the BezDim campaign have been documented by statements and articles that have been posted on the campaign's website. I have also provided a first-hand account of the initiative's formation and its members' goals in a lengthy essay (Antonov 2010).
3   Source: Field notes H0037 from 31 March 2010.
4   Source: Field notes H0042 from April 2010.
5   All the raw and processed research data have been collected and stored securely in physical and electronic form in line with the ethical research requirements applied by the Open University.
6   Source: Field notes H0011 from February 2010.
7   Source: Field notes H0053 from April 2010.
8   Source: Field notes H0001 from February 2010.
9   Source: Field notes H0025 from March 2010.
10 Source: Field notes H0061 from April 2010.
11 Source: Field notes H0025 from March 2010.
12 Source: Field notes H0053 from April 2010.
13 Source: Field notes G054 from April 2010.
14 Source: Field notes H0061 from April 2010.

Chapter 5

Discourse Communities as Catalysts for Science and Technology Communication

Hedwig te Molder

In the spring of 2009, there was a wave of public unrest in the Netherlands in response to a government vaccination campaign against the human papillomavirus (HPV), an important cause of cervical cancer. There were countless reports of side-effects of the vaccine that were being hushed up, of the alleged lack of effectiveness and of the undue influence of pharmaceutical companies. Parents were not sure whether they should let their daughters be vaccinated and young women posted criticisms of the vaccination on a wide variety of social media. Policymakers, scientists and civil servants jostled with one another to assure the public that there was nothing to be worried about. 'That chap from the RIVM [the Dutch National Institute for Public Health and the Environment – the person referred to was Roel Coutinho, Director of the Centre for the Control of Infectious Diseases] keeps on saying that it's all old wives' tales, but the more he says it the less I believe him', wrote one of the mothers in question in an online discussion forum.

This is not an isolated example. It looks as if science is under attack from all sides. Climate change sceptics raise their voice on the Internet, nutritionists are accused of being the lackeys of industry and population groups that used to follow government directives docilely are now increasingly failing to respond to cervical cancer or swine flu vaccination campaigns. Scientists look back nostalgically to the time when they could make bold statements without being continually weighed in the balance and found wanting. The days when the label 'scientific expert' would guarantee faith in any pronouncement they made seem long gone.

But while the public debate about science has definitely become more intense, its root causes are less clear (see also Dijstelbloem and Hagendijk 2011). I will argue that the apparent opposition to the statements of scientific experts is diffuse in nature and not simply rooted in a dislike of science and experts. As part of the substantiation of my claim I will introduce a new perspective on science communication – one that aims to expose the dynamics of the interactions between science and society and may thus provide a new point of departure for communication.

This chapter is divided into three main parts, followed by a conclusion. I shall start by sketching the changing role of science and technology in our society and arguing that the implications of these changes for the practice of communicating science and technology have hardly been thought through yet. We are brought up with what I shall call happy science, and later in the public domain mainly confronted with constructions of grim technology – both of which are expressions of a limited vision of the social significance of science and technology.

In the public domain, fierce criticism of scientific knowledge is coupled with the almost unassailable position of this same science. As I shall argue in the second part of this chapter, this phenomenon can be understood if we view it in the light of the question: what is an expert opinion, and how is this expertise – consciously or unconsciously – deployed? In order to understand what is at stake in the interactions – sometimes noisy, sometimes less so – between consumer-citizens and scientific experts, we need to dissociate expertise from the traditional roles of expert and layperson, and look at the way in which knowledge and experience are mobilised in real-life settings and what effects this can have.

Research, mainly in science and technology studies, has shown interest in the performative dimension of dialogue between citizens and scientific experts, for example by looking at publics 'doing being a public' (Michael 2009), or the actual construction of publics in public engagement exercises (Felt and Fochler 2010). Also, there has been some consideration of the interactional dynamics of laying claim to different forms of expertise in public dialogue (for example, Kerr, Cunningham-Burley and Tutton 2007). My plea here is both for more detailed studies of interaction, and for paying more – but not exclusive – attention to communities that 'self-organise' in the public arena, thereby going beyond the dominant focus on forums regarding emerging science and technologies that are organised by governments or government institutions. To this end I shall draw on the related traditions of ethnomethodology, conversation analysis and discursive psychology, and use the term 'discourse communities'. Finally, I will illustrate the value of an interactional perspective on science communication through analysis of interactions about a new technology (a gluten-neutralising pill) in an online discussion forum for patients suffering from celiac disease and in face-to-face meetings between scientists and patients.

Science and technology from a social perspective

It was more than thirty years ago that sociologists and anthropologists of science decided to take a look in the kitchen of sciences (Latour and Woolgar 1986; Latour 1987; Knorr-Cetina 1981). Scientists were no longer interviewed *post facto* about how they had arrived at their results but were observed at work in their laboratory like some exotic tribe in the jungle. Latour and co-workers concluded that scientific knowledge did not merely describe reality but actually helped to constitute it. Scientific facts only become facts after they have been fashioned to withstand the storms of criticism they will encounter both inside and outside the laboratory. Scientists are handymen, fact-builders, not just random passers-by in the garden of reality.

Nowotny, Scott and Gibbons (2001) do not talk about science in relation to society, but about a co-evolution of science *and* society. They claim the emergence, alongside the age-old academic 'Mode-1 science', of a problem-driven, interdisciplinary 'Mode-2 science'. Mode-2 science blurs the boundaries between the private and the public domains, and is publicly called to account at unexpected moments. As a result, the production of knowledge is no longer the sole province of an elite in their ivory tower: the agora, the new public space where science is put to the test, now furnishes an important measure of the robustness of that knowledge (for a critical discussion of perspectives on 'new knowledge production', see Hessels and van Lente 2008).

Latour and his constructivist colleagues did not claim so much that the ivory tower of science was slowly crumbling away but rather that it had never existed, since the construction of facts always requires a network of allies, not just in the laboratory but perhaps above all in the outside world. Nowotny and colleagues showed that this activity is increasingly played out in the public gaze. It is more visible to society, and is sometimes intentionally organised to be so, for example in the form of public debates and hearings. In a complex and uncertain society like ours, it is inevitable that the type and number of actors engaged in knowledge production should grow: 'not only does science speak to society (it always has), but … conditions are established in which society can "speak back" to science', according to the authors of *Rethinking Science* (Nowotny, Scott and Gibbons 2001: 245).

In this way, different generations of constructivist work have taken us beyond ready-made science – the congealed facts dished up to us in the science columns of the newspaper or the blogs written by science journalists – to science-in-the-making and science as social controversy. They show us that science in various ways contains more society, and *vice versa*, than we might at first sight have been tempted to think. Note however that these social influences are not always identifiable as well-defined interests. The above-mentioned studies of scientists in the laboratory undermine the idea that facts arise ineluctably from an unambiguous reality. Their construction often involves subtle room for discussion about what constitutes an observation or a reproducible experiment. This room for negotiation is the basis for the constructivist claim that scientific knowledge does not differ *essentially* from other forms of knowledge production. It will be clear that this claim, which challenges the superiority of scientific expertise, has not been greeted equally enthusiastically by everyone.

The findings of the first generation of constructivist studies elicited various reactions in the field of science and technology studies – and in that of the public communication of science and technology. In the first instance, they gave rise to questions about just how essential the differences are between scientific expertise and other forms of expertise, and the frictions between them. One of the main protagonists of this line of research is the sociologist of science Brian Wynne (1996; see also Marris et al. 2001). Wynne draws a distinction between various types of lay knowledge. These include knowledge about the – often inadequate – past behaviour of institutions responsible for scientific developments, and the knowledge that formal rules and regulations will not be fully applied in the real world. The idea here is that lay knowledge may differ from scientific expertise, but is not inferior to it. Wynne (2006; see also Irwin 2001) further shows that despite the increasing involvement of citizens in public debate, the tendency of scientists to engage in 'deficit thinking' remains undiminished. According to this line of thought, citizens reject scientific expertise because they do not know enough about the facts in question or about the processes leading to these facts, or they have little confidence in scientific activity as such. Scientists are not keen to engage in critical self-reflection, but they have no hesitation in pointing out the weak points of the lay public. Wynne revalues lay knowledge by giving it a clearly recognisable face, and showing what it may consist of. But on the same grounds, the approach can be seen to maintain the distinction between technical and lay expertise and partly reify it (see also Potter 1996: 38–39). In doing so, the interest is less in what precisely is at stake in the interaction between scientific experts and citizens. I shall be returning to this point later on in the chapter.

Partly in reaction to studies of this type which may be seen as upgrading lay knowledge, we see the more recent emergence of initiatives aimed at rehabilitating technical expertise. In a study of expertise in our society, the sociologists of science Harry Collins and Robert Evans (2002: 271) state that the urge to add more and more members to the class of expert involves significant risks. They write in this connection: 'The romantic and reckless extension of expertise has many well-known dangers – the public can be wrong.' Collins and Evans mention the successful campaign by the environmental organisation Greenpeace to block the dumping of the Brent Spar oil platform in the Atlantic Ocean, after which Greenpeace had to admit that their actions had been based on incorrect figures, and the drop in measles vaccinations in the UK due to reports of a supposed link between MMR (measles, mumps and rubella) vaccines and autism in children. A key question here, however, is what precisely these examples show. Is it simply a case of non-scientists or pseudo-scientists who were unable to judge the true significance of the facts?

Collins and Evans suggest that the boundary between scientific and lay expertise – they call it experience-based expertise – should be maintained to ensure that we are not left with a big grey lump of mush that gives us no leg to stand on when we want to reach a definitive decision about the rights and wrongs of a scientific issue. It is not that experience-based expertise is not useful; it is more that it is not useful nor legitimate in every stage of decision-making. According to Collins and Evans, current debates on science and technology are handicapped by the 'Problem of Extension' (2007: 10, my italics): 'How do we know how, when, and why, to limit participation in technological decision-making *so that the boundary between the knowledge of the expert and that of the layperson does not disappear?*'

In other words, it is the boundary between expert and lay knowledge that is at issue here in the first place, and that needs to be rehabilitated. Collins and Evans do not themselves use the terms 'expert' and 'layperson' without qualification, but distinguish between various types of omnipresent and specialist expertise. While certain types of expertise, such as experience-based knowledge, are important in political decision-making, another more specialised expertise is needed to make a contribution in the domain of science and technology.

But the pre-assignment of certain types of expertise to certain domains and stages in decision-making creates a new issue to be solved: who is to be the judge when the boundary between the political and scientific stages has to be defined? Collins and Evans apparently assume this to be a relatively unproblematic matter. In many public discussions, however, scientists claim that the scientific and technological phase has already reached a definitive conclusion – think, for example, of the old wives' tales ascribed to opponents of HPV vaccination – while other parties to the discussion claim that there are still plenty of factual uncertainties that need to be cleared up.

As constructivist research has shown, the boundary between science and society is not a clear-cut dividing line but one of the main points of discussion – perhaps the most important one – in debates between scientists and non-scientists. The sociologist of science Thomas Gieryn (1983, 1999) demonstrates that the answer to the question of where science ends and politics or society begins is not a simple side issue, but is key to the quest for intellectual authority and the denial of such authority to others. *Boundary work* in this context refers not to the policing of fixed boundaries but to the flexible setting and resetting of such boundaries with the aim of achieving key objectives. The distinction that Collins and Evans make between a scientific and a political phase ignores the difficulty of determining beforehand what knowledge is useful when, and the risk of missing out on valuable knowledge at a stage where that knowledge is neither expected nor permitted.

Probably more important than the question of the feasibility of the policing of the borders is the observation that this activity hardly ever seems to be useful in practice. We see examples nearly every week of debates about science and technology where the hammering on the facts and the discounting of the other party's facts seem to lead to little more than a stalemate. Apparently, 'hard' facts do not carry enough authority to end the debate or to get the right on your side – irrespective of whether the facts really are hard and whether the debate really needs to be ended.

In the Machiavelli Lecture to which I have already referred, Roel Coutinho (2009: 6) concluded that it would have been better in the vaccination campaign against cervical cancer if: 'we had not felt the need to refer to old wives' tales in the heat of the discussion about the HPV vaccine but had patiently explained, point by point, where all the counter-arguments went wrong'. While this statement is obviously an expression of good will, the question is whether this analysis of the problem is fruitful in the long run. It tends to lead in practice to undue stress on 'the facts', which are assumed to bear the main load of the argument. This does not mean that facts are not important, simply that the 'bare facts' do not provide an adequate basis for better interaction between scientists and the other parties concerned.

Boundary work, the laying of dividing lines between science and society, is neither good nor bad in itself. The assumption that the two are interrelated does not mean that we have to accept all mutual influences. What is important here, however, is the goals that are consciously or unconsciously served by this division and more generally what all participants in the debate – not just the scientific experts – achieve by deploying certain sources of knowledge or experience at given moments. Statements on online forums that HPV vaccination can lead to paralysis can be characterised as examples of lay expertise, but that does not tell us precisely what these statements are a reaction to or how they, intentionally or unintentionally, affect other people.

It should be noted here that when I use the term 'goals' above, I am not referring to the everyday definition that ascribes an intentional strategic purpose to the activities in question – at any rate not on the part of the researchers concerned. The goals in question are those oriented to by the participants in the discussion themselves, and that gain significance through the interaction between the participants, ranging from the construction of a particular identity to the assigning of responsibilities.

Our interest in the interaction between science and society should not limit itself to the organised arenas of debate. In this context, the question posed by Collins and Evans – how can we give participation such a form as to maintain the boundary between expert and layperson – is no longer so relevant. The one-sided decision as to who may or may not participate in the debate has long been taken out of the hands of the authorities or the bodies that organise such debates. *Society talks back*, say Nowotny, Scott and Gibbons (2001). I argue that society not only talks back but may actually initiate the talking.

However, we see relatively little of this dynamic picture of science and technology in current practices of popularising science. Happy science is still a dominant picture of science presented to us from our very first science lessons in primary school. I call it happy science – not to be confused with Nietzsche's concept of 'gay science'[2] – because this science is a finished product, with little or no evidence of the turbulent events that may have been involved in its creation. It has had the rough edges rubbed off before we catch sight of it. Mitroff (1974) put this idea in a slightly different way when he talked of *the storybook image of science*.

In contrast to this image of happy science, the technology we encounter in the organised public debates on emerging technologies is usually characterised as 'grim'. I use the term 'grim' here to refer to the fact that these debates – on such topics as biotechnology, cloning or more recently on nanotechnology – focus primarily and sometimes exclusively on the risks to health, safety, the economy and the environment that are involved (see also Swierstra and te Molder 2012). The happy science is transformed from a black box full of happy truths into a landscape crowded with potential hazards – a minefield. 'Happy science' and 'grim technology' contain a grain of truth but both have their limitations. For example, they do not reflect the interactional dynamic through which science and technology emerge. An understanding of this dynamic is crucial, for example, in order to explain why people seem to hate science at some moments and love it at others. To this end, you need to examine not so much the nature and content of expertise as such, but rather the relationships between the participants in the debate and what they achieve in these relationships by making use of the knowledge and experience available to them at particular moments.

Uncoupling the debate on science and technology from the roles of expert and layperson in the first instance will widen the playing field of science and technology communication. We will expand our perspective to cover not only the arena of organised debate but also everyone who has something to say, directly or indirectly, about science and technology.

This wider arena includes self-organising *discourse communities*, which sometimes claim or capitalise on their right to speak at unexpected moments. The *Verontruste Moeders* (Concerned Mothers, a Dutch online forum campaigning for 'more honest information about vaccination') is a good example, but so are the scientific experts taking part in the vaccination debates – not so much because they *are* a community, but because they present themselves as such in a certain context, claiming a right to speak on the basis of a specific expertise, for example expertise that non-scientists in the debate have no direct access to, and achieving particular goals in doing so.

In a study on activist health groups that have emerged from online discussion groups, Akrich (2010) points to the fact that non-scientific epistemic communities (Haas 1992), which engage themselves in policy enterprises in which knowledge plays a major role, often emerge out of opposition. They 'are created in response to/oppose other epistemic communities mainly formed by professionals, or at least groups that have a dominant position due to the authority conferred on them by knowledge' (Akrich 2010: 31). While these communities do not necessarily manifest themselves online, it is clear that the online environment offers unique opportunities for mobilisation.

In order to understand what is going on between and within these communities, we need to go beyond the mere arguments that they exchange and provide a fine-grained analysis of arguments-in-context. Consumer choice, for example, is often presented as an opportunity for the consumer to emancipate, but the 'choice argument' can also be used to define difficult questions as private issues and to remove them from the public agenda (see also Swierstra and te Molder 2012). Likewise, the statement that certain kinds of food are unnatural seems at first sight to be merely an argument against new food technologies but can also be drawn upon by citizens to claim new territory: I have the right to decide on this issue, not you. For insight into this action-oriented dimension of talk, the (often standard) cognitive perspective needs to be replaced with a truly interactional approach. As I will illustrate in the third section, such an interactional perspective shifts the focus from merely looking at evaluations of the pros and cons of a given technology to also analysing, in detail, what the participants *achieve* by introducing these evaluations into the debate at given moments.

From cognition to (inter)action

Let us have a closer look at this interactional perspective. It makes use of discursive psychology as developed by Edwards and Potter (e.g. Edwards 1997; Potter 1996), an approach that has its roots in ethnomethodology and conversation analysis. The basic assumption of ethnomethodology (Garfinkel 1967) is that members of society continually order reality so as to give it a rational, legitimate form. This ordering is not some kind of random sideline but constitutive for each interaction. If a question is not followed by an answer, or a greeting by a counter-greeting, the situation is given meaning by treating it as a departure from a certain rule or expectation. The participants in the conversation judge whether a given action constitutes an implicit accusation or is free from hostile intent by determining the status of this action with reference to a given norm. Norms are thus seen as reflexively *constitutive* of actions rather than standards that behaviour simply has to *comply with*.

We constantly attribute meaning to utterances by declaring that certain rules or expectations apply to them. It follows that language is not an objective reflection of reality but rather a toolbox that can be used to *do* things. Suppose a mother walks into the kitchen and tells her daughter, 'There's a whole pile of dirty dishes there', to which the daughter responds, 'Well, I've been too busy to wash them up.' It is clear that the girl treats her mother's comment not simply as a statement of fact but also as a complaint, since she responds by defending her actions (or rather lack of action). The pile of dishes has now become an accountable phenomenon; that is, it is treated as such by the girl.

This normativity can take various forms and is not always predictable. For example, we observed in a study of the new technology of nutrigenomics that participants held themselves and others accountable not only for activities that were associated with an unhealthy lifestyle, but also and particularly for those that were associated with a *healthy* lifestyle (Komduur and te Molder 2011). In other words, they treated the choice of a healthy lifestyle as behaviour that required explanation, not simply as something that could be taken for granted. The normativity of interactions is ever-present but not always observed – it is '*seen but unnoticed*' in the words of Harold Garfinkel, the founder of ethnomethodology.

Conversation analysis reveals the continual focus on what is 'normal' and 'correct', and the assigning of significance to language in this way, by studying the structure of everyday conversations. Conversation analysts prefer to work on detailed transcripts of natural conversations – in other words, conversations that are not brought about through the intermediacy of the researcher. They may vary from phone calls between friends to conversations between a doctor and his or her patient. One of the most striking characteristics of conversation analysis is that it does not confine itself to the study of 'important' conversations – such as political debates – but is also interested in seemingly inconsequential chit-chat. It takes work to determine what is normal and correct, and to assign significance to language, even in the most innocent of conversations. The ordering of our life is a task that is always with us, according to the founder of conversation analysis Harvey Sacks. The researcher should want to understand what this work consists of, and what it is consciously or unconsciously applied to. In a study that has become a classic in this field, Sacks (1984: 415) focuses on '*doing being ordinary*': the pursuit of ordinariness as a task that demands continuous effort, not just something that you simply are. For example, an emotional outburst from an expert in a public debate may require explanation, while a layperson who is invited to the same discussion would be allowed more leeway. Apparently negligible details not only make the conventional framework that we call 'society' visible and relevant, but also keep it in existence: '*institutions are ultimately and accountably talked into being*', according to the conversation analyst John Heritage (1984: 290).

Conversation analytic studies demonstrate that what people *do* with language, such as building up expertise or assigning responsibility, is not brought about on the basis of a single turn of the conversation but involves a whole series of turns. The meaning of an utterance can never be assessed without taking its interactional context into consideration. This may be a commonplace, but there are few disciplines within the field of the social sciences that take it as seriously as conversation analysis does.

Conversation analysts look at the things people do with their language – the interactional effects – through the eyes of the participants in the conversation themselves. 'Those facts don't add up' becomes an accusation if it is treated as such, for example by replying, 'I never said they did.' This is a theoretical principle, but it is also of methodological importance. The interpretations of what is said and done, which are available not only to the participants in the conversation but also to the researcher, form the main input for an understanding of the course of the interaction. Although I use the term 'interpretations' here for the sake of convenience, a conversation analyst would prefer to speak of the way a particular expression is *treated* by one of the people taking part in the conversation. This seems like a complicated way of describing the matter, but it can be ascribed to an important analytical principle: the researcher refrains from making judgements about the truth or authenticity of the thoughts and feelings expressed.

Assumptions about the truth or falsehood of descriptions mainly impede the understanding of the *course* of interactions. By putting reality between brackets (Heritage 1984: 228–229; see also Edwards 1997: 62) and temporarily suspending judgement on the truth or falsehood of statements about the world, we clear the way for what Whalen and Zimmerman (1990) call *practical epistemology*. This approach allows us, without prejudging the issues involved, to examine the way the participants in social intercourse use their expertise and to what ends, consciously or unconsciously.

Such an agnostic attitude towards cognition – motives, intentions, attributions, perceptions etc. – forms the point of departure of discursive psychology (for an elaborate discussion on the status of cognition in interaction analysis, see te Molder and Potter 2005). I will draw upon this non-cognitivist perspective on interaction to put flesh on the claim that I made in the introduction of this chapter, namely, that critical statements about science and technology are not necessarily evidence of an anti-scientific attitude. In the next section, I will illustrate the empirical application of this perspective with examples from a study of an online discussion forum for patients focusing on a gluten-neutralising pill.

Towards an interactional perspective on science communication

In a conversation analytic study of how members of focus groups talk *about* experts, and *as* experts, Greg Myers (2004) shows that there is no single source of authority that they blindly accept, or that puts an end to the discussion. Scientific expertise – referring to risks in this study, for example the risks of spreading mad cow disease (BSE) – is cited very frequently, and rejected just as often. This applies equally to the experience of the focus group members. However, unlike claims of experience-based knowledge, claims of scientific expertise often come with a built-in assumption that once they are put forward, this will immediately preclude the need for any further discussion. It is precisely this expectation, Myers argues, that seems to be challenged in debates.

These observations are in line with what I mentioned previously in connection with the discussion about vaccination against cervical cancer: scientific certainties are introduced into the debate in the expectation that they will put an end to the discussion. We could encapsulate this idea in a variation on the closing words of the *Rijdende Rechter* [*The Travelling Judge*, a popular Dutch TV programme modelled on the American TV show *The People's Court*]: 'These are the facts, and you'll just have to accept them.' Unfortunately – or not – however, 'the facts' often do not close the discussion but rather mark a new beginning.

Myers argues that expertise should not be seen as a fixed characteristic of certain persons, but rather as an *entitlement to speak* (see also Heritage and Raymond 2005; Sacks 1984; Whalen and Zimmerman 1990) This entitlement is reinforced – and not just by scientists – in all possible ways and by all available means, including an appeal to an authority based on scientific knowledge. The same entitlement is however undermined by a claim that the knowledge introduced is the alpha and omega of the discussion. The fact that expert knowledge is so often challenged seems due not so much to any doubts about its correctness per se – this also applies to other sources of knowledge – but rather to its claim of precedence, of a decisive voice in the debate that is not open to question.

Let us assume for the moment that expertise can be defined as 'entitlement to speak'. The conversation analysts John Heritage and Geoff Raymond (2005) argue that the right to speak and the responsibilities of speakers are regulated not just sometimes and in a random manner, but always and everywhere. If I, as the first speaker, say 'Science delivers hard facts', I am claiming the primary right to make this statement. Someone who replies, 'Yes, I think so too', not only agrees with my statement but also confirms my primary rights to make it. If, however, the answer is, 'That is indeed what science does', this lays claim to an independent opinion that existed before I made my statement. In this way, speakers show not only *what* they agree about but also *who* agrees with *whom* (Heritage and Raymond 2005). This example simplifies the interactional reality, but also illustrates the indirectness of negotiations about entitlement to speak.

The following examples from a study of an online discussion forum dealing with a gluten-neutralising pill provide detailed illustrations of what may be at stake in talk among patients and medical experts about a technology introduced by medical experts (te Molder et al. 2011; see also Veen et al. 2011). The discussion on the gluten-neutralising pill was part of an online forum for celiac disease patients (www.celiac.com). Celiac disease is a genetic disorder that causes an auto immune reaction to the wheat protein gluten, which results in serious damage to the small intestine. At the moment, a lifelong diet is the only remedy. This not only requires discipline, but is also difficult to implement as gluten is found in many daily foods.

The analysis below demonstrates that patients did not so much reject the technology on offer (a pill), but rather the assumptions indirectly underlying this offer. The question 'how much would you be willing to pay each day if you could take a pill that would let you eat a normal diet?' presupposes among other things that the patients definitely want such a pill and that the only potential problem is the price. Extract 1 shows a (self-reported) scientific expert introducing the pill. The analytic focus is on what the expert's question is *doing* – in terms of discursive action – by looking at how the participants in the online discussion forum *treat* the contribution:

Extract 1

How Much Would You Pay For A Pill? Cost of therapy

1   *Researcher (Sept 6 2004, 09:38 AM)*
2   *Newbie*
3
4   I am doing some research on developing potential new therapies for celiac
5   disease and am wondering, how much would you be willing to pay each day if
6   you could take a pill that would let you eat a normal diet? How much would
7   you pay per year?
8   (9 lines omitted)
9
10 *Sammy (Sept 9 2004, 08:04 PM)*
11 *Member*
12
13 I wouldn't give one red cent for a pill. I have taken pills all of my life
14 because of this disease. I would just keep on with the diet as is. I feel
15 better than ever and have more energy than most 60 year olds should have.
16 Pills? Thanks any way. Sammy.

The topic is initiated by a researcher, obviously not a celiac patient and in this respect an outsider in the forum. Notice how, by inquiring into the amount of money that patients would be willing to pay each day (5–7), the need or desire to have this pill is already presupposed. Second, the pill is presented as an *easy solution* to the disease in comparison to the current treatment ('a pill that would let you eat a *normal* diet', 6). Sammy's contribution (10–16) challenges the validity of both presuppositions. By saying that she 'wouldn't give one red cent for a pill' (13), she claims to reject the pill irrespective of the price. She grounds the rejection in her elaborate experience with pills (13–14). If you have used pills all your life, and the disease has ultimately been treated effectively by a diet, it makes no sense to go back on a pill and give up the diet and its pay-off ('better than ever' and 'more energy than…', 15). Sammy's reply thereby questions the assumption in the researcher's post that the pill will change her life for the better, and is therefore obviously needed and desirable.

In the introduction to another discussion thread, the possibility is raised that a pill 'may come'. Note how this introduction evokes a response that is very different from the one in the first thread:

Extract 2

If they came out with an anti-gluten pill thingy, It may come ... eventually

```
132   If they found a pill that would neutralize the effects of gluten on your body
133   (sort of like the pill people take who are lactose intolerant), would you use it?
134
135   Yes, definitely – all the time                              [ 18 ]   [43.90%]
136   Sometimes, but only when I am eating out                    [ 12 ]   [29.27%]
137   Sometimes, maybe once or twice a week                       [ 4 ]    [9.76%]
138   No, I'd be afraid that it wouldn't work                     [ 4 ]    [9.76%]
139   No, I don't think I could ever look at wheat the same way   [ 3 ]    [7.32%]
140   Total Votes: 41
141
142
143   Ronald (Apr 9 2004, 12:35 PM)
144   Advanced Member
145
146   It could happen, eventually.
```

The title of the discussion thread is formulated in terms of a possible future: 'It may come ... eventually'. Furthermore, the introduction does not presuppose a need or desire of celiac patients to have a pill; instead, participants are invited to answer a hypothetical question: 'If they found a pill ..., would you use it?' (132–133). While the responses to this question (135–140) point in the direction of a generally positive attitude regarding the pill, the question itself sets up an environment in which different options, including non-use, are inquired into rather than presupposed. The response pattern found in this thread, as exemplified by Ronald's cautiously optimistic response 'It could happen, eventually' (146), indeed treats the question as a possible scenario that is worth further exploration (for more on this, see te Molder et al. 2011).

This then illustrates that it is not the pill *itself*, but the assumption that patients will need and use it *as a matter of course* that is dealt with as disputable. Sammy (in Extract 1) rejects being characterised as a passive patient. She presents herself as a healthy individual, who is able to maintain her vitality in the face of adverse circumstances. By resisting the notion that they would straightforwardly accept the pill, patients constructed themselves as proactive, thoughtful people with a healthy way of living. Presenting new possibilities as cure-alls made the gluten-free diet appear as a hardship, and undermined the complexity of the patients' relation to their disease, including the positive values embedded in that relation. The study shows that an apparent straightforward rejection of a new medical technology is drawn upon by patients to display a concern not so much about the pill's impact on their health but about how the presentation of this innovation impacts their sense of achievement, or more precisely, their primary rights to speak in first position about their own lives (see also Veen et al. 2012).

A study of face-to-face meetings between scientific experts and celiac patients about a gluten-neutralising pill in the making (Veen et al. 2012) shows strikingly similar results. The meetings were organised by the Celiac Disease Consortium (CDC), a Dutch innovative genomics cluster consisting of representatives of scientific research, patient associations, dieticians, general practitioners and industry. The CDC organised the meetings to inform patients about current research developments and receive feedback on those developments from patients. Interestingly, the predominant yes/no interrogatives used by the scientific experts to ask patients about the future of the pill, such as 'Will you use that pill?', systemically biased the patient's reply in favour of acceptance of the use of the pill in question, including acceptance of presuppositions regarding the patients' quality of life (problematic) and the safety of the pill (100%) that appeared in the question's preface.

An example of this pattern is shown in the following extract that takes place after an elaborate answer to a patient's question about the pill. One of the patients observes a transition from information giving in the meeting to requiring patients' input:

Extract 3[3]

Group 1, 24:26-26:20

```
1 P1    So you really want to know what we ↓think of such a pill. (1.5)
2 Ex    Yes for us that is a eh very relevant question. (.)°Yes° (0.7) I
3       can imagine ↑right. What I hea:r here is of course like yes, the
4       diet is fine but it is hard. Hard to accept. Ehhh↓hh. (.)
5       Holiday a drag. Ehhh well the question is just (1.8) say such a
6       pill is coming. And this pill turns out to be completely safe.
7       (2.1) Will patients then ↑use it or ehhh (.) are we just sitting
8       around here ehhh developing [some-
9 P4                                [I guess we'll see how it ↑turns
10      out, hehehehhh
11      ((laughter))
12 P4   Yea [hhh]
13 P2       [Yes] I think it that it really depends
14      Because I think that the diet in the sense of eh (.) excuse me
```

15   not right now, that (0.4) seems much harder to me than that you

16   (.) know, well, >not↑allowed< that's clear, ↓done. So I will

17   ehhhh yes, for con<u>ve</u>nience's sake, that is (.) for yourself it's

18   difficult, °because something like° yes you don't really need

19   to, I don't need to be so-g loyal, because I <u>have</u> an

20   alternative, that feels different than I know what I'm up

21   against I cannot ↓eat it because >if I eat it< I get sick. (1.0)

22   So then I'm like <u>if</u> there is something then I would like to have

23   something that helps me get rid of it ↑across the- because eh

24   (.)>once in a while< tha- that doesn't do it for me.

25   (1.0)

26 **Ex** Yes.

27 **P3** Yes all the time or not all the time.

28 **P2** Yes <u>all</u> the time or not at all.

The patient's turn establishes what patients '↓think of such a pill' (1) as a new topic on the agenda. Although acknowledging the relevance of this question (2), after a preface (3–5), the innovator-expert ends up asking a different set of questions (5–8) that shift the focus to patients' *use* of the pill. This reformulation is achieved by a description of dietary practice as a burden ('hard to accept', 'a drag', 4–5). Furthermore, this description is presented as something the patients *themselves* have said ('What I hea:r here'). So the question the expert finally asks is accounted for as occasioned by the patients' own presentation of the diet as difficult.

The question offered by the patient in line 1 explicitly constructs the innovators as requiring information from the patients (*you* want to know what *we* think), and asserts no knowledge concerning a likely answer. In the question the expert poses, however, this information gap is much smaller. It is prefaced by a description of the situation of the addressees, implying that the questioner knows their situation, as well as the possible reactions they might have to it. It is just a matter of knowing which reaction is relevant here. This leaves much less room for epistemic maneuvering on the part of the respondent.

There is also a difference in the presuppositions set up by the patient's turn and the innovator-expert's. Wanting to know 'what patients think of such a pill' (1) presupposes that patients have an opinion about the pill but it does not make any assertions about how to frame this opinion or what it means for the development of the pill. The expert, on the other hand, asks patients to assume in their answers that a particular pill is on its way. The preface to his question (2–5) is set up as a first part of a contrast in which either the pill will be used by patients or it will have been a waste of time for its designers. The patient's turn invites patients' responses in terms of *asserting opinions*, the innovator's turn in terms of making a *choice*. This invokes a fundamental difference in the relationship between patients and innovators. In the first case, patients are involved in terms of their thoughts and opinions about the innovation process in general; in the second case, in terms of choosing between available options that have already been decided.

The first response to the expert's question (9–11) is constructed jokingly, followed by the patient's laughter and that of others, including the expert's. P4 displays reluctance to answer the question by not providing a type-conforming 'Yes' or 'No' response. This reluctance can be seen as resisting the constraining character of the expert's question. The joke is, of course, that this patient gives a literal answer to the question '*will* patients use it', by taking it up as a request to make a prediction about the future of patients' behaviour. By withholding an affirmative response to the expert's question, she also resists affirming what the expert constructs as being at stake in the question regarding use of the pill: 'are *we* just sitting around' suggests that if the pill is not accepted, it is the innovators who will be negatively affected.

The second response (13–24) starts with a type-conforming 'Yes' but proceeds to qualify this affirmation by making the response to the question contingent on another factor: 'it really depends on how you use it' (13). P2's description of a pill alongside the diet as 'much harder' than the current situation challenges the presupposition in the expert's question that the pill would make things easier for patients. Her account is a departure from what was asked for – namely, an answer to the question of whether patients would use the pill or not. Rather than taking the pill as a given, and evaluating it, P2 poses conditions on the *kind* of pill that she would want: '*if* there is something, *then* I would like to have something that…' (22–23). She treats the version of the pill that the expert is presenting as only one of more possibilities, thereby challenging the terms of the expert's question, in which the only choice is between affirming the option presented by the innovators and discarding it entirely.

The analysis shows how, in both settings, the innovators' questions build 'offers you can't refuse' by presupposing the absolute safety and/or efficacy of the pill, in contrast to the patient's problem-ridden life. In doing so, however, the innovators claim direct access to the patients' everyday life – thereby failing to treat them as having privileged access to their own experiences and having specific rights to narrate them. By resisting the question format and/or unpacking its assumptions one by one, patients are shown to (re-)claim epistemic ownership.

Conclusion

'The regulation of knowledge is among the most basic mechanisms by which social relationships are managed and constituted', says Raymond (2010: 104) on the relationship between expertise and identity. Opinions, truths and half-truths do not so much follow from a particular identity but rather form an integral part of it (cf. Myers 2004: 178). If we add to this the claim that science is the epitome of true knowledge, it is easy to understand why the reactions to scientific and technological pronouncements are often so fierce. It is not just the truth but our own identity that is at stake here.

It is no easy matter to look beyond the arguments as such and to widen one's perspective to include *how* these pronouncements are understood by those who take part in the discussion – for example, as an accusation or an infringement of one's entitlement to speak. But such an effort often makes the difference when we want to gain a better understanding of the interactions between science and society: an utterance that at first sight looks like a rejection of technology may then be revealed as a reaction to an infringement of someone's entitlement to speak.

Hobson-West (2007) showed in a study of childhood vaccination in the United Kingdom that rejection of the vaccination campaign set up by the authorities was targeted not so much at the vaccination itself but rather at the suggestion that what the authorities really wanted was blind trust from the population – and these were the same authorities who had in the first place trained the population to make independent choices and above all to learn to think critically.

There is a great risk, however, that such interactional concerns will not be recognised or acknowledged either by scientific experts and technologists or by the potential users of the technology themselves. The philosopher of technology Tsjalling Swierstra talks in this context of 'soft impacts' – foreseen or unforeseen consequences of technology that are treated as 'soft' and that elicit no response (Swierstra and te Molder 2012). While some concerns are difficult to recognise, as we have just mentioned, others stand out quite clearly but it is difficult to assess their real significance. A preliminary study (ibid.) of soft impacts in food technology has shown how concerns about whether food is natural or not can relatively easily be sidetracked. Scientific experts and technologists treated the issue of naturalness as a well-known, prototypical public concern that required no further examination. This may explain why the precise meaning of 'natural', and to what purposes it is put to use in, for example, public debates, remain unclear.

One of the important tasks of science communicators is to raise awareness of interactional concerns in people who are taking part in debates about science in the widest sense of the term. These concerns cannot be met or eliminated by concentrating solely on the 'literal' content of the arguments. The historian of science Steven Shapin (2007: 185) expressed this insight as follows: 'You cannot use better logic or more evidence to refute a different kind of concern'. Logic and facts are not used solely to transmit information; they are also drawn upon to perform different sorts of interactional business. This business may relate to *what* is and may be said, but also to *who* is the first, or the only, one allowed to address the issue in question. Such negotiation about the entitlement to speak is directly related to the identities we ascribe to others and to ourselves.

Our analysis shows that these concerns are often not or only indirectly available for the debate facilitator. Likewise, participants themselves tend not to have direct access to interactional concerns although, when confronted with them, they will recognise them immediately. The discursive action method (Lamerichs and te Molder 2011) is a method that aims to turn participants into analysts of their own discourse by making these interactional concerns visible and open for discussion. This is not only relevant for expert-designers or policymakers but just as much for users of technologies. Natural food may be reshuffled into a private consumer concern with which a food expert should not be preoccupied, but 'naturalness' may just as well be drawn upon by consumers to delineate their territory such that no expert is allowed in.

The method enables participants to reflect, consciously or not, not only on what they say but also on the effects of saying certain things, in certain ways, at certain moments – for example, what their questions convey irrespective of their intentions. Previous applications of the method in the context of adolescents' health-related behaviour (Lamerichs, Koelen and te Molder 2009) have shown that adopting a non-cognitive stance offers a non-threatening and attractive point of entry for participants. The questions asked by the facilitators – as part of guiding the participants through their own talk – invite them to look at what is *achieved* with people's utterances rather than to reflect on themselves as a person, or judge the behaviour of fellow participants. By providing a safe environment in which highly recognisable topics can be discussed and critical comparisons with alternative discursive strategies can be made, the method is also able to unlock participants' motivation to develop their own activities and enhance a sense of ownership in developing and implementing them.

The question '*Why that now?*', as conversation analysts so elegantly put it (Heritage 2010) – why that particular remark, at this particular moment? – should be part of the permanent armoury of the science communicator. He or she should learn to put it to different discourse communities – scientists, groups of citizen-consumers, members of industry etc. – and to (help) answer it, also, or perhaps especially, when accounts of science and technology are treated as 'old wives' tales'. This brings us beyond happy science by looking at facts in context and beyond grim technology by talking about more than the risks attendant on emerging technologies.

References

Akrich, M., 'From Communities of Practice to Epistemic Communities: Health Mobilizations on the Internet'. *Sociological Research Online*, 15:2 (2010).

Collins, H. and Evans, R., 'The Third Wave of Science Studies: Studies of Expertise and Experience'. *Social Studies of Science*, 32:2 (2002), pp. 235–296.

——— *Rethinking Expertise*. Chicago and London: The University of Chicago Press, 2007.

Coutinho, R., 'Het Gezag van de Wetenschap in Gedrang [The Authority of Science in Risk]'. Machiavelli Lecture 2009, The Hague. Available: http://www.stichtingmachiavelli.nl [Accessed 10 August 2011].

Dijstelbloem, H. and Hagendijk, R., *Onzekerheid Troef. Het Betwiste Gezag van de Wetenschap [Uncertainty Trumps. The Disputed Authority of Science]*. Amsterdam: Van Gennep, 2011.

Edwards, D., *Discourse and Cognition*. London: Sage, 1997.

Felt, U. and Fochler, M., 'Machineries for Making Publics: Inscribing and De-scribing Publics in Public Engagement'. *Minerva*, 48:3 (2010), pp. 219–238.

Garfinkel, H., *Studies in Ethnomethodology*. Englewood Cliffs, NJ: Prentice-Hall, 1967.

Gieryn, T. F., 'Boundary-work and the Demarcation of Science from Non-science: Strains and Interests in Professional Ideologies of Scientists'. *American Sociological Review*, 48:6 (1983), pp. 781–795.

——— *Cultural Boundaries of Science: Credibility on the Line*. Chicago: University of Chicago Press, 1999.

Haas, P. M., 'Introduction: Epistemic Communities and International Policy Coordination'. *International Organization*, 46:1 (1992), pp. 1–35.

Heritage, J. C., *Garfinkel and Ethnomethodology*. Cambridge: Polity, 1984.

——— 'Questioning in Medicine'. In A. Freed and S. Ehrlich (eds), *"Why Do You Ask?" The Function of Questions in Institutional Discourse*. Oxford, Oxford University Press, 2010, pp. 42–68.

Heritage, J. C. and Raymond, G., 'The Terms of Agreement: Indexing Epistemic Authority and Subordination in Assessment Sequences'. *Social Psychology Quarterly*, 68:1 (2005), pp. 15–38.

Hessels, L. and van Lente, H., 'Re-thinking New Knowledge Production: A Literature Review and a Research Agenda'. *Research Policy*, 37 (2008), pp. 740–760.

Hobson-West, P., 'Trusting Blindly Can Be the Biggest Risk of All': Organized Resistance to Childhood Vaccination in the UK'. *Sociology of Health & Illness*, 29:2 (2007), pp. 198–215.

Irwin, M., 'Constructing the Scientific Citizen: Science and Democracy in the Biosciences'. *Public Understanding of Science*, 10:1 (2001), pp. 1–18.

Kerr, A., Cunningham-Burley, S. and Tutton, R., 'Shifting Subject Positions: Experts and Lay People in Public Dialogue'. *Social Studies of Science*, 37:3 (2007), pp. 385–411.

Knorr-Cetina, K., *The Manufacture of Knowledge: An Essay on the Constructivist and Contextual Nature of Science*. Oxford: Pergamon, 1981.

Komduur, R. and te Molder, H., 'The Role of Genes in Talking about Overweight: An Analysis of Discourse on Genetics, Overweight and Health Risks in Relation to Nutrigenomics' (2011). Manuscript submitted for publication.

Lamerichs, J., Koelen, M. and te Molder, H., 'Turning Adolescents into Analysts of Their Own Discourse: Raising Reflexive Awareness of Everyday Talk to Develop Peer-based Health Activities'. *Qualitative Health Research*, 19:8 (2009), pp. 1162–1175.

Lamerichs, J. and te Molder, H., 'Reflecting on Your Own Talk: The Discursive Action Method at Work'. In C. Antaki (ed.), *Applied Conversation Analysis: Intervention and Change in Institutional Talk*. Basingstoke: Palgrave Macmillan, 2011, pp. 184–206.

Latour, B., *Science in Action*. Milton Keynes: Open University Press, 1987.

Latour, B. and Woolgar, S., *Laboratory Life: The Construction of Scientific Facts*, second edition. Princeton, NJ: Princeton University Press, 1986.

Marris, C., Wynne, B., Simmons, P. and Weldon, S., 'Public Perceptions of GMOs: Focus Group Results'. In *PABE* [Public Perceptions of Agricultural Biotechnologies in Europe]. *Final Report of the PABE Research Project*, Research project funded by EC-DG12, (2001), pp. 46–70.

Michael, M., 'Publics Performing Publics: Of PiGs, PiPs and Politics'. *Public Understanding of Science*, 18:5 (2009), pp. 617–631.

Mitroff, I. I., *The Subjective Side of Science*. Amsterdam: Elsevier, 1974.

Myers, G., *Matters of Opinion. Talking about Public Issues*. Cambridge: Cambridge University Press, 2004.

Nietzsche, F., *The Gay Science: With a Prelude in German Rhymes and an Appendix of Songs*, edited by B. Williams, translated by J. Nauckhoff, poems translated by A. del Caro (Cambridge Texts in the History of Philosophy). Cambridge: Cambridge University Press, 2001 (Original version *Die Fröhliche Wissenschaft ('la gaya scienza')*, 1882).

Nowotny, H., Scott, P. and Gibbons, M., *Rethinking Science: Knowledge in an Age of Uncertainty*. Cambridge: Polity, 2001.

Potter, J., *Representing Reality: Discourse, Rhetoric and Social Construction*. Sage: London, 1996.

Raymond, G., 'Grammar and Social Relations: Alternative Forms of Yes/No-type Initiating Actions in Health Visitor Interactions'. In A. Freed and S. Ehrlich (eds), *"Why Do You Ask?" The Function of Questions in Institutional Discourse*. Oxford: Oxford University Press, 2010, pp. 87–107.

Sacks, H., 'On Doing "Being Ordinary"'. In J. M. Atkinson and J. C. Heritage (eds), *Structures of Social Action: Studies in Conversation Analysis*. Cambridge: Cambridge University Press, 1984, pp. 413–429.

Shapin, S., 'Expertise, Common Sense and The Atkins Diet'. In P. W. B. Phillips (ed.), *Public Science in Liberal Democracy*. Toronto: University of Toronto Press, 2007, pp. 174–193.

Swierstra, T. and te Molder, H., 'Risk and Soft Impacts'. In S. Roeser, R. Hillerbrand, M. Peterson and P. Sandin (eds), *Handbook of Risk Theory. Epistemology, Decision Theory, Ethics, and Social Implications of Risk*. Dordrecht: Springer, 2012, pp. 1050–1066.

te Molder, H. and Potter, J. (eds), *Conversation and Cognition*. Cambridge: Cambridge University Press, 2005.

te Molder, H., Bovenhoff, M., Gremmen, B. and van Woerkum, C., 'Talking Future Technologies: How Celiac Disease Patients Neither Accept Nor Reject "a Simple Pill"'. (2011). Manuscript submitted for publication.

Veen, M., Gremmen, B., te Molder, H. and van Woerkum, C., 'Emergent Technologies Against the Background of Everyday Life: Discursive Psychology as a Technology Assessment Tool'. *Public Understanding of Science*, 20:6 (2011), pp. 810–825.

Veen, M., te Molder, H., Gremmen, B. and van Woerkum, C., 'Competing Agendas in Upstream Engagement Meetings between Celiac Disease Experts and Patients'. *Science Communication*, 34:4 (2012), pp. 460–486.

Whalen, M. R. and Zimmerman, D. H., 'Describing Trouble: Practical Epistemology in Citizen Calls to the Police'. *Language in Society*, 19:4 (1990), pp. 465–492.

Wynne, B., 'Misunderstood Understandings: Social Identities and Public Uptake of Science'. In A. Irwin and B. Wynne (eds), *Misunderstanding Science? The Public Reconstruction of Science and Technology*. Cambridge: Cambridge University Press, 1996a, pp. 19–46.

—— 'Public Engagement as a Means of Restoring Public Trust in Science – Hitting the Notes, but Missing the Music?' *Community Genetics*, 9:3 (2006), pp. 211–220.

Notes

1   This chapter is partly based on the inaugural address that I gave at the University of Twente, the Netherlands, on 15 September 2011, entitled 'Beyond Happy Science and Grim Technology: Science Communication in an Interactional Perspective'.

2   In his book *Die fröhliche Wissenschaft* (1882) – translated into English as *The Gay Science* – Friedrich Nietzsche advocates radical modification of the efforts and results of science, to make it more life-affirming. The modifications I propose are less radical and are derived from other motives.

3   Transcription Notations

P1, P2, and so on are patients, Ex is the expert. Based on Jeffersonian transcription (Jefferson 2004).

[text]	Overlapping speech
(x.x)	Pause of x.x seconds
(.)	Micro pause, less than 0.2 seconds
(text)	Speech unclear
↑word, ↓ word	Onset of noticeable pitch rise or fall
wo:rd	Colons show that the speaker has stretched the preceding sound
word	Signals sound stress
°text°	Material between degree signs is quiet
((text))	Transcriber's remarks
=	No pause between words
>text<	Fast speaking

Chapter 6

Online Talk: How Exposure to Disagreement in Online Comments Affects Beliefs in the Promise of Controversial Science

Ashley A. Anderson, Dominique Brossard, Dietram A. Scheufele and Michael A. Xenos

One clear limitation of formal public engagement exercises with respect to public participation is that the number of participants tends to be relatively small and often has an underrepresentation of subordinate groups (Scheufele 2011). Mass media are viewed as sources of scientific knowledge for potentially a much wider range. Several studies have demonstrated the role mass media play in fostering perceptions of scientific issues and participation in science-related issues, such as joining a political demonstration or public discussion (e.g. Becker et al. 2010; Ho et al. 2011; Nisbet et al. 2002). However, mass media are changing with the establishment of an online media environment characterised by the integration of news stories and interactive, interpersonal communication (Walther et al. 2011). Comments from other individuals online populate mass media stories, with 25 per cent of Internet users in the United States reporting that they have posted comments to a news story (Purcell et al. 2010). People share and discuss news stories on social media sites. In the United States, 37 per cent of online users post news items or comments on stories via social media sites (Purcell et al. 2010). Bloggers insert mass media stories into their own commentary. One early content analysis of blogs demonstrated that approximately 12 per cent of blogs are 'filter' blogs, or blogs about content such as current events rather than personal diaries or spaces for self expression (Herring et al. 2004). In short, mass media stories are placed within a social context of a wide range of online activities in which media consumers participate.

In this chapter, we argue that with respect to public participation in science communication, researchers need to explore the impact of exposure to online discussion about science. Beliefs about science – whatever their valence – play a role in public participation in scientific issues (e.g. Horlick-Jones, Rowe and Walls 2007; Kleinman, Delborne and Anderson 2011). In this chapter we examine how exposure to disagreement in reader comments regarding a blog news post about a controversial scientific topic affects beliefs about the promise of controversial science. In this study, we conceptualise participation in science as engagement in dialogic exchange among citizens and experts, which allows citizens to construct meaning about scientific issues (Einsiedel and Eastlick 2000) and inform policy about science (Joss and Durant 1995). Thus, participation becomes a space 'where the actors involved in decision-making processes are positioned towards each other through power relationships that are (to an extent) egalitarian' (Carpentier 2011: 31).

Individuals' beliefs in controversial science, either in terms of its promises or in terms of reservations about it, play a role in motivation to participate in related communication activities (e.g. Kleinman, Delborne and Anderson 2011; Becker et al. 2010). For instance, although organisers of formal public engagement exercises related to nanotechnology, such as consensus conferences, attempt to select participants who are not already invested in the topic of the conference, attendees tend to have a personal interest in the topic that acts as a motivation for participation (Kleinman, Delborne and Anderson 2011). In another example, participants in a public debate on genetically modified foods in the United Kingdom tended to hold stronger concerns and negative opinions about the issue than the general population (GM Public Debate Steering Board 2003; Horlick-Jones, Rowe and Walls 2007). Other research shows that for a controversial scientific issue, such as stem cell research, attitudes are related to participation in activities such as joining a demonstration or writing a letter to the editor about the issue (Becker et al. 2010). In short, research has demonstrated that attitudes and beliefs about science are related to participation in science communication.

In light of the connection between beliefs about science and participation in scientific issues, in this chapter we explore how exposure to a new form of dialogue – online comments – impacts beliefs about the promises of controversial science. We present empirical evidence from an experiment with a nationally representative sample of the population of the United States that shows that disagreement in online comments of a newspaper blog post affects how people perceive controversial science. We also show how the impact of disagreement in online comments is different for those who regularly engage in online activities, such as blog reading, blog writing and comment reading. Finally, we discuss what this means for the role of online discussions in public engagement with science and discuss possible reasons why more frequent online users respond differently to disagreement in online comments.

Dialogue, public engagement and science

Science communication scholars have begun emphasising dialogue among scientists and citizens as an important dimension for public engagement with science. As a result of a shift to dialogue in science/society relations (see Chapter 1 and 7), there has been a proliferation of public engagement exercises in which the public engages in discussion with scientists with the official aim of including the public in decision-making processes about the direction and content of controversial scientific and technological developments. These formal, institutionalised public engagement exercises are intended as sites for dialogue between science and the rest of society. For instance, consensus conferences are public forums designed to facilitate discussions among citizens and between citizens and experts, with the goal of producing informed judgements among citizens to create policy recommendations about technical issues (Joss and Durant 1995). Consensus conferences originated in Denmark in the late 1980s but have since been held in many countries with various adaptations (Einsiedel, Jelsøe and Breck 2001; see also Chapter 7). In some countries – such as in the case of Denmark, which implements consensus conferences as an institutionalised process – public engagement exercises occasionally have direct policy impacts (Joss 1998). In other countries where engagement exercises are not institutionalised, the impacts are often gauged through media coverage (Glasmeier 1995).

Judged in terms of models of deliberative democracy on which they are based, citizen deliberations on scientific issues provide other benefits in addition to media coverage and policy impact. In consensus conferences, citizens gain substantive knowledge about the topic at hand, as well as procedural knowledge about the role of citizens in public decision-making on scientific issues, and reflexive knowledge about themselves and their place in society (Guston 1999). Previous research on one consensus conference showed that participating individuals felt more efficacious about scientific issues and participated in longer-term discussion groups following the conclusion of the consensus conference (Powell and Kleinman 2008). People who participate in organised discussion engagement exercises report that they discuss the issue later outside the exercise (Besley et al. 2008). Thus, formal discussion settings provide benefits to participating individuals, indicating the importance of dialogue with other citizens for public engagement with science.

Scholars have also raised critiques of deliberative public engagement exercises. For instance, Rogers-Hayden and Pidgeon (2007) question if dialogic exercises actually foster the engagement of citizens who then help guide the development of technology, or whether they function as exercises to familiarise the public with scientific issues early in their development in order to prevent controversy. Public engagement exercises are also critiqued for their representativeness, as organisers do not always draw a sample that represents the broader public (Rowe et al. 2005). Furthermore, deliberative exercises about scientific issues often begin with the goal of consensus, thus inhibiting possibilities for participants to share plural perspectives (Irwin 2006). The potential for exposure to a range of ideas and arguments in public engagement exercises is limited.

Despite the extensive number of public engagement exercises for scientific issues in both the interpersonal and online realms, scholars have noted that these exercises tend to have limited reach – involving relatively small numbers of citizens with socio-demographically narrow background – and instead call for a 'long term infrastructure for a balanced public debate in mediated and interpersonal channels' (Scheufele 2011: 2). On this basis, we argue in this chapter that researchers need to better understand the effects of exposure to dialogue in which potentially larger numbers of citizens participate on beliefs in controversial scientific issues. We focus in this chapter on interpersonal discussions that occur in online mass media stories about controversial science and their effects on citizens' beliefs about the promise of such science. Do people tend to see more potential benefits than risks in scientific issues that entail technical, but also ethical and social, dimensions after being exposed to different types of blog comments?

Science and society relations in online media

The advent of user-generated content, such as blogs, has created a social context for news media sources. While empirical research has demonstrated the positive effects of various forms of online communication on participation in civic life (e.g. Shah, Cho and Eveland 2005; Gil de Zuñiga et al. 2010), scholars have questioned whether the individualised nature of online communication detracts from participation (Dahlgren 2011). In the case of scientific issues, scholars have noted that online media such as blogs provide a new setting for interaction among scientists and members of the public (Butler 2005). Thus, online communication about science potentially encourages participation in the traditional public engagement exercises we mention above which occur in face-to-face settings as well as online settings (Delborne et al. 2011).

One approach to science in online media highlights the potential of blogs as spaces for scientists to engage members of the public in scientific issues. For instance, blogs are an opportunity for scientists to communicate their research directly to the public (Batts, Anthis and Smith 2008; Bonetta 2007; Secko 2005; Wilkins 2008). This approach tends to be focused on one-way communication, with scientists aiming to transfer their knowledge and information about science to the public. Hence it has been argued that the potential for science blogs to reconfigure relations between scientists and the public by serving as sites for dialogue and collaborative knowledge-sharing rather than knowledge transfer has not been realised (Trench 2012).

Others perceive online media to be more dialogic, with websites acting as an intermediary between scientists and the public (Minol et al. 2007). For instance, online media enable new forms of formal dialogue among members of the public and scientists through venues such as the question-and-answer sections of science museum websites (Falchetti, Caravita and Sperduti 2007). Online media have the potential to further behaviour changes and widen the public's access to new information about science via key characteristics of online media, including inclusivity, information and interactivity (O'Neill and Boykoff 2011).

Approaches that perceive online communication as dialogic also focus on audience comments in various online spaces, such as news organisation websites, discussion forums, and blogs about science. For instance, audiences can shape how scientific issues are portrayed in online news media by contributing their own frames in reader comments in addition to those frames presented in the media story (Laslo, Baram-Tsabari and Lewenstein 2011). Additionally, discussion forums that are linked to podcasts about science act as spaces for feedback between listeners and media producers and as spaces of dialogue among listeners which can include scientists (Birch and Weitkamp 2010).

While the approach to dialogic communication among scientists and citizens is ideal, actual participation in dialogue online via posting comments or other forms of user-generated content is selective. For instance, in their interviews with science podcast listeners, Birch and Weitkamp (2010) noticed that people report that they often read the comments posted by other listeners but do not usually contribute their own comments. Research on online comments about scientific issues is scant. However, more general research about online comments and informal conversations happening in social media sites demonstrates at least modest participation in social contexts online. More than three in ten Americans online report posting comments to an online news group, website, blog or photo site, and 65 per cent of online Americans use an online social networking site, such as Facebook (Pew Research Center 2011). Thus, individuals are at least encountering forms of online discussion posted by other media consumers online.

This proliferation of user-generated content online and exposure to it raises the question of how dialogue in the context of news media about science affects beliefs about science. Traditional public engagement exercises about science typically feature a setting that allows for disagreement among participants. These exercises are often based on ideas about deliberative democracy that assume that exposure to a variety of opinions, including conflicting ones, encourages or supports the formation of an informed opinion about the issue under discussion. Taking this assumption as our point of departure in this chapter, we explore how disagreement in audience comments following a newspaper blog post about science influences beliefs about science. We also examine whether disagreement in those comments affects beliefs in the promise of controversial science differently for people who are frequent or regular participants in online discussion activities such as blog writing, comment reading, and status update posting.

Methods of data collection and analysis

In order to examine the effects of online disagreement on beliefs in the promise of controversial science, we relied on a carefully designed online experiment given to a representative sample of the United States population, funded by the National Science Foundation (NSF). The online experiment was administered by Knowledge Networks, a trustworthy public opinion and market research firm in the United States, and participants were selected from KnowledgePanel, a probability-based web panel. Knowledge Networks initially selects households for their panel using random digit dialing (RDD) sampling and address-based sampling (ABS) methodology. Households that do not already have Internet access are provided a laptop computer and Internet access. The sample for this study was drawn at random from the active panel members. Descriptive statistics and results reported in this chapter use a post-stratification weighting of the sample to ensure that the demographic distribution of the sample is similar to that of the population. Those contacted who did not consent to participate were eliminated from the survey. The completion rate was 54.20 per cent. Knowledge Networks made efforts to enhance survey completion, including e-mail reminders to non-responders on two different dates during the field period. In total, 2,338 people completed the survey.

In the experiment, participants saw one of two newspaper blog posts about nuclear energy or nanotechnology on a generic fictional science blog in the *Vancouver Sun* newspaper, which was held constant across experimental conditions and chosen because Americans tend not to have any preconceptions about it. Each post presented risks and benefits equally, and both posts were about the issue of water toxicity. We chose controversial scientific topics as context of inquiry, and more particularly two that have very distinct cultural resonance with the American public: nuclear power and nanotechnology. Scientific expertise and lay expertise, as well as dialogue between scientists and citizens, are particularly important for these issues that include not only technical, but also social and ethical elements. The issues of nanotechnology and nuclear energy are different in how they are perceived by members of the general public.

While social factors, such as power plant disasters or how close one lives to a nuclear power plant, guide attitude formation about nuclear energy (Bolsen and Cook 2008; Vleeming 1985), cognitive heuristics – or mental shortcuts, such as exposure to mass media framing about scientific issues or existing value predispositions – guide attitude formation about nanotechnology (Brossard et al. 2009; Scheufele and Lewenstein 2005). Demonstrating that our results are valid for two very different controversial scientific issues provides more external validity to our study and bolsters our claims about the influence of the experimental manipulation, which had to do with the tone of the reader comments – in which the readers disagreed with each other – and not the actual content of the blog or the comments, on beliefs about controversial science.

The primary goal of the experiment was to assess how people respond to reader comments in a newspaper blog post. Thus, underneath each blog post, six comments were presented. The content of each of the comments was the same, while the tone of the comments changed. Approximately half of the participants received comments in which the commenters disagreed with each other, while the other half received comments in which the commenters agreed with each other. For example, a comment expressing explicit disagreement was, 'KLJones, I don't agree that this technology is that harmful at all ... Just think of all the benefits.' Alternatively, a comment expressing explicit agreement was, 'Look, KLJones, I agree that this technology could be harmful ... We just need to think about all the benefits, too.' Thus, each of the six comments addressed the previous comment, producing an iterative conversation among the six commenters. The commenters each had a screen name that would not identify any identity or gender connected to the commenter. This study is part of a broader experiment examining other communicative elements in addition to agreement and disagreement, including civility and incivility, as well as reason and emotion. However, the analysis in this chapter only examines the effects of agreement and disagreement. We created an independent variable that categorises all participants into either *agreement* exposure ($n = 1,161$) or *disagreement* exposure ($n = 1,177$).

Prior to the experimental manipulation, the participants were asked a number of. pre-item measures, measuring various forms of online activity. The three online activity items were used as independent variables to assess whether online disagreement impacts regular online users differently than those who conduct these online activities less

126

frequently. The first activity, *read comments*, asked participants how often they read comments in newspaper and blog posts on a 10-point scale. The item was recoded into two categories, infrequent comment readers and frequent comment readers, based on a median split ($M = .50$, $SD = .50$). The second online activity measure, *read blogs*, was created using the means of two items measured on a 10-point scale that asked participants how often they read blogs about politics and blogs about science (*Pearson's r* = .76, $p \leq$ .001).[1] The combined item was recoded into two categories, infrequent blog readers and frequent blog readers, based on a mean split ($M = .34$, $SD = .47$). The third online activity item, *write blogs*, was measured using a single item on a 10-point scale asking people how often they write blog posts. This item was recoded into two categories, infrequent blog writers and frequent blog writers, based on a median split ($M = .18$, $SD = .38$). The item on writing blog posts did not ask participants to report the type or general content of blog posts.

Following the experimental manipulation, participants were asked on a 5-point scale whether they thought that the risks outweighed the benefits, the benefits outweighed the risks or the benefits and risks were about the same about the issue they had just seen (nanotechnology or nuclear energy). We recoded this item into *beliefs in the promise of controversial science* so that those who think the benefits outweigh the risks are coded as high, and those who think the risks outweigh the benefits are coded as low. We used this as our dependent variable to test the main effects of agreement and disagreement and online activities, including comment readership, blog readership and blog writing, on beliefs in the promise of controversial science. We also tested the interaction effects of agreement and disagreement with these online activities on beliefs in the promise of controversial science. We conducted these tests using Analysis of Variance (ANOVA), a statistical procedure used to compare the means of more than two groups in an experimental analysis. The next section of this chapter presents the results of these analyses. Prior to presenting the main results, we provide basic descriptive statistics about who frequently participates in various online activities.

Manipulation check

We conducted a manipulation check to ensure that the participants in the agreement condition perceived more agreement in the comments of the post than those in the disagreement condition. Participants were asked to rate their agreement with the statement, 'Many people who posted comments in the blog disagreed with each other' on a 10-point Likert scale with 1 equal to 'do not agree at all' and 10 equal to 'agree very much'. Participants in the disagreement condition perceived significantly more disagreement ($M = 6.38$, $SD = 2.54$) than did participants in the agreement condition ($M = 6.16$, $SD = 2.44$), t(2280) = -2.14, $p \leq .05$.

Results: Who participates in online discussion activities?

Various forms of online discussion have been developed over time, and adoption of online activities varies. Our survey data demonstrates how often people participate in these activities. Slightly more than 32 per cent of respondents in our survey reported that they post comments to news stories or blog posts at least sometimes, and nearly a quarter of people reported that they read comments about online news stories or blog posts at least sometimes. Nearly three in ten people reported that they post status updates in social networking sites such as Facebook or Twitter at least sometimes. Slightly more than 15 per cent of people reported they read blogs about science or politics at least sometimes. People reported a much lower frequency when it came to writing blog posts. Only 7 per cent responded they write blog posts at least sometimes. Thus, significant numbers of individuals are taking part in discursive activities online, and particularly those discussion activities that are interactive.

Results: Effects of disagreement and online activities on beliefs in the promise of controversial science

First, our study examined the effect of disagreement in the comments section of a newspaper blog post on beliefs in the promise of controversial science. Our findings reveal a significant difference in beliefs in the promise of controversial science between those who saw agreement in the comments and those who saw disagreement in the comments, $F(1, 2282) = 5.84$, $p \leq .05$. Those who saw agreement were more likely ($M = 3.27, SD = .92$) than those who saw disagreement ($M = 3.17, SD = .97$) to report belief in the promise of controversial science. Therefore, disagreement in the comments of a newspaper blog post decreases beliefs in the promise of controversial science.

Second, our study examined the effects of online activity usage on beliefs in the promise of controversial science. Our findings reveal a significant difference in beliefs in the promise of controversial science between those who frequently read comments and those who do not frequently read comments, $F(1, 2282) = 53.29, p \leq .001$. Those who frequently read comments ($M = 3.36, SD = .95$) are more likely to report beliefs in the promise of controversial science than those who infrequently read comments ($M = 3.08, SD = .92$). Also, our findings reveal a significant difference in perceptions of the promise of controversial science between those who frequently read blogs and those who do not frequently read blogs, $F(1, 2295) = 34.80$, $p \leq .001$. Those who frequently read blogs are more likely to report beliefs in the promise of controversial science ($M = 3.38, SD = .96$) than those who are infrequent blog readers ($M = 3.14, SD = .93$). These results indicate that those who frequently read comments blogs are more likely to report beliefs in the promise of controversial science than those who read them less frequently. It should be noted that we do not know the nature of the comments frequently read by those believing in the promise of controversial science which may be in line with their attitudes towards science.

Our analysis reveals interaction effects in relation to beliefs in the promise of controversial science between the different types of online activities (comment reading, blog reading and blog post writing) and disagreement. First, we found a significant interaction between *comment* readership and disagreement on beliefs in the promise of controversial science, $F(3, 2282) = 6.33$, $p \le .05$ (see Figure 6.1). In other words, frequent comment readers and infrequent comment readers are impacted differently by agreement or disagreement in the comments. For frequent comment readers, exposure to agreement or disagreement in the comments does not make a difference in terms of beliefs in the promise of controversial science. However, infrequent comment readers are significantly more likely to report beliefs in the promise of controversial science if they are exposed to agreement ($M = 3.17$, $SD = .88$) rather than disagreement ($M = 2.98$, $SD = .96$). We found a similar interaction between disagreement in the comments for frequent *blog* readers (in contrast to *comment* readers) on beliefs in the promise of controversial science, $F(3, 2295) = 5.81$, $p \le .01$ (see Figure 6.2). Disagreement or agreement in the comments does not affect frequent blog readers' beliefs in the promise of controversial science. However, beliefs in the promise of controversial science are significantly higher among infrequent blog readers if those individuals are exposed to agreement ($M = 3.36$, $SD = .97$) rather than disagreement ($M = 3.40$, $SD = .95$) in the comments. Finally, we also found a significant interaction effect between *blog post writing* and disagreement on beliefs in the promise of controversial science, $F(3, 2266) = 5.26$, $p \le .05$ (see Figure 6.3), with different effects for the two groups. On the one hand, those who write blog posts regularly are significantly more likely to report beliefs in the promise of controversial science if they are exposed to disagreement ($M = 3.34$, $SD = .97$) rather than agreement ($M = 3.24$, $SD = .96$) in the comments. On the

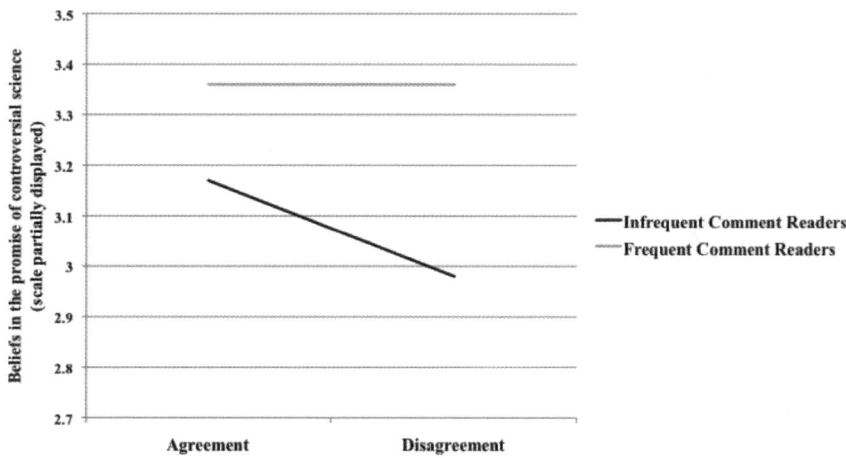

Figure 6.1: Those who frequently read comments are more likely than those who infrequently read comments in news and blog posts to report beliefs in the promise of controversial science when exposed to disagreements in online comments.

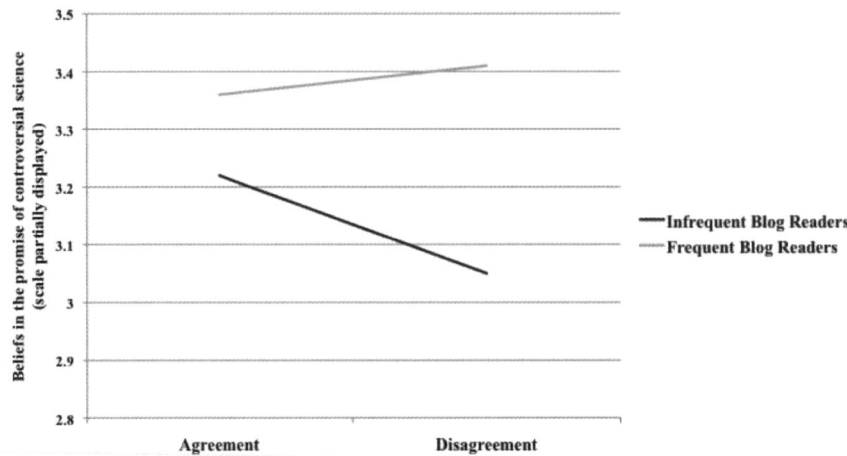

Figure 6.2: Those who frequently read blogs are more likely than those who infrequently read blogs to report beliefs in the promise of controversial science when exposed to disagreements in online comments.

other hand, those who infrequently write blog posts are less likely to report beliefs in the promise of controversial science if they are exposed to disagreeable (M = 3.14, SD = .97) rather than agreeable (M = 3.27, SD = .92) comments. In summary, people who regularly conduct expressive online activities (reading comments, reading blogs, writing blog posts) are less likely to be influenced by the disagreement they encounter online when developing beliefs in the promise of controversial science.

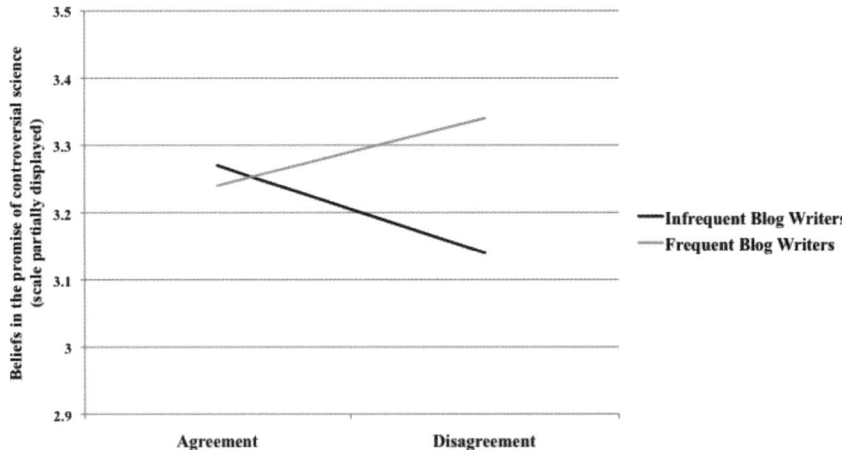

Figure 6.3: Those who frequently write blogs are more likely than those who infrequently write blogs to report beliefs in the promise of controversial science when exposed to disagreements in online comments.

Discussion and conclusion

Disagreement and debate are important dimensions of public engagement exercises that use deliberative approaches requiring individuals to carefully consider diverse points of view in order to arrive at a well-reasoned solution (Gastil and Black 2008). Exposure to disagreement in those deliberative settings enables participants to arrive at informed opinions about science, and people often change their attitudes about the topic under discussion after participating in deliberative exercises. Our research shows that exposure to disagreement in a new discussion setting – comments connected to a newspaper blog – affects individuals' beliefs about science.

Our results show that exposure to disagreement in the comments of a newspaper blog post do indeed have an effect on beliefs in the promise of controversial science, with those exposed to disagreement less likely to develop beliefs in the promise of controversial science. However, disagreement does not have an effect on these beliefs for people who regularly conduct online activities, including reading comments and reading blogs. Furthermore, disagreement actually increases beliefs in the promise of controversial science among people who write blog posts regularly.

Our analyses also provide evidence that those who frequently engage in online activities are initially more likely to believe in the promise of controversial science than those who do not frequently engage in online activities. These findings are not surprising considering that previous research shows that people who regularly turn to the Internet for news and information are heavier consumers of science and technology news and likely to be biased towards science (Pew Research Center 2008). However, they are interesting considering the differences exposure to disagreement had for those who frequently engage in online discussion activities. Our analyses indicate that these regular online users are less likely to be affected by disagreement than people who are less frequent online users. Since our results show that these online users also already tend to believe more in the promise of controversial science, it is likely that those beliefs are predispositions for online users. Thus, they are not affected by the exposure to disagreement because of the strength of these predispositions. Future research should examine whether those who hold strong preexisting attitudes about science are less affected by exposure to disagreement in online comment spaces.

As we described earlier, empirical research has demonstrated a connection between beliefs about science and public participation in science (e.g. Becker et al. 2010; Kleinman, Delborne and Anderson 2010). The relationship between online social discussions and beliefs about the promises of controversial science identified in our study suggests that those online discussions may therefore also have an impact on participation in science. The results presented in this chapter show that online comments in a newspaper blog post do have an impact on how people perceive controversial science and suggest that exposure to disagreement in blog comments may ultimately influence public participation in science communication and public engagement with science. The quantitative approach used for this study is therefore an important complement to qualitative analyses of the dynamics of public participation in science communication.

Those who go online for news and information are not only exposed to online versions of traditional media outlets' stories, but also to conversation occurring among other online users. People are increasingly using online communication tools, such as social networking sites, to share science and technology related news and information with others. Online news consumers are participating in, and exposed to, online discussions amongst other online users regularly in the comments sections of websites. The effect of these types of interaction on perceptions of science, and ultimately in public engagement with science should continue to be given careful attention.

References

Batts, S. A., Anthis, N. J. and Smith, T. C., 'Advancing Science through Conversations: Bridging the Gap between Blogs and the Academy'. *Plos Biology*, 6:9 (2008), pp. 1837–1841.

Becker, A. B., Dalrymple, K. E., Brossard, D., Scheufele, D. A. and Gunther, A. C., 'Getting Citizens Involved: How Controversial Policy Debates Stimulate Issue Participation during a Political Campaign'. *International Journal of Public Opinion Research*, 22:2 (2010), pp. 181–203.

Besley, J. C., Kramer, V. L., Yao, Q. J. and Toumey, C., 'Interpersonal Discussion Following Citizen Engagement about Nanotechnology What, If Anything, Do They Say?' *Science Communication*, 30:2 (2008), pp. 209–235.

Birch, H. and Weitkamp, E., 'Podologues: Conversations Created by Science Podcasts'. *New Media & Society*, 12:6 (2010), pp. 889–909.

Bolsen, T. and Cook, F. L., 'The Polls-Trends – Public Opinion on Energy Policy: 1974–2006'. *Public Opinion Quarterly*, 72:2 (2008), pp. 364–388.

Bonetta, L., 'Scientists Enter the Blogosphere'. *Cell*, 129:3 (2007), pp. 443–445.

Brossard, D., Scheufele, D. A., Kim, E. and Lewenstein, B. V., 'Religiosity as a Perceptual Filter: Examining Processes of Opinion Formation about Nanotechnology'. *Public Understanding of Science*, 18:5 (2009), pp. 546–558.

Butler, D., 'Joint Efforts'. *Nature*, 438:7068 (2005), pp. 548–549.

Carpentier, N., 'The Concept of Participation: If They Have Access and Interact, Do They Really Participate?'. Communication Management Quarterly, 21:4 (2011), pp. 13–36.

Dahlgren, P., 'Parameters of Online Participation: Conceptualising Civic Contingencies'. *Communication Management Quarterly*, 21:4 (2011), pp. 87–110.

Delborne, J. A., Anderson, A. A., Kleinman, D. L., Colin, M. and Powell, M., 'Virtual Deliberation? Prospects and Challenges for Integrating the Internet in Consensus Conferences'. *Public Understanding of Science*, 20:3 (2011), pp. 367–384.

Einsiedel, E. F. and Eastlick, D. L., 'Consensus Conferences as Deliberative Democracy – A Communications Perspective'. *Science Communication*, 21:4 (2000), pp. 323–343.

Einsiedel, E. F., Jelsoe, E. and Breck, T., 'Publics at the Technology Table: The Consensus Conference in Denmark, Canada, and Australia'. *Public Understanding of Science*, 10:1 (2001), pp. 83–98.

Falchetti, E., Caravita, S. and Sperduti, A., 'What Do Laypersons Want to Know from Scientists? An Analysis of a Dialogue between Scientists and Laypersons on the Web Site Scienzaonline'. *Public Understanding of Science*, 16:4 (2007), pp. 489–506.

Gastil, J. and Black, L. W., 'Public Deliberation as the Organizing Principle of Political Communication Research'. *Journal of Public Deliberation*, 4:1 (2008), Article 3.

Gil De Zuñiga, H., Veenstra, A. S., Vraga, E. and Shah, D. V., 'Digital Democracy: Reimagining Pathways to Political Participation'. *Journal of Information Technology & Politics*, 7 (2010), 36–51.

Glasmeier, A., 'Consensus Conferences, the Media and Public Information in the Netherlands'. In S. Joss and J. Durant (eds), *Public Participation in Science: The Role of Consensus Conferences in Europe*. London, UK: Science Museum with the support of the European Commission Directorate General XII, 1995, pp. 67–73.

GM Public Debate Steering Board, *GM Nation? The Findings of the Public Debate*. London: UK Department of Trade and Industry, 2003.

Guston, D. H., 'Evaluating the First US Consensus Conference: The Impact of the Citizens' Panel on Telecommunications and the Future of Democracy'. *Science Technology & Human Values*, 24:4 (1999), pp. 451–482.

Herring, S. C., Scheidt, L. A., Bonus, S. and Wright, E., 'Bridging the Gap: A Genre Analysis of Weblogs'. Paper presented at the 37th Hawaii International Conference on System Sciences 2004.

Ho, S. S., Binder, A. R., Becker, A. B., Moy, P., Scheufele, D. A., Brossard, D. and Gunther, A. C., 'The Role of Perceptions of Media Bias in General and Issue-Specific Political Participation'. *Mass Communication and Society*, 14:3 (2011), pp. 343–374.

Horlick-Jones, T., Rowe, G. and Walls, J., 'Citizen Engagement Processes as Information Systems: The Role of Knowledge and the Concept of Translation Quality'. *Public Understanding of Science*, 16:3 (2007), pp. 259–278.

Irwin, A., 'The Politics of Talk: Coming to Terms with the 'New' Scientific Governance'. *Social Studies of Science*, 36:2 (2006), pp. 299–320.

Joss, S., 'Danish Consensus Conferences as a Model of Participatory Technology Assessment: An Impact Study of Consensus Conferences on Danish Parliament and Danish Public Debate'. *Science and Public Policy*, 25:1 (1998), pp. 2–22.

Joss, S. and Durant, J., 'Introduction'. In S. Joss and J. Durant (eds), *Public Participation in Science: The Role of Consensus Conferences in Europe*. London: The Science Museum, 1995, pp. 9–13.

Kleinman, D. L., Delborne, J. A. and Anderson, A. A., 'Engaging Citizens: The High Cost of Citizen Participation in High Technology'. *Public Understanding of Science*, 20:2 (2011), pp. 221–240.

Laslo, E., Baram-Tsabari, A. and Lewenstein, B. V., 'A Growth Medium for the Message: Online Science Journalism Affordances for Exploring Public Discourse of Science and Ethics'. *Journalism: Theory, Practice and Criticism*, 12:7 (2011), pp. 847–870.

Minol, K., Spelsberg, G., Schulte, E. and Morris, N., 'Portals, Blogs and Co.: The Role of the Internet as a Medium of Science Communication'. *Biotechnology Journal*, 2:9 (2007), pp. 1129–1140.

Nisbet, M. C., Scheufele, D. A., Shanahan, J., Moy, P., Brossard, D. and Lewenstein, B. V., 'Knowledge, Reservations, or Promise? A Media Effects Model for Public Perceptions of Science and Technology'. *Communication Research*, 29:5 (2002), pp. 584–608.

O'Neill, S. and Boykoff, M., 'The Role of New Media in Engaging the Public with Climate Change'. In L. Whitmarsh, S. O'Neill and I. Lorenzoni (eds), *Engaging the Public with Climate Change*. London: EarthScan, 2011, pp. 233–251.

Pew Research Center, 'Audience Segments in a Changing News Environment', *Pew Internet & American Life Project*, 2008. Available: http://people-press.org/reports/pdf/444.pdf, [Accessed on 6 November 2010].

——— 'Trend Data (Adults)', 2011. Available here: http://www.pewinternet.org/Static-Pages/ Trend-Data-(Adults).aspx, [Accessed on 9 June 2012].

Powell, M. and Kleinman, D. L., 'Building Citizen Capacities for Participation in Nanotechnology Decision-Making: The Democratic Virtues of the Consensus Conference Model'. *Public Understanding of Science*, 17:3 (2008), pp. 329–348.

Purcell, K., Rainie, L., Mitchell, A., Rosenstiel, T. and Olmstead, K., 'Understanding the participatory news consumer: How Internet and cell phone users have turned news into a social experience', *Pew Internet & American Life Project*, 2010. Available here: http://www. journalism.org/sites/journalism.org/files/Participatory_News_Consumer.pdf, [Accessed on 12 July 2010].

Rogers-Hayden, T. and Pidgeon, N., 'Moving Engagement 'Upstream'? Nanotechnologies and the Royal Society and Royal Academy of Engineering's Inquiry'. *Public Understanding of Science*, 16:3 (2007), pp. 345–364.

Rowe, G., Horlick-Jones, T., Walls, J. and Pidgeon, N., 'Difficulties in Evaluating Public Engagement Initiatives: Reflections on an Evaluation of the UK GM Nation? Public Debate about Transgenic Crops'. *Public Understanding of Science*, 14:4 (2005), pp. 331–352.

Scheufele, D. A., 'Modern Citizenship or Policy Dead End? Evaluating the Need for Public Participation in Science Policy Making, and Why Public Meetings May Not Be the Answer'. Joan Shorenstein Center on the Press, Politics and Public Policy Research Paper Series, 2011.

Scheufele, D. A. and Lewenstein, B. V., 'The Public and Nanotechnology: How Citizens Make Sense of Emerging Technologies'. *Journal of Nanoparticle Research*, 7:6 (2005), pp. 659–667.

Secko, D., 'The Power of the Blog'. *The Scientist*, 19:15 (2005), p. 37.

Shah, D., Cho, J. and Eveland, W., 'Information and Expression in a Digital Age: Modeling Internet Effects on Civic Participation'. *Communication Research*, 32:5 (2005), pp. 531–565.

Trench, B., 'Scientists' Blogs: Glimpses Behind the Sciences'. In S. Rödder, M. Franzen and P. Weingart (eds), *The Sciences' Media Connection – Public Communication and Its Repercussions*. The Netherlands: Springer, 2012, pp. 273–290.

Vleeming, R. G., 'Factors Affecting Attitudes Toward Nulcear-Power in the Netherlands'. *Journal of Social Psychology*, 125:1 (1985), 119–125.

Walther, J. B., Carr, C. T., Choi, S. S., DeAndrea, D. C., Kim, J., Tong, S. T. and Van Der Heide, B., 'Interaction of Interpersonal, Peer, and Media Influence Sources Online: A Research Agenda for Technology Convergence'. In Z. Papacharissi (ed.), *A Networked Self: Identity, Community, and Culture on Social Network Sites*. New York: Routledge, 2011, pp. 17–38.

Wilkins, J. S., 'The Roles, Reasons and Restrictions of Science Blogs'. *Trends in Ecology & Evolution*, 23:8 (2008), pp. 411–413.

Note

This chapter is based upon work supported by a grant from the National Science Foundation to the UW-Madison Nanoscale Science and Engineering Center in Templated Synthesis and Assembly at the Nanoscale (Grant No. SES-DMR-0832760). Any opinions, findings and conclusions or recommendations expressed in the chapter are those of the authors and do not necessarily reflect the views of the National Science Foundation.

1   Controversial scientific topics are generally politico-scientific in that they include political as well as scientific regulations and discourse often centres around safety and regulations regarding these topics. Readers interested in these issues will encounter them in political, as well as scientific, blogs.

PART II

Public Participation and Formal Public Engagement Initiatives

Chapter 7

Communicating about Climate Change in a Citizen Consultation: Dynamics of Exclusion and Inclusion

Louise Phillips

A starting point for this book is that the global proliferation of exercises of public engagement in science and technology over the past two decades is part of a new mode of scientific governance in which relations between policymakers, science and publics are apparently democratised along the lines of principles of participatory democracy (see Chapter 1). Within the terms of participatory models of democracy, communication is conceptualised as *dialogue* between science and publics; here, publics are construed as *scientific citizens* with a legitimate role to play as active agents in policymaking about the direction of scientific and technological developments. In line with the loose use of the term 'dialogue' in other social fields (see Phillips 2011), 'dialogue' in the context of public engagement is a vaguely defined construction, signifying some kind of interaction and exchange of knowledge between science and publics. A rhetorical contrast is set up between public engagement with its conceptualisation of communication as *dialogue* and the public understanding of science tradition with its conceptualisation of communication as the *diffusion* of scientific knowledge to the public. While the discourse of dialogue constructs publics as scientific citizens who participate actively in democratic forums that shape scientific policymaking, the discourse of diffusion constructs the 'public' as consumers of scientific knowledge. The conceptualisation of communication as dialogue stands in opposition to the 'deficit' models of public understanding of science that sought, through the dissemination of scientific knowledge, to cure the public's ignorance and thus gain their acceptance of scientific and technological developments. Often the model of democracy underpinning public engagement initiatives is one of deliberative democracy (see e.g. Dryzek 2000; Gastil and Levine 2005); in models of deliberative democracy, 'dialogue' is presented as the means through which deliberation takes place, frequently leading to the formation of consensus.

Within Science and Technology Studies (STS), there is growing scepticism among researchers for public engagement, founded on the criticism that public engagement practices do not live up to their professed ideals of dialogue and democracy. This criticism builds on empirical analyses of tensions and contradictions arising from the partial, incomplete nature of the shift to dialogue (e.g. Delgado et al. 2010; Hornig Priest 2005; Irwin 2001, 2006; MacNaghten, Kearnes and Wynne 2005; Rogers-Hayden and Pidgeon 2007; Trench 2008; Wynne 2006). More specifically, much of this work judges engagement practices from within the terms of the model of democracy and concludes that the practices fall short of democratic ideals as a result of the lingering presence of the diffusion model and the dominance of scientific agendas in the design of engagement practices (e.g. Kurath and Gisler 2009; Trench 2008; Wynne 2006).

In this chapter I align myself with the position taken by Felt and Fochler who point out that research has concentrated on the design and outcome of engagement exercises and neglected issues of how participants 'inhabit and appropriate [the] discursive spaces offered to them' (Felt and Fochler 2010: 220). Felt and Fochler analyse *both* how public engagement designs construct particular identities for the participants *and* how those participants appropriate, transform and challenge those identities in relation to wider publics. While I have carried out research with this double focus on the case presented in this chapter elsewhere (see Agger et al. 2012; Phillips 2011), in the present chapter I refrain from analysis of the design and focus exclusively on how participants in deliberation processes perform the identity of 'scientific citizen' in the light of how they are positioned by facilitators.

The case I analyse in this chapter is the global citizen consultation World Wide Views on Global Warming (WWViews), which was organised by the Danish Board of Technology (DBT) and took place on 26 September 2009 in advance of the UN Climate Change Conference (COP15), Copenhagen, 7–18 December 2009. As a case of public engagement, WWViews is innovative in its global reach, representing the first-ever attempt at a global citizen consultation. It took the form of 44 one-day, local deliberations in 38 countries (across six continents), including Denmark, in which invited citizens were brought together to engage in processes of deliberation about their views on climate change. In this chapter, I analyse the local deliberations in Denmark which took place in Copenhagen Town Hall.[1]

The organisation of all 44 citizen deliberations was co-ordinated by the DBT and their basic structure was the same, with some local variations. This chapter has as its object of analysis the Danish deliberations that took place at the town hall in Copenhagen. The stated purpose of WWViews was 'to give a broad sample of citizens from across the world the opportunity to influence the COP15 negotiations and thereby the future of global climate policy' and 'to demonstrate that political decision-making processes on a global scale can benefit from the participation of ordinary people'.[2] The official conclusion was that WWViews achieved the aims of communicating the 'voice' of citizens to decision-makers: 'WWViews did send vital messages about climate policy from citizens to decision-makers. [..] And it set a path-breaking precedent by demonstrating that ordinary people merit, and can have, a voice within global political processes'.[3]

In common with other public engagement exercises based on deliberative democracy, the participants in WWViews were constructed as 'citizens' and expected to form a 'citizen voice' through dialogue. How the DBT define the 'citizen voice' is a vexed question, which the DBT have been asked repeatedly. Given the restricted number of participants in their consensus conferences and citizen consultations, it is impossible for participants to be representative of the population in statistical sense (in consensus conferences, panels of 14–16 participants, and in WWViews, 100 citizens in each country participated). The position of the DBT is that the participants in their public engagement exercises represent the voice of the citizens by virtue of the broad spread of backgrounds and values that ensures that they 'reflect as many different views as possible' (Klüver 1995: 46).

In this chapter, I present an empirical analysis of how principles of deliberative democracy are played out in communication processes in the deliberations of the participating citizens at the Danish WWViews event in Copenhagen. My analysis focuses both on the ways in which the deliberations open up for multiple citizen voices – articulating plural knowledge forms and identities – and on the ways in which they exclude voices and construct a singular 'citizen voice' through the application of a procedure for rational argumentation based on principles of deliberative democracy. A central analytical focus is the *performativity* of the construction of the participants as 'citizens' who, through the deliberations, can produce a 'citizen voice' capable of shaping decision-making at COP15. I argue for the value of this kind of empirical analysis as a foundation for reflexive discussions of how to further develop practices of public engagement, taking intoaccount the inexorable workings of dynamics of exclusion in relation to citizen participation.

My analytical strategy is based on three main components: an approach to the analysis of public engagement developed in the field of STS; dialogic communication theory, building on the work of Bakhtin on multi-voicedness; and Chantal Mouffe's post-structuralist critique of deliberative democracy's emphasis on the need for, and possibility of, reasoned political consensus.

I begin with a brief outline of the DBT as an institution that emerged out of a particular democratic tradition characterised by a particular form of deliberative democracy. This outline is followed by an account of my analytical strategy. Then I present an empirical analysis of how the principles of deliberative democracy are played out in the ways in which participants perform 'scientific citizenship' in the deliberations themselves. Again, analysis revolves around relations between top-down and bottom-up dynamics. In the concluding section of the chapter, I reflect on the nature and significance of the Copenhagen WWViews event as a political construction that circumscribes public participation in particular ways.

Founding public engagement on deliberative democracy: The case of the DBT

Established in 1986, the DBT has played a role as one of the pioneers of consensus-oriented, deliberative public engagement, their methods providing a main source of inspiration for public engagement initiatives outside Denmark. The most influential and widely exported of the DBT's methodologies is the consensus conference model (Einsiedel and Eastlick 2000; Einsiedel, Jelsøe and Breck 2001; Guston 1999; Seifert 2006). WWViews incorporates many of the elements of the consensus model as well as drawing on other methods used by the DBT.[4] The establishment of the DBT in 1986 can be understood as a product of the politicisation of technology assessment in the 1970s, arising from concerns for the consequences of new technologies. The DBT organised the first citizen participation process based on the consensus conference model in 1987, adapting the solely expert-based consensus conference model formulated in the US (Einsiedel, Jelsøe and Breck 2001).

Applying principles of deliberative democracy under the specific political conditions peculiar to Denmark, the public engagement methods developed by the DBT contain features that, on the one hand, are common to deliberative democracy theory in general and, on the other hand, are peculiar to Danish politics. I will briefly sketch out both the common and the peculiar features.

Common to all deliberative democracy theories is the assumption that the use of political power depends for its legitimacy on its expressing the public good – defined as 'the interest of all considered as free and equal moral beings' (Benhabib 1994: 29). To achieve that legitimacy, deliberative processes must adhere to three procedural rules: participation must follow the norms of equality and symmetry, with all participants being given equal opportunity to initiate speech acts, to question, and to start debate; all participants have the right to question the designated topics for deliberation; and all participants have the right to present reflexive arguments about the procedural rules themselves, including how they are implemented (Benhabib 1994: 31). 'Deliberation' refers to careful consideration of the topic in question as a basis for decision-making and, in the context of deliberative democracy, that decision-making is carried out by reference to the public good (Dryzek 2000). Conducted correctly, deliberation involves reflection and, on the basis of that reflection, processes of mutual learning and education. A core assumption is that preferences can be transformed in the process of deliberation as participants are amenable to changing their minds when presented with other points of view in a non-coercive way.

Proponents of deliberative democracy single out four particular qualities of deliberation (e.g. Button and Ryfe 2005). First, deliberation is claimed to produce *civic virtue*. Through education in the process of collective deliberation and the topic under deliberation, deliberative processes create more informed, active and cooperative citizens with 'better' democratic capabilities. Second, it is claimed to generate *governance virtue*. By adhering to fair procedures for public reasoning that are open to all, the outcome of deliberation will be equally in the interests of all and thus will have political legitimacy. Third, it is argued that deliberation creates *cognitive virtue*. By bringing different perspectives to the issue, clarifying substantive controversies and allowing the clear articulation of arguments, deliberative processes encourage participants to discover and develop their own standpoints. Fourth, deliberative democracy promotes *deliberative accountability* since participants in deliberative processes are encouraged to give justifications for their arguments and decisions (Gutmann and Thompson 1996: 129). By virtue of these four qualities, citizen participation in deliberation exercises – according to proponents - produces a more democratic and effective policymaking process (Guttman 2007).

The particular ideals of deliberative democracy espoused by the DBT have their roots in the particular democratic tradition developed in Denmark. An iconic figure in that tradition is the priest, poet and politician N. F. S. Grundtvig (1783–1872). Central to Grundtvig's perspective is a vision of national consensus politics founded on 'folkelig' democracy – that is, popular democracy, a democracy of the people, in which the people engage in processes of deliberation that generate an understanding of the public good (Horst and Irwin 2010).

The people bring to these processes their practical, experience-based knowledge of life and a sense of national identity rooted in a shared culture and language. Grundtvig's recognition of the value of the people's practical, experiential knowledge represents an anti-elitist position that challenges the taken-for-granted superiority of academic, research-based knowledge and justifies the involvement of the people in deliberation oriented to producing a consensus about the common good that then shapes national decision-making (Horst and Irwin 2010). However, while the participation of the people is a prerequisite for a *folkelig* democracy, another prerequisite is the enlightenment of the people through education; according to Grundtvig, the people lack the education necessary in order to be able to participate as responsible citizens in deliberation about society (Horst and Irwin 2010). Grundtvig's perspective was developed further by other thinkers and practitioners, contributing to the establishment of *both* institutions of representative democracy such as the national parliament and local government structures *and* institutions of participatory democracy such as the DBT.

Within the context of public engagement in science and technology, the Grundtvigian perspective leads to an approach to public engagement in which lay people and experts engage in dialogue about science and technology. Following along this path, the DBT treat lay people as legitimate actors in the dialogue on the grounds that they contribute practical, experience-based knowledge and cultural, social and moral reasoning beyond the scope of expert knowledge (Andersen and Jæger 1999). Thus consensus conferences are designed specifically in order to open up for 'broader social values and concerns over and above expert and technical knowledge based on instrumental rationality' (Eisendel, Jelsøe and Breck 2001: 85). And as the DBT put it in their online description of the WWViews method, 'As non-specialists, citizens are in a unique position to weigh the pros and cons of different technological and political initiatives and to evaluate scientific progress from moral, social and cultural perspectives'.[5] Thus it can be said that expertise is *de-monopolised* (Eisendel, Jelsøe and Breck 2001: 95) or indeed *democratised* in the sense that scientific knowledge and scientific knowers relinquish their monopoly on expertise (Blok 2007). Scientific experts are enlisted as partners in dialogue with citizens: expert input provides the lay participants with the education that allows them to exercise the rights of *scientific citizenship* responsibly (Irwin 2001). If they exercise those rights responsibly, lay participants act as competent *scientific citizens*, who deserve the voice they have been given in decision-making about the direction and content of developments in science and technology (Elam and Bertilsson 2003).

As in other forms of public engagement involving 'citizens', an underlying assumption is that recruitment among, for example, environmental activists would represent a threat to the legitimacy of the results of the exercise. This assumption can be challenged from a pluralist understanding of multiple publics. It could be argued that if the participating citizens are supposed to represent the population, some of the participants ought to be activists. Moreover, the figure of the 'ordinary citizen' and the notion of the unified voices of the citizens can be criticised for romanticising the public and presenting them as a homogeneous, unitary entity (e.g. Horst 2008: 262), and, from a post-structuralist perspective, for implying that it is possible for groups of citizens to speak with a singular voice without excluding alternative voices in the move towards consensus (as was the case in the final session of the deliberations but not in the prior sessions).

Analytical strategy

In constructing a strategy for analysing how processes of inclusion and exclusion are at work in the participation of 'citizens' in practices based on principles of deliberative democracy, I build, as noted earlier, on STS work on public engagement, Mouffe's post-structuralist critique of deliberative democracy and Bakhtinian dialogic communication theory.

As outlined in Chapter 1 and noted in the introduction to this chapter, STS researchers argue that the shift to dialogue in scientific governance has been only partial, with the result that public engagement practices are riddled with tensions and contradictions. Many researchers question 'the story of progress from deficit to dialogue' (Trench 2008: 120) and point out discrepancies between the rhetoric and the actual practices and the gap between theory and practice (Delgado et al. 2010; Irwin 2001, 2006; Wynne 2006). Often criticism is raised of the tight institutional framing of exercises in order to achieve predefined, instrumental aims (e.g. Bickerstaff et al. 2010; Goven 2003; Irwin 2001, 2006). And, in some cases, the exercises are castigated as technologies of legitimatisation, rubber-stamping primarily top-down decision-making about science and technology (e.g. Harrison and Mort 1998 cited in Stirling 2008: 264; Wynne 2006). The claim of mutual learning is often empty, critics contend: diffusion based on the deficit model is a central component of many practices defined as dialogic (Kurath and Gisler 2009; Trench 2008), and scientists impose their own techo-scientific knowledges rather than listening to, and thus genuinely hearing, the other participants (Kerr et al. 2007; Wynne 2006).

Irwin, like other STS researchers, identifies the lingering presence of the deficit model and the operation of top-down management in ostensibly dialogic scientific governance but, in contrast to many other researchers, adopts an open, empirical approach rather than a heavily normative one. Irwin's position is that we should analyse public engagement practices as social experiments as opposed to condemning them from a normative perspective (Irwin 2006: 317), concentrating instead on how processes of inclusion and exclusion in relation to citizen participation are at work in the articulation of principles of deliberative democracy. I analyse these processes through a focus on the tensions between top-down dynamics designed to achieve *closure*, on the one hand, and the bottom-up *opening up* for the emergence of a plurality of different knowledge forms among the participants, on the other (Carolan 2008; Stirling 2008). I attempt an approach that is open and empirical and, at the same time, normatively addresses the possibilities and limitations of engagement practices with respect to their dialogic ambitions. Here, I follow an approach that focuses on how participants actively construct, perform and negotiate identities as 'citizens' in the communication processes at the core of public engagement exercises (Felt and Fochler 2010).

In conceptualising communication as a constitutive force in the relational construction of objects and subjects, this approach is based on a *model of emergence*, which Horst (2012) has identified as the most recent model developed in studies of public understanding of science. According to the model of emergence, it is in communication processes that social categories such as 'knowledge', 'citizens' and 'publics' emerge, are brought into being or made (see, for example, Felt and Fochler 2010; Horst 2008; Horst and Irwin 2010; Irwin and Michael 2003; Michael 2009). In this respect, the model of emergence stands in contrast to both the model of diffusion underpinning public understanding of science and the model of democracy underpinning public engagement, with their shared understanding understanding of communication as a channel in which predefined actors (scientists, citizens and the public) convey pre-formed scientific knowledge and lay opinions.

In order to theorise processes of inclusion and exclusion, I draw on Mouffe's post-structuralist critique of the emphasis in deliberative democracy on the need for, and possibility of, reasoned political consensus. Mouffe challenges two related assumptions of models of deliberative democracy: the rationalist assumption that rational decisions on political questions can be arrived at through reasoned consensus; and the universalist assumption that consensus is the expression of 'a democracy of mankind' based on the operation of universal principles of liberty and equality (Mouffe 2000). Here, Mouffe draws on the view of the critic of liberal democracy Carl Schmitt that the liberal ideal of the equality of mankind clashes with the democratic ideal of an identity grounded in homogeneity (2000: 39). Owing to the political logic of democracy and contrary to the liberal ideal, there can never be a democracy of mankind; '[d]emocracy can exist only for a people' (2000: 41).

The political logic of democracy, then, entails a moment of 'closure' involving relations of inclusion and exclusion as a 'we, the people' is constructed in opposition to a 'them' (Mouffe 2000: 43). Thus the ideal underpinning deliberative democracy of 'consensus without exclusion' (Mouffe 2000: 48) and of a 'fully inclusive political community' (Mouffe 1993: 114) is illusory since power is always at play and is always exclusionary. Consensus is always 'the expression of a hegemony and crystallization of power relations' (Mouffe 2000: 49). Moreover, the notion basic to models of deliberative democracy that rational decisions can be reached through reasoned consensus entails an individualistic view of politics that reduces it to a competition between interests resolvable through rational argumentation (Elam and Bertilsson 2003: 244). For Mouffe, politics is 'a power struggle between collective identities' (Rummens 2009: 377). Models of deliberative democracy, by treating reason and rational argumentation as central to politics, underestimate the centrality to politics of power struggles (Mouffe 2000: 46). The notion of a 'democracy of mankind' has a depoliticising effect by implying that it is possible to bracket relations of power out of politics.

On the basis of this critique, Mouffe argues instead for an *agonistic pluralism* that recognises the centrality of political struggle and acknowledges that consensus is the product of the hegemonic articulations of power relations and not a universal rationality. Mouffe distances herself here from what she dubs an extreme pluralism that valorises all differences and advocates that pluralism should operate without limits; for Mouffe, a pluralism without limits is deeply problematic as some differences entail relations of subordination that we ought to identify and challenge from a democratic political perspective (Mouffe 2000: 20). And she also argues against Schmitt's conclusion that the contradiction between the democratic and liberal ideals of equality (which represents the 'constitutive paradox' of liberal democracy [Mouffe 2000: 45]) will lead to the self-destruction of liberal democracy. Her position, rather, is that the conflict is a source of tension that can serve as a positive dynamic.

In developing my analytical strategy, I take on board Mouffe's critique of deliberative democracy, conceptualising deliberation processes as sites for power struggles entailing tensional processes of inclusion and exclusion. To analyse these processes of inclusion and exclusion in detail, I draw on Bakhtin's notion of voice and the struggle between the centrifugal and centripetal tendencies towards, respectively, difference and unity (Bakhtin 1981, 1984, 1986). According to Bakhtin, meanings – including understandings of self and other – are produced dialectically in the tension between different and often contradictory and opposing voices. Bakhtin understands each voice as a discourse, ideology, perspective or theme and not just as the medium for speech or the uttered speech of an individual, embodied person (Bakhtin 1981). Meaning-making is dialogic as it is produced through the interplay of multiple voices; in that interplay, a unity is formed but, as a result of the play of difference across voices, that unity is a multivocal one, full of contradictions. Bakhtin asserts that the unity that emerges in meaning-making is the product of the two competing tendencies, the centrifugal tendency towards difference and the centripetal tendency towards unity. While the centrifugal movement pushes towards the Other, it is counterbalanced by the centripetal movement 'towards a common word, a shared text, a unifying topic and an orchestration of the many into a culture or a literary piece' (Gurevitch 2000: 247). I assume in formulating my analytical strategy that processes of inclusion and exclusion work through the articulation of different voices, such that particular voices, articulating particular identities as 'citizens' and particular forms of knowledge, dominate and others are marginalised or silenced. Combining Mouffe and Bakhtin, I hold that the tension identified by Mouffe between the liberal and democratic logics can be understood and analysed in terms of Bakhtin's understanding of communication as a struggle between the centrifugal tendency towards difference and the centripetal tendency towards unity in the interplay of multiple voices: the liberal logic opens up for difference based on inclusion while the democratic logic entails a gravitation towards unity based on exclusion.

My focus is on the ways in which the deliberations open up for a plurality of different voices and for dialogue across those voices and the ways in which they exclude voices through the application of a procedure for rational argumentation and through the move towards consensus in the ultimate stage of the event when each table is given the task of formulating a common message for the decision-makers at COP15.

The focus is on the tension between the *opening up* for social contestation among diverse voices, on the one hand and, on the other hand, the management of the process and the attainment of *closure* in reaching individual and collective decisions (Carolan 2008; Stirling 2008).

It is not my goal to come up with suggestions for how to eradicate relations of dominance and subordination since eradication is an impossibility. Drawing on Mouffe and Bakhtin, I see such relations as products of tensions between the centrifugal and the centripetal processes which are necessary and integral components of meaning-making; for Bakhtin, it is this tension that renders all meaning-making dialogical. Since both sides of the tension are intrinsic to meaning-making, it does not make sense to attempt to eradicate the centripetal forces that lead to the dominance of certain voices and the exclusion of others. Aside from the futility of an attempt to alleviate the tension between centripetal and centrifugal forces, it would not be the right thing to try to do normatively, from the perspective of both Mouffe and Bakhtin. For Mouffe, as noted above, the conflict at the heart of the tension serves as a positive dynamic: the democratic logic leads to a grounding of the principles of liberalism in concrete practice-contexts and the liberal logic challenges the workings of exclusion intrinsic to the democratic logic. And, for Bakhtin, the monologisation of communication whereby attempts are made to replace dialogic, multivocal meaning-making with a singular voice, is a politically undesirable, totalitarian move.

Instead of aiming to eradicate the tensions, I argue for the value of empirical analysis of *how* the tensions operate in the *opening up* for deliberation among diverse voices and in the *closing down* through framing in terms of a predefined set of questions in the case of the first four sessions and in the orientation towards consensus in the final session. Empirical analysis has this value, I assert, because it can provide a qualified, informed basis for reflexive consideration of the dynamics of inclusion and exclusion in the performance of public participation in deliberative practices.

My assumption is that such reflexive consideration can generate ideas for refining practices of public engagement by indicating alternative ways of negotiating the balance between opening up and closure. Here, I align myself with Delgado et al. (2010: 7), who argue for 'open recognition of challenges, pitfalls and tensions' in the institutional uses of public engagement as a first step in countering the co-optation of public engagement practices for instrumental, technocratic purposes.

The main methods of data production in my overarching of WWViews as follows: participant observation of the full WWViews event in Copenhagen on 26 September 2010, including participation observation of deliberations at three of the 16 tables and audio recording of the deliberations at those three tables (three times six hours); the material distributed to the citizens in advance of, and during, the Copenhagen event; the guidelines formulated for organising the event; the oral presentations given by the organisers and the films presented on the day; the collated results of participants' votes; brief interviews with citizen participants at the end of the event; one group interview with three citizen participants two weeks after the event; and one group interview with three organisers of WWViews at the DBT two months after the event.[6] With respect to the analysis presented in this chapter, the data analysed are transcriptions of the audio recordings of the deliberations at three of the 16 tables on the day and field notes from participant observation on the day.

Enacting 'deliberative democracy' in the citizen deliberations: Empirical analysis

In this section, I present an empirical analysis of how the principles of deliberative democracy are articulated in the performance of 'scientific citizenship' in the deliberations. My account has two main themes. The first theme concerns relations between top-down and bottom-up dynamics, addressing the analytical question: What part do facilitators play in managing the tension between, on the one hand, creating space for a plurality of citizen voices and, on the other hand, steering the process in order to achieve a form of closure in line with pre-formulated aims? In the case of the first four sessions, the closure takes the form of individual answers to the set of questions deliberated upon; in the case of the final session, the closure constitutes consensus formation in the form of a shared message per table to be relayed to COP15 negotiators. The second theme concerns the nature of the deliberations as spaces in which expertise appears to be democratised such that citizen participants can lay claim to expertise and expert authority (based, for instance, on experiential knowledge forms). The focus here is on the extent to which, and how, those spaces are politicised such that claims to expertise and expert authority are subject to social contestation, with some knowledge claims being given more weight than others by the participants and some participants being positioned as more authoritative than others.

The role of the facilitators

The facilitators framed and managed the interaction at their tables in adherence with the principles of deliberative democracy through a number of different rhetorical strategies (applied deliberately or not). One strategy was to summarise the ongoing discussion and to present it in terms of an opposition between two different positions:

> *Facilitator: But I think that I'm hearing two different things a bit. Some are saying that we have in some way or another to extend the negotiation project or continue in some or other way to involve these countries. On the other hand, there are also some who're saying we also have to continue in some way or another.*
>
> *(8306, lines 413–417)*

The facilitator's characterisation of the discussion in terms of two opposing positions is obviously in line with the deliberative principle that participants should form a considered judgement on the basis of a weighing up of different perspectives. It can be criticised as a reduction of complexity that narrows down the discursive field to fit the terms of the facilitator's own interpretative lens and thus constrains what can be said in line with the facilitator's perspective. Alternatively, it can be understood as a constructive move that helps the participants to position themselves in the debate and take a clear stance.

Another strategy in play was the point that views were not fixed but open to change through the meeting of different perspectives in deliberation with others:

Jørgen: [...]And I also think that our first discussion about the degree of concern means that all of us around the table would say that something has to happen, so that's in line with the first theme.
Facilitator: And what about the last two themes[...]
Jørgen: Yes. Well, now I was one of them who answered 'a bit concerned' so for me it would suit me fine with two degrees. On the basis of the material I've seen and the discussion, that would be the level that I would vote for, now I'm going to hear the debate so.
Facilitator: Yes, you may well arrive at something else.

(3806, lines 53–63)

Here, the participant, Jørgen, makes the metacomment that the debate so far has indicated a consensus around the table. He then asserts the particular position he has arrived at in the debate partly as a result of input from the information material, but implies that his position is not fixed but may be open to change on the basis of the debate to follow ('now I'm going to hear the debate'). The facilitator makes this openness explicit in stating 'Yes, you may well arrive at something else'. Thus both the participant and the facilitator express the ideal of deliberative democratic debate that participants should be open to the different arguments presented in the information material (designed to provide an informed starting point for discussion) and in the discussion itself and then form a final position on the basis of hearing those arguments.

A requirement of processes of deliberative democracy is that everyone has the right to question the designated topics of discussion and to initiate reflexive arguments about the procedural rules and how they are implemented (Benhabib 1994: 31). Analysis of the WWViews event indicates that the deliberations did provide space for reflexive questioning. This can be understood in the terms of Bakhtin as a centrifugal opening up for a plurality of different, and potentially oppositional, voices and, in the terms of Mouffe, as an inclusionary move. The following is an example of the articulation of a reflexively questioning voice and how it was heard and tackled by the facilitator. Here, a participant expresses frustration based on reflexive recognition of a process in which the complexities of the issue – on which the deliberative process has up until that point concentrated – are set aside in the move towards formulating a single plan for action:

Josephine: Well, I'm sitting here thinking a bit about, well the statement we have to come up with at some point and it has to be max 30 words. And if I now [...] could imagine this responsible politician who really takes this seriously, note that I'm saying 'responsible politician', what is needed in order to influence this responsible politician? Well, does it just have to be a white piece of paper with 30 words or should we fold it like a paper airplane and make a sum? What is needed exactly to say to this politician, this is what we've got to do

[…]. What should the form be? Well, 30 words, yes. But a long sentence has to be formulated which may tend to be very general, so you read, 'yeah, we have to stop global warming, we have to have alternative energy, we have to have this and that'. Well, Primary 6 could also come up with that.
Marie: Yes, they could. […]
Facilitator: Well, Connie Hedegaard she asked for a signal for her negotiations, what she's got a mandate for. What will we as citizens accept.

(3804, lines 676–714)

Josephine's reflexive critique of the shift from deliberative consideration of the complexities of the issue to discussion of how to communicate a simple, singular message is met by the facilitator's attempt to justify the exercise – restating the purpose of WWViews whereby citizens are treated as central agents in the participatory political process: 'Well, Connie Hedegaard asked for a signal for her negotiations, what she has got a mandate for. What will we as citizens accept'. Also later on (about five minutes or so), the facilitator reiterates the need for simplicity on pragmatic grounds: 'Yes, that's really the way we'll get the most messages across in practice'. The participants proceed to perform the task without further questioning:

Martin: We'll gladly pay, that's a good statement, I think, because it's a pledge.
Lisbeth: Yes
Martin: It's a point of view. It's a citizen point of view, if we say, we really will!
Lisbeth: We're giving them a message that it's okay, well.
Martin: It's okay.

(3804, lines 771–779)

Here, the participants accept the premises of the exercise and the position as active citizens who are contributing to participatory democracy by bringing a message to COP15. Thus, the tension between the centrifugal tendency towards opening up for diverse voices and the centripetal tendency towards closure was at work here in the articulation of reflexive questioning voices and the defensive response. There were several other instances of the operation of the tension in this way whereby participants put forward reflexive, metacomments about the design of the debate, including raising questions about the formulations of the questions, and were met by explanations by the facilitators, defending the design on the grounds that it furthered the pragmatic aim of sending a message to COP15 that would have a direct impact on policymaking.

The democratisation of expertise and expert authority in practice

As expertise is democratised in the sense that scientific expertise and scientific experts relinquish their monopoly on truth, negotiations between different knowledge claims and identities take place and a tension often occurs between an opening up to a plurality of voices, on the one hand, and a move towards consensus formation, on the other. Here is an example:

> *Jakob: It's also a question of putting on the pressure so that we can get developments that mean that we save fuel.*
> *Peter: That's correct but you can't change fuel from A to B with a lorry.*
> *Christina: But what about something like ethanol, does that not pollute less?*
> *Peter: No, it doesn't pollute less.*
> *Christina: It doesn't?*
> *Peter: That's because you can say well if it is bio-ethanol, then it's CO_2 neutral ... but making it, isn't cheap.*
> *Christina: No, not cheap, but isn't it CO_2 neutral? It doesn't produce so much CO_2.*
> *Peter: Yes it does at first, but the green plant you plant, it absorbs it so it evens out. That's why it's called CO2 neutral.*
>
> *(3806, lines 732–751)*

In the next part of the discussion, Peter positions himself as an authority in relation to ethanol, but Christina does not give up and capitulate. First, Christina challenges Peter again:

> *Christina: It's the whole system we should look at.*

Peter appeals here to an implied consensus based on a unanimous 'we':

> *Peter: No but, it's the same that happens with the cost of moving a good from A to B, it goes up. We don't want that do we?*

But Christina challenges the consensus status of the claim:

> *Christina: Well actually, I don't know if we don't want that.*

Peter recognises Christina's position (*'Well but, well okay'*) and then argues against it:

> *Peter: Well but, well okay. It's the same as putting the price of oil up. Well, oil gets dearer [..].*

Christina meets this argument with a counter-argument:

> *Christina: Yes, yes. But the price difference won't be so big if we raise the price of fossil fuels.*

Jakob backs up Christina's position:

Jakob: Well, it's the fossil fuels you should raise the price of in order to encourage people to
Christina: use something else.

Peter challenges Christina's position and is then backed up by Anna:

Peter: But that's what I'm getting at, it'll also become dearer to move from A to B, because
it's more expensive today to produce that bio-ethanol.
Anna: And that's exactly what I meant when I said that somehow or another, it's got to be
sustainable in some or other way, because it's something we exploit.

(3806, lines 753–775)

This example illustrates how deliberative interactions are dynamic, and expert authority is not something that is fixed and tied to particular individuals but subject to social processes of negotiation. One participant, Christina, can be said to be ascribed, and to ascribe herself, a subordinate position and less authority; but, at the same time, there is space here for her to challenge this positioning and to be heard by the others. Although there is no symmetry or equality between the voices, this points at a relatively open process in line with the principle of deliberative democracy that deliberations should make room for a plurality of voices.

The information material distributed to the participants was occasionally drawn on explicitly as a source of expert knowledge:

Henrik: But I think you can say, I read something about it, that we use 25% of our CO_2 on
heating. And we use about 15–20% on transport. So if we started with these two central
questions or areas, we could maybe reduce a lot that way.
Conrad: a significant amount.
Henrik: yes.
Marianne: 25% is a lot, I thought a lot of it was production. It'll be less in the future.
Conrad: Isn't there something or other about this in here. Now I can't remember at all, but I
think it was in the material we were sent. Have none of you read it?
Tina: Yes, but we can't remember it.
Marianne: I can't remember that I received it.
Tina: I think I read it, but I can't remember how much it was.
Conrad: heating takes place in factories too.
Marianne: Yes, if you include that heating in production.
Anders: But we can say generally that the standard of living we have at home, it must be us
that have been contributing to making, we've got it by using a whole lot of CO_2 and that must
mean that we're now willing to pay the bill.

(3803, lines 895–922)

The information material is brought in as a source of factual knowledge as the group is concerned about facticity. However, it is not positioned unequivocally as the authoritative source that they are duty-bound to draw on: Tina states that she has read it but that 'we' cannot remember it; and Marianne states that she does not remember getting it. Thus, a casual stance towards this source of expert knowledge appears legitimate, in line with the popular/*folkelig* understanding of democracy with its privileging of experiential knowledge. At the same time, the participants do not invoke experiential knowledge forms; rather, they seek factual knowledge about the emissions of CO_2 and all statements are based on statistical information.

In some cases, participants presented expert knowledge from external sources as constructive contributions to the debate. In the following example, Anders suggests 'expert' material as something from which the others could benefit:

> Anders: Have any of you read the little 'The trip goes to the hot countries'?
> Caroline: No.
> Martine: What is it?
> Anders: It's a book you get free at libraries and bookshops which is about climate issues.
> Martine: Is it made just like, design-wise, just like 'The trip goes to...'?[7]
> Anders: Yes, totally. It is very enlightening I think. It's free. It's Politiken's (broadsheet daily newspaper) publishers who have made it, so it's the same people who make the others.
> Martine: But who has written it?
> Anders: Well, it's people from Politiken's publishers who have made it, and of course the Climate Ministry, all the experts have been part of it, Danida [Danish Government development agency] and the Foreign Ministry have primarily been those who have been responsible for publication. It can be found both in the bookshop and at the library.
> Martine: Yes, I thought it was a guidebook, ha ha.
> Konrad: Now I live in such a small town that there isn't even a bookshop.
> Anders: Okay, but just down on the corner, there's Politiken's bookshop. I could actually almost just go down there and smoke a fag at the same time. What's happening with the programme?
> Mathias (facilitator): Yes, well, now we're going to discuss a bit more and then there will be voting in half an hour.

> *(3803, lines 94–130)*

In line with the principle that expert knowledge provides the level of information necessary for participants to act as informed and enlightened scientific citizens, Anders implies that the book he is offering is useful for debate as it is 'very enlightening'. When the others say that they have not heard of the book and one says that he comes from a town without a bookshop, Anders offers to go and get it for them. Thus Anders provides expertise from a source other than that of the WWViews material and positions himself as teacher/mediator.

Negotiations of knowledge also occurred in which there were disagreement and the formation of consensus around one view:

> *Emma: There may be a problem with some of those countries in the middle group which have some nature which is getting destroyed and is emitting CO_2 which in reality isn't their industry. How do you subtract that from their quota? Well, Brazil can help having a huge rainforest.*
> *Josephine: No but they're involved in cutting it down.*
> *Emma: Or that the tundra is drying up [...]*
> *Josephine: Well*
> *Emma: That country cannot help it.*
> *Josephine: No I don't think that that is part of the calculations. Do you know that, Jonathan?*
> *Jonathan (facilitator): I don't think so.*
> *Josephine: No, I don't think so either. It's hard to take into account.*
> *Emma: You can't.*
> *Josephine: You can't work it out.*
> *Jonathan (facilitator): It's based on human activities.*
> *Emma: Yes, but it's a consequence of human activities.*
> *Jonathan (facilitator): Yes, I think it's to the power of 1.*
> *Josephine: Well it must be the CO_2 that comes from creating energy which you take into account, right?*
> *Jonathan (facilitator): Industrial production and transport etc.*
> *Josephine: Yes, but you have to in these annex-1 countries or in all the countries that are not annex 1 but are growing a lot now, you have to think of them.*
>
> *(3805, R1_0012, lines 1498–1531)*

In the negotiation of meanings here, Josephine expresses uncertainty and positions the facilitator as a source of knowledge capable of providing knowledge that will alleviate the uncertainty: 'Do you know that, Jonathan?' In response, the facilitator himself echoes Josephine's position: 'I don't think so'. Josephine uses this to confirm her position – 'No, I don't think so either' – and this leads to the co-construction of consensus. Thus, the facilitator contributes to the formation of consensus by providing support for the initial point of view around which consensus forms. Again, it is expert, scientific knowledge that is articulated rather than knowledges based on wider experiential and moral perspectives.

This focus on scientific expertise can be seen in the light of the organisers' deliberate framing of the event in terms of the standard set of questions. This set of questions closely follows the agenda of COP15, the questions having been selected as the agenda for WWViews in order to maximise the possibility of WWViews having an impact on the negotiations at COP15. In addition, it was decided that standardisation was necessary in order to reduce the occurrence of differences in the organisation of the different events that would hinder generalisability and threaten the construction of a unitary, coherent 'voice' transmittable to the negotiators at COP15.[6] The mirroring of the COP15 agenda may have led to deliberations revolving around issues relatively detached from people's everyday life. And thus the relevance of people's experiential knowledges may have been minimised.

Concluding discussion

The above analysis focused, then, on how 'scientific citizenship' was played out in the enactment of deliberative principles through the facilitators' management of the citizen deliberation processes and through the participants' articulation of the subject position of 'citizen' representatives. A key theme was the 'democratisation of expertise' at work in participants' negotiation among different forms of knowledge and expert authority. The examples point at the complex dynamics of 'opening up' for deliberations among a plurality of diverse voices and 'closing down' in reaching individual and collective decisions. In those dynamics, the tension between centripetal and centrifugal tendencies was clearly at work.

Judged from *within* the terms of deliberative democracy, WWViews can be said to have given agency to participants by treating them as scientific citizens and opening up for a plurality of citizen voices in the deliberations themselves. One way in which an opening up took place was through the articulation of voices in individual table deliberations that reflexively questioned the premises of the deliberations. Additionally, in treating participants as scientific citizens, the practices may well have contributed to creating more informed and active citizens – or, in the terms of deliberative democracy, the practices had *civic virtue*.

At the same time – and still judged in its own terms – the lack of visible, direct impact on COP15 is a weakness for WWViews, given that the event was presented to participants as giving them the possibility to influence decision-making at COP15 and thus satisfy the democratic ideals of public engagement with respect to relations between science, expertise and citizens. Crucially, this objective was communicated clearly to the participants in official material and in the plenum talks and facilitators' instructions and comments.

'Dialogue' between policymakers and citizens, then, served as a promise that played a constitutive role in discursively constructing the event as a site for public participation in environmental governance. This is line with Felt and Fochler's point that participation can be understood as part of an 'economy of promises' whereby the *promise*, implicit in public engagement practices, of a more democratic form of politics appears to suffice, irrespective of how 'participation' is actually ascribed meaning and enacted in practice (2010: 236).

In this chapter I have also judged WWViews from *outwith* the model of deliberative democracy – and more specifically from a post-structuralist perspective combining a Bakhtinian focus on the dialogic interplay of voices and the tension between the centrifugal tendency towards difference and the centripetal tendency towards unity and a Mouffian critique of the ideal of 'consensus without exclusion' (Mouffe 2000: 48). Inevitable dynamics of inclusion and exclusion necessarily entail the marginalisation or silencing of voices, articulating particular forms of knowledge and identities.

My point is not that these dynamics are necessarily problematic. Also, bottom-up activities are not *a priori* preferable; from the perspective of the strategic goal of the organisers – the formation of a 'citizen voice' that is communicable to decision-makers – top-down management of the deliberation processes is necessary. And in relation to WWViews as an experiment in global public engagement, the attempt at standardisation allows for the production of social practices on a cross-national scale. Moreover, it can be argued that higher status should be given to relevant scientific expertise as opposed to other knowledge forms on the grounds that it is scientifically valid. (Collins and Evans 2002). However, it *is* problematic not to acknowledge the operation of the dynamics of inclusion and exclusion and not to reflect on how top-down management circumscribes practices of deliberation by excluding certain voices that articulate particular knowledge forms and identities.

I argue, then, for the value of engaging in reflexive discussion of the dynamics of exclusion and inclusion and the (contextually justifiable) conditions that circumscribe the scope for action by the participating citizens. Reflexivity provides a base for considering how to refine engagement practices within the terms of what is practically possible. Here, the ideals can be held up against the complexities of practices of deliberation, circumscribed as they are by socially and politically specific conditions for action.

Reflexive discussion could fruitfully build on pre-existing elements of reflexivity in public engagement. As analysed above, reflexive moments, involving a centrifugal opening up for dissident voices, took place at the WWViews event, as participants in individual table deliberations were able to question the reduction of complexity that occurred in the move towards the construction of a common message. But the closure that occurred in the facilitators' defence of the reduction in complexity, in my view, was too abrupt; I would propose the systematic integration of spaces for reflexive consideration of the processes of inclusion and exclusion in the event itself.

In addition, while dynamics of exclusion and inclusion are inevitable and top-down management is necessary in order to produce a global event with a clear identity, my view, building on Mouffe's critique of deliberative democracy, is that the figure of the 'ordinary citizen' basic to the deliberative model of engagement underestimates the centrality of political struggle and thus leads to practices that are more heavily exclusionary than they need be. The construction of the 'purified' public of ordinary citizens works to further the exclusion of different voices articulating a diversity of knowledge forms.

To open up to more diverse voices, it could be argued that the interests of different stakeholders and interest groups ought to be acknowledged in deliberations and links ought to be cultivated between WWViews activities and the activities of grassroots activists and NGO's. As Gaventa and Cornwall assert, the spaces for change that large-scale participatory exercises create from above should be filled partly by voices from social movements 'from below' (2006). 'Otherwise', they warn, 'there is always the danger that these openings for participation will simply mirror the status quo and serve to strengthen and reinforce more dominant voices at every level' (Gaventa and Cornwall 2006: 79).

Given its organisation 'from above' by an institution connected to institutions of established politics, there is also the danger that the discourse of dialogue and participation works to further dominant knowledge forms and, in the terms of subaltern studies, maintain the subjugation of marginal voices (Dutta and Pal 2010). Thus, the WWViews event could be said to represent a space for elitist knowledge production (Dutta and Pal 2010: 364). When participants are positioned as 'ordinary citizens', who represent a national 'we' of Danish citizens and contribute to the formation of a global citizen voice to be heard by politicians at COP15, other voices – articulating alternative knowledge forms and identities – are excluded and the centripetal tendency towards unity overpowers the centrifugal tendency towards difference.

References

Andersen, I. E. and Jæger, B., 'Scenario workshops and consensus conferences: towards more democratic decision-making', *Science and Public Policy*, 26:5 (1999), pp. 331–340.

Agger, A., Jelsøe, E., Jæger, B. and Phillips, L., 'Deliberating Climate Change: The Creation of a Global Voice for Citizens – the Case of Denmark'. In M. Rask, R. Worthington and M. Lammi (eds), *Citizen Participation in Global Environmental Governance*. London: Earthscan, 2011.

Bakhtin, M., *TheDialogic Imagination: Four Essays*, edited by Michael Holquist, trans. Caryl Emerson and Michael Holquist. Austin and London: University of Texas Press, 1981.

—— *Problems of Dostoevsky's Poetics*, edited by and trans. Carly Emerson. Minneapolis: University of Minnesota Press, 1984.

Bakhtin, M., *Speech Genres and Other Late Essays*. Austin: University of Texas Press, 1986.

Benhabib, S. , 'Deliberative Rationality and Models of Democratic Legitimacy', *Constellations*, 1 (1994), pp. 25–53.

Bickerstaff, K., Lorenzoni, I., Jones, M. and Pidgeon, N., 'Locating Scientific Citizenship: The Institutional Contexts and Cultures of Public Engagement'. *Science, Technology, Human Values*. OnlineFirst, published on 3 March 2010, pp. 1–27.

Blok, A., 'Experts on Public Trial: On Democratizing Expertise through a Danish Consensus Conference'. *Public Understanding of Science*, 162:2 (2007), pp. 163–182.

Button, M. and Ryfe, D., 'What Can We Learn from the Practice of Deliberative Democracy?' In J. Gastil and P. Levine (eds), *The Deliberative Democracy Handbook Strategies for Effective Civic Engagement in the 21st Cetury*. San Francisco: Jossey-Bass, 2005, pp. 20–33.

Carolan, M., 'Democratizing knowledge: sustainable and conventional agricultural field days as divergent democratic forms', *Science, Technology and Human Values,* 33:4 (2008), pp. 508–528.

Collins, H. M. and Evans, R., 'The Third Wave of Science Studies: Studies of Expertise and Experience'. *Social Studies of Science*, 32:2 (2002), pp. 235–296.

Delgado, A., Kjølberg, K. and Wickson, F., 'Public Engagement Coming of Age: From Theory to Practice in STS Encounters with Nanotechnology'. *Public Understanding of Science*, pp. 1–20. Published online ahead of print, 11 May 2010.

Dryzek, J. S., *Deliberative Democracy and Beyond – Liberals, Critics, Contestations*. Oxford: Oxford University Press, 2000.

Dutta, M. and Pal, M., 'Dialog Theory in Marginalized Settings: A Subaltern Studies Approach'. *Communication Theory*, 20:4 (2010), pp. 363–386.

Einsiedel, E. and Eastlick, D., 'Consensus Conferences as Deliberative Democracy: A Communications Perspective'. *Science Communication*, 21:4 (2000), pp. 323–343.

Einsiedel, E., Jelsøe, E. and Breck, T., 'Publics at the Technology Table: The Consensus Conference in Denmark, Canada and Australia'. *Public Understanding of Science*, 10:1 (2001), pp. 83–98.

Elam, M. and Bertilsson, M., 'Consuming, Engaging and Confronting Science: The Emerging Dimensions of Scientific Citizenship'. *European Journal of Social Theory*, 62:6 (2003), pp. 233–251.

Felt, U. and Fochler, M., 'Machineries for Making Publics: Inscribing and de-scribing publics in public engagement', *Minerva*, 48:3 (2010), pp. 219–238.

Gastil, J. and Levine, P. (eds), *The Deliberative Democracy Handbook Strategies for Effective Civic Engagement in the 21st Century*. San Francisco: Jossey–Bass, 2005.

Gaventa, J. and Cornwall, A., 'Power and Knowledge'. In P. Reason and H. Bradbury (eds), *Handbook of Action Research*. London: Sage, 2006, pp. 71–82.

Goven, J., 'Deploying the Consensus Conference in New Zealand: Democracy and De-problematization'. *Public Understanding of Science*, 12:4 (2003), pp. 423–440.

Gurevitch, Z., 'Plurality in Dialogue: A Comment on Bakhtin'. *Sociology*, 342:2, pp. 243–263.

Guston, D., 'Evaluating the First US Consensus Conference: The Impact of the Citizen's Panel on Telecommunications and the Future of Democracy'. *Science, Technology and Human Values*, 24:4 (1999), pp. 451–482.

Gutmann, A. and Thompson, D., *Democracy and Disagreement*. Cambridge: The Belknap Press of Harvard University Press, 1996.

Guttman, N., 'Bringing the Mountain to the Public: Dilemmas and Contradictions in the Procedures of Public Deliberation Initiatives that Aim to Get "ordinary citizens" to Deliberate Policy Issues'. *Communication Theory*, 17:4 (2007), pp. 411–438.

Harrison, S. and Mort, M., 'Which Champions, Which People? Public and User Involvement in Health Care as a Technology of Legitimation'. *Social Policy & Administration*, 32:1 (1998), pp. 60–70.

Hornig Priest, S. 'Commentary - Room at the Bottom of Pandora's Box: Peril and Promise in Communicating Nanotechnology', *Science Communication* 27:2 (2005), pp. 292–299.

Horst, M., 'In Search of Dialogue: Staging Science Communication in Consensus Cconferences'. In D. Cheng, M. Claessens, T. Gascoigne, J. Metcalfe, B. Schiele and S. Shi (eds), *Communicating Science in Social Contexts: New Models, New Practices*. New York: Springer, 2008.

Horst, M., 'Caring for Discomfort: Science Communication Experiments between Diffusion, Dialogue and Emergence'. In L. Phillips, M. Kristiansen, M. Vehviläinen and E.Gunnarsson (ed.), *Knowledge and Power in Collaborative Research: A Reflexive Approach*. London: Routledge, 2013.

Horst, M. and Irwin, A., 'Nations at Ease with Radical Knowledge: On Consensus, Consensusing and False Consensusness'. *Social Studies of Science*, 40:1 (2010), pp. 105–126.

Irwin, A., 'Constructing the Scientific Citizen: Science and Democracy in the Biosciences'. *Public Understanding of Science*, 10:1 (2001), pp. 1–18.

———— 'The Politics of Talk: Coming to Terms with the 'New' Scientific Governance'. *Social Studies of Science*, 36:2 (2006), pp. 299–330.

Irwin, A. and Michael, M., *Science, social theory and public knowledge*. Maidenhead: Open University Press, 2003.

Kerr, A., Cunningham-Burley, S. and Tutton, R., 'Shifting Subject Positions: Experts and Lay People in Public Dialogue'. *Social Studies of Science*, 37:3 (2007), pp. 385–411.

Klüver, L., 'Consensus Conferences at the Danish Board of Technology'. In S. Joss, and J. Durant (eds), *Public Participation in Science: The Role of Consensus Conferences in Europe*. London: Science Museum, 1995, 41–49.

Kurath, M. and Gisler, P., 'Informing, Involving or Engaging? Science Communication, in the Ages of Atom-, Bio- and Nanotechnology'. *Public Understanding of Science*, 18:5 (2009), pp. 559–573.

MacNaghten, P., Kearnes, M. and Wynne, B., "Nanotechnology, Governance and Public Deliberation: What Role for the Social Sciences", *Science Communication*, 27:2 (2005), pp. 268–291.

Michael, M., 'Publics performing publics: of PiGs, PiPs and politics', *Public Understanding of Science*, 16:3 (2009), pp. 279–297.

Mouffe, C., *The Return of the Political*. London and New York: Verso, 1993.

———— *The Democratic Paradox*. London and New York: Verso, 2000.

Phillips, L., *The Promise of Dialogue: The Dialogic Turn in the Production and Communication of Knowledge*. Amsterdam: John Benjamins Publishing, 2011.

Rogers-Hayden, T. and Pidgeon, N., 'Moving engagement "upstream"? Nanotechnologies and Royal Society and Royal Academy of Engineering's inquiry', *Public Understanding of Science*, 16:3 (2007), pp. 345–364.

Rummens, S., 'Democracy as a Non-Hegemonic Struggle? Disambiguating Chantal Mouffe's Agonistic Model of Politics', *Constellations*, 16:3 (2009), pp. 377–389.

Seifert, F., 'Local steps in an international career: A Danish-style consensus conference in Austria', *Public Understanding of Science*, 15:1 (2006), pp. 73–88.

Stirling, A., '"Opening up" and "closing down": Power, Participation and Pluralism in the Social Appraisal of Technology'. *Science, Technology and Human Values*, 33:2 (2008), pp. 262–294.

Trench, B., 'Towards an Analytical Framework of Science Communication Models'. In D. Cheng, M. Claessens, T. Gascoigne, J. Metcalfe, B. Schiele and S. Shi (eds), *Communicating Science in Social Contexts: New Models, New Practices*. New York: Springer Publishing, 2008.

Wynne, B., 'Public Engagement as a Means of Restoring Public Trust in Science – Hitting the Notes but Missing the Music?', *Community Genetics*, 9:3 (2006), pp. 211–220.

Notes

1   This chapter is based on Phillips (2011). For a lengthier discussion and analysis, see Chapter 4 of Phillips (2011).

2   From the WWViews website: http://www.wwviews.org.

3   From the WWViews website: http://www.wwviews.org.

4   One key difference between the WWV format and that of consensus conferences relates to the role of consensus formation. At the WWViews event, the first four deliberation sessions ended in each participant individually answering a set of questions and placing them in a ballot box; formal consensus formation took place only in the final session when the participants at each table carried out the task of formulating a common message from their table to the negotiators at COP15. In consensus conferences, in contrast, consensus is sought in two phases – first, the citizen panel's selection and formulation of the main questions to be asked of the experts, which then forms the agenda for the conference, and second, the conclusions and recommendations of the citizen panel's final document (Andersen and Jæger 1999: 335).

5   From the WWViews website: http://www.wwviews.org.

6   The empirical research presented in this chapter was conducted in collaboration with Annika Agger, Birgit Jæger and Erling Jelsøe. The collaboration encompasses both data production and data analysis – see Agger et al. (2011) for an account of our joint research.

7   *The trip goes to...* is a series of travel guides published by the Danish publishers Politiken.

8   Interview with organisers, 24 November 2009, lines 2166–2173.

Chapter 8

Public Engagement as a Field of Tension between Bottom-up and Top-down Strategies: Critical Discourse Moments in an 'Energy Town'

Anders Horsbøl and Inger Lassen

In the ongoing debate about climate change, *public engagement* is given increasing prominence as a way of encouraging citizens to participate in climate change mitigation efforts. This is part of a surge in public engagement initiatives in many countries in the western world. At a rhetorical level, it seems that bottom-up approaches concerned with public participation and dialogue with citizens have replaced the older, increasingly denigrated 'knowledge deficit model' and the related paradigm of 'public understanding of science'. In practice, however, as several studies document (for instance, Felt and Fochler 2010; Irwin 2006; Kurath and Gisler 2009; Phillips 2011), top-down approaches concerned with educating and convincing the public are still very much alive, and initiatives of public engagement often seem to be characterised by tension between top-down and bottom-up strategies.

Whereas this general insight is already well established, more concrete and in-depth studies of the nature of these tensions in public engagement processes are needed. This is not least the case for climate change mitigation and environmental sustainability efforts, where many of the more promising initiatives take place at a local, as opposed to national, scale, in the form of initiatives by towns, communities and regions around the world. These local initiatives pose new challenges when it comes to public participation. Crucially, they may entail the articulation of new tensions between top-down and bottom-up approaches. This ought to be more fully explored, both in the interest of substantial public participation, and in the interest of effective climate change mitigation. This chapter contributes to this aim by a study of a series of meetings between (invited) citizens and municipality representatives in the context of an energy transition project in a Danish town. Methodologically, we address the issue from a discourse analytical perspective (Fairclough 2003; van Leeuwen 2009; Wodak 2000), paying particular attention to critical discourse moments (Chilton 1987; Gamson 1992), that is, moments where discursive constructions are challenged, and the purpose or the trajectory of the public engagement process is opened up for discussion and decision-making. Our analysis thus focuses on the ways in which citizenship and public participation are negotiated and enacted interactionally in those critical moments. We thereby aim to assess central tensions between top-down and bottom-up approaches in the engagement process and point to factors constraining public participation in the context of local climate change mitigation and environmental sustainability initiatives.

We begin this chapter by offering information about the context in which our case is situated. This is followed by an overview of relevant literature within the fields of climate change, public engagement and scientific citizenship. Then we explain our methods for the collection and analysis of data, and finally we analyse and discuss a selected number of examples of critical discourse moments in which citizen positions are negotiated. This is followed by a brief conclusion on our empirical study of the practice of public participation and tensions between top-down and bottom-up strategies.

Contextual background

At a local level, several municipalities in Denmark have taken action to prevent climate change by, for instance, developing renewable energy sources. By August 2011, out of 98 municipalities in Denmark, a total of 70 had declared themselves 'Climate Municipalities',[1] thereby committing themselves to persistent reductions in carbon dioxide emission over the next years. Among the front runners in this initiative is the municipality of Frederikshavn in northern Denmark, which has set the goal of 100 per cent reliance on renewable energy sources by the end of 2015 for the 25,000 inhabitants of the town Frederikshavn and its vicinity.[2] In this context, it is important to note that Frederikshavn is commonly referred to in Denmark as a marginalised and in some ways disenfranchised community, partly as a result of its location on the periphery of the Global North. Ever since the closing down of two shipyards in the 1980s, the town has been at risk of being abandoned by people who migrate to other areas in Denmark for jobs. In a so-called Energy Camp, which took place in 2006 with the purpose of discussing how Denmark could make a transition from fossil fuels to renewable energy, Frederikshavn was chosen as a test site because of its windy and sunny location by the sea, but also because there has been a tradition of strong political commitment and a will to survive adverse conditions of local recession resulting from the many job losses. By promoting the aims of building a sustainable environment without using fossil fuels and by focusing on green technology and 'green growth', Energy Town Frederikshavn[3] hopes to create an attractive municipality where people wish to live. One of the major concerns to be addressed to ensure the success of the energy town project relates to the degree to which citizens participate in the process. Energy Town Frederikshavn raises this issue in their introduction material (NY) as follows: 'If we are clever enough to convince the citizens about the perspectives in this magnificent project for sustainable prosperity, the politicians on all levels will support it too and the investors will see the business possibilities. … This is why the involvement of the citizens is so important'.

Public engagement and scientific citizenship

For citizens to engage with sustainable growth, some level of 'scientific citizenship' is needed. Scientific citizenship may be subsumed in what Mejlgaard (2007: 38) refers to as *competence* and *participation*. Briefly explained, *competence* – also known as *public competence* – refers to knowledge among the general public about matters of science and technology, subsumed in the acronym PUS (Public Understanding of Science). *Public participation*, on the other hand, characterises 'organized processes adopted by elected officials, government agencies, or other public- or private-sector organizations to engage the public in environmental assessment, planning, decision making, management, monitoring and evaluation' (Dietz and Stern 2008: 17). PUS is a tradition of research and practice, which gained its name from a report from the Royal Society of London (1985) aiming at 'bringing science to citizens'. The ambition of the report was to 'empower citizens to deal successfully with the science and technologies of their everyday lives', but, at the same time, it was assumed that more knowledge about science and technology would lead to the greater acceptance and appropriation of science (ibid.: 39) and thereby reduce the impacts of what science perceived as a legitimation crisis (Irwin 2006: 317). However, surveys (e.g. EU-barometer reported in Bauer and Gaskell 2002) have demonstrated that narrowing the knowledge gap between science and citizens does not necessarily lead to higher acceptance of science and technology; perhaps surprisingly, increased levels of knowledge have instead often led to polarised attitudes (Allum, Boy and Bauer 2002), to which interest gradually emerging among scholars critical of the PUS research direction bears witness. Rather than dissemination of knowledge from science to passive citizens, a new participatory approach known as PES (Public Engagement with Science) emerged. This approach aimed at direct interaction, dialogue and two-way communication. In PES research the focus is on public participation rather than on public competence (Mejlgaard and Stares 2010: 545).

In line with new directions of research in science communication, more recently subsumed under the umbrella term of the *participatory turn*, literature on climate change issues has addressed the limited public response, which has been variably explained with reference to 'lack of information', 'media distortion' or 'lack of concern', implying that 'if people only knew' they would act (Norgaard 2011: 1). As these explanations have partly failed and seeing that more knowledge and information about climate change has not significantly led to stronger commitment among citizens (termed by Giddens as the 'Giddens's Paradox', Giddens 2009: 2), alternative approaches have taken over. A study by Norgaard (2011) of climate change issues and everyday practices among Norwegians indicated that '[….] what we can observe in the public silence on climate change in United States and around the world – is not in most cases a rejection of information per se, but the failure to integrate this knowledge into everyday life or to transform it into social action' (ibid.: 11). As suggested by Norgaard (ibid.) a lack of knowledge does not seem to be the problem – rather, how to transform knowledge into action seems to be the stumbling block (see also Wolf 2010).

In response to mounting public scepticism towards science, following a number of controversies over risk-prone technologies such as nuclear power, pharmaceuticals, food technologies, electromagnetism, genetic modification and nanotechnology, the PUS paradigm was, if not replaced, then supplemented by a *participatory* paradigm that called for more democratic involvement of citizens (Felt and Fochler 2010). Some catchwords frequently associated with the 'participatory turn' are *participation, empowerment, public engagement, dialogue and public consultation* (Irwin 2006; Kurath and Gisler 2009; Phillips 2011; Wynne 2006). Instruments for engaging the public in what Irwin (2006) has referred to as 'new' scientific governance were developed, for example *consensus conferences, public consultations, citizens meetings* and *focus group discussions*. In Denmark, the Danish Board of Technology (DBT), which was established in 1986, has played a central role in the development of participatory methods of public engagement with science and technology (see Phillips, this volume, for an analysis of a global consultation on climate change organised by the DBT). However, although citizen participation in scientific governance would seem to be a truly democratic approach that allows citizens access to decision-making processes, scholars seem to be increasingly critical of aspects of the 'participatory turn'. Wynne (2006: 212) refers to public engagement as 'a means of restoring public trust in science'. Suggesting that science has 'failed to respond constructively to the experience of public engagement' (ibid.: 218), he argues for the need for a more reflective diagnosis of the causes of public mistrust of science. In a study of a series of official reports in Britain, Irwin (2006: 314) cautions us against accepting concepts such as *consultation, dialogue* and *engagement* at face value because such concepts are open to variable interpretation. As a second reservation, Irwin (ibid.: 315) voices concern over how citizens are selected and represented in public debates. This concern is shared by Wynne (2007) (in Felt and Fochler 2010: 221), who argues that by 'focusing on invited publics as the most authoritative and "true" representation of public interests', the voices of other uninvited publics are excluded.

To Dietz and Stern (2008: 14), the dichotomy of invited or uninvited is important from the point of view of participation. In other words, how strong is the effort made by participants to participate and by the conveners to enable and support participation? However, the dichotomy of invited versus uninvited may represent an oversimplistic construction of citizens and the general public, as also indicated by our data (see *Analysis*). A third caveat that Irwin (ibid.) refers to is the design of the engagement initiative. The institution that invites citizens is bound to have an agenda, and might thus preempt the outcome of the discussions. One might ask with Irwin: 'What scope can there be for dialogue when the direction is already set?' (Irwin 2006: 316).

In a similar vein, and taking inspiration from Foucault (2003), Phillips (2011: 13) addresses the issue of knowledge and power, and challenges the taken for granted positive value that is ascribed to dialogue, arguing that the discourse of 'dialogue' may mask the operation of knowledge–power in dialogue-based practices by offering 'a false promise of egalitarian, democratic processes of mutual learning and knowledge co-production or, at best, a promise that is only partially met'. Recognising that there is a need for 'reflexive analysis of how the tension between controlling the process in order to achieve strategic ends and opening for a multiplicity of voices is negotiated', Phillips (2011: 41–42) develops a model for analysing the production and communication of knowledge which addresses the tensions inherent in the enactment of 'dialogue' and 'participation' in the specific contexts of practice. Here she draws on critique that asserts that the use of 'dialogue' is often heavily circumscribed through the top-down design and management of the processes; in the worst cases, it functions 'instrumentally to pass off "top-down", decision-making processes as bottom-up, democratic ones' (Phillips 2011: 13).

As we have seen, much literature on citizen participation has primarily focused on risk issues relating to genetic modification and nanotechnology (e.g. Bauer and Gaskell 2002; Wynne 2006; Irwin 2006; Kurath and Gisler 2009) and the extent to which members of the public have confidence in science (Wynne 2006). Addressing the topic of citizen participation in relation to nanotechnology, Delgado, Kjølberg and Wickson (2010: 1) support the view that, rather than focusing on how to generate public acceptance of new technology, public engagement should assist the active involvement by citizens 'in the development of socio-technical trajectories'. Following Wynne (2006), they argue that there is a 'gap' between theoretical ideals of public engagement and their practical implementation, a problem that needs to be tackled (Delgado, Kjølberg and Wickson 2010: 2).

To conclude, the participatory turn in science communication has not simply replaced the paradigm of PUS; rather, 'participatory' science governance is characterised by tensions and contradictions resulting from the lingering presence of the deficit model and the operation of both top-down and bottom-up dynamics. Thus it is important to explore empirically how public engagement is being practised with sensitivity towards the articulation of those tensions and contradictions (Irwin 2006; Phillips 2011). Facing this challenge, we take a discourse approach and ask how participants position themselves in discursive struggles over what counts as legitimate talk, who controls the framework of engagement (Irwin 2006: 315–16) and how participants 'inhabit and appropriate' discursive spaces offered to them (Felt and Fochler 2010: 220).

We will do so in relation to climate change mitigation initiatives, acknowledging that although there are many similarities in the ways in which public engagement is approached within the fields of bio-science and climate change, there are also marked differences. An important difference is that while there may be ways of opting out of using GMO or nanotechnology products, climate change is likely to affect us all. Also, GMO and nanotechnology have generally been met with public scepticism, whereas the scientific account of global warming is now widely, although not entirely, trusted among the general public, and global warming is often represented in spectacular ways in the news media (Cottle 2009; Doyle 2011). But nevertheless, public measures seem to be lagging behind. In addition, as noted above, climate change mitigation initiatives increasingly seem to be initiated on a local scale by towns, cities, communities and regions, acting without control or coordination by the nation state. Examples include the transition town movement (Hopkins 2011), or the 'climate municipalities' and 'energy towns' of our case. These local initiatives pose new challenges when it comes to public participation and the discursive construction and negotiation of citizen identities, and particular tensions between top-down and bottom-up approaches seem to emerge.

Data and methodology

Our data are based on a series of meetings between citizens and representatives from Energy Town Frederikshavn[4]. The energy town secretariat initiated the meetings by inviting citizens to help realise Energy Town Frederikshavn and contribute to the project. After the first meeting in January 2009, local citizens signed up as citizen participants and most of them took part in the five meetings that followed. The meetings took place approximately once a month until August 2009 in Frederikshavn and typically lasted around two hours. Apart from the citizens, two to four representatives of Energy Town Frederikshavn took part in each meeting. The meetings were audio recorded by the authors and subsequently transcribed.

The series of meetings provide an opportunity to study public engagement as a local, situated practice, which is enacted in the ongoing interaction in the group. We aim to study public engagement with a focus on the tensions between bottom-up and top-down approaches, as discourse-in-action. In line with Linell and Marková (1993), who draw on Bakhtin (1986), we take a *dialogical* approach to the citizen meetings. This does not imply that we consider the citizen meetings to be dialogical in a normative sense, but that we consider the discursive construals in the meetings as socially co-produced and realised by the participants' responsive and anticipatory (projective) orientation to each other. In line with ethnomethodology (Garfinkel 1967), and partly inspired by conversation analysis, we shall thus focus on the ways in which the participants orient towards each other's prior and subsequent contributions, including 'a retrospective interpretation of a prior contribution and a prospective anticipation (projection) of what is going to follow, or of what would be a relevant continuation' (Linell and Marková 1993: 183). We understand this dialogical approach in an all-encompassing way, such that the retrospective interpretation may orient to contributions by the previous speaker as well as to contributions at a much earlier stage of the interaction. Thus, participants continuously negotiate whether topics are exhausted and problems solved, or whether they need to be picked up and discussed anew. Similarly, the prospective anticipation may orient not only to the very next contribution, but also to questions to be addressed at a much later stage of the interaction. Within the framework of our dialogical approach, we draw on analytical concepts from systemic functional linguistics, critical discourse analysis, rhetorics and argumentation analysis, in order to analyse the participants' interactional orientations and the co-production of meaning in terms of both discursive objects and identities.

Moreover, the dialogical approach can be expanded beyond the singular interaction. The series of meetings makes it possible to study how the practice of citizen involvement traverses the individual interaction and unfolds on a larger time scale (Lemke 2000), that is, how the participants intertextually refer back to former discussions or decisions at prior meetings, or refer ahead to future meetings and things to be accomplished later in the process. In that sense, *recontextualisation* of discourse from one meeting to another (Bernstein 1990; Chouliaraki/Fairclough 1999; Wodak 2000; van Leeuwen 2009) forms a central way of studying public engagement as it unfolds over time.

The analysis will centre on a selection of *critical discourse moments* (Chilton 1987; Gamson 1992; Carvalho 2007) in the series of meetings. The term has been used in media studies to signify incidents 'that make discourse on an issue especially visible' (Gamson 1992: 26), but we find it applicable also to a course of interpersonal interactions as in this case. In line with Carvalho, we understand critical discourse moments as incidents 'that could bring challenges to discursive constructions of the issue' (Carvalho 2007: 226). Critical discourse moments, in our use of the term, are moments where discursive constructions are challenged, and where the purpose or the trajectory of the process is called into question and opened up for discussion and decision-making. Critical discourse moments are decisive moments in which different perspectives are articulated and (potential) conflicts appear. These moments emerge when different voices diverge and challenge a given representation of the common will of a group, that is, challenge a *translation* of the many individual voices into one (Callon 1986; Latour 2005). Critical discourse moments thus call for a re-negotiation of the way in which to translate the diverging voices into one representation of the trajectory of the group. This may also involve attempts to establish connections or even *discourse coalitions* (Hajer 1995) with other actors in which attempts are made to discursively construe common projects and enroll third parties in these. In the analysis, we will trace some of these processes *of challenging, negotiating, coalition-building* and *translation*.

We thereby aim to make visible important tensions between bottom-up and top-down discursive strategies in the citizen meetings and point to factors that limit or constrain citizens' participation. Our analysis focuses on two critical discourse moments. First, an exchange between a citizen and the energy town representatives at the second meeting where the tasks and obligations of the participants are challenged and negotiated, and second, an interaction leading up to and including a meeting with a guest from the local utility at which an attempt is made to form a discourse alliance with the utility.

Analysis

Setting the scene

The first part of the analysis focuses on the second citizen meeting in the series of six meetings. Before we enter the analysis, we will give a brief account of the way in which the participating citizens were recruited and positioned by the invitation letter and press release from Energy Town Frederikshavn, which preceded the series of meetings. First, in the invitation letter, published on the website of the energy town project, the term *activist* was used to refer to the potential participating citizens. The headline of the letter read 'Energy Town Frederikshavn is looking for activists'. Commonly, the notion of 'activists' refers to people engaged in grassroots movements, who are *uninvited* citizens and operate outside established systems of power and often in opposition to these. In the invitation letter, however, the energy town as a municipal authority explicitly invited 'activists' and thereby appropriated the term within an institutional frame in a seemingly paradoxical way. The citizen reader of the invitation letter was thus called upon to act as an activist, but obviously in a new, modified sense of the word, which had yet to be negotiated in subsequent meetings. Secondly, both the invitation letter and the press release were characterised by a tension between representing Energy Town Frederikshavn as a given entity in terms of purpose and overall roadmap, which was to be communicated by the participating citizens to other citizens in the area, and as a more open entity to be influenced and shaped by the participating citizens. In that sense, there was a tension between positioning citizen participation as the implementation of a roadmap, within the terms of a discourse of green governmentality, and as bringing about ideas and activities that could take a less predictable path, more in line with a discourse of civic environmentalism (Bäckstrand and Lövbrand 2007; see Lassen et al. 2011 for a full analysis of the invitation letter and press release). In that sense, two very different citizen (or 'activist') identities were made available in the invitation letter and press release.

Information about the first citizen meeting was also diffused through local media, and the energy town secretariat used a word-of-mouth method to invite people who had formerly participated in citizen-driven activities. About 50 people turned up at the meeting. Its main aims were to inform the participants about Energy Town Frederikshavn, brainstorm about ideas for the energy town and recruit citizens for the 'activist' group. The first meeting brought about a large number of ideas, drawing on diverse discourses such as ecology, branding and green growth, and 31 local citizens signed up as 'activists'.

The second meeting was the first time representatives of Energy Town Frederikshavn met with the participating citizens. After a word of welcome, a presentation round and other initial steps, the group entered a discussion about the planning of the further process. The discussion was launched by one of the representatives of the energy town project (E-Ann[5]), who asked the group for 'suggestions as to how we deal with this now ... if there are any suggestions for or if you have any personal suggestions as to how we best do this'. A citizen (C-Julia) immediately responded to the invitation and the following exchange took place between her and another representative of the energy town project (E-Peter), here represented in a slightly shortened version[6]:

C-Julia: I would like to ask you if you have done (.) I mean (.) one may as well steal left, right and centre the good ideas (.) and there is as you know so much going on in Denmark eh and that is also what I hear when I visit different places you know [...] do you have some sort of or is there some sort of (.) eh where these things are gathered where one can go and get inspired and then say (.) is there something we can take right away and then implement up here or where we can say exactly that we want to work with that (.) is there some sort of overview because that could be an easy way to get started that could be adjusted to the local conditions (.) that was just a suggestion.

E-Peter: yes (.) eh there is not like a central register over (.) these about this about this group of interested partners that that is called 'My municipality' as such […] but as far as I know most municipalities work (.) exactly as you say (.) in these areas especially Odense (.) Sønderborg (.) this absorption and citizen involvement this is also what we weight that is why it figures in our organization as an equal theme in relation to all the others so that's it (.) it is just a question of (.) using the internet if I may say so.

C-Julia: yes but then I would perhaps like to call on you to go and say eh how have they organized or what kinds of initiatives have there been maybe at some other places that where they have already had some success and where we may already now go in and be successful very very fast because we can you know just as well take what is easy.

E-Peter: the thought [overlapping talk] the thought was you know that we wouldn't come and dictate anything (.) we really want this to be an autonomous group that you on your own (.) out of your own desire and enthusiasm and interest (.) will bring contributions otherwise we can list a LOT of things (.) but but we are (.) again to practise democracy that means that everyone should have a right to say something and to leave a mark on on a developing process (.) and this is what we would like to promote by keeping ourselves a bit in the background and let this be an autonomous group who find out their own how to put it (.) solutions.

In her first turn, C-Julia presumes the position of a well-informed citizen in that she refers to a shared knowledge ('as you know') as well as to a knowledge she has acquired 'when I visit different places'. Yet, she does not assume to be an expert on the matter; on the contrary, she poses a question about the existence of more authorised knowledge ('some sort of overview'), which assumes superior knowledge, relevant to the organising of the involvement process, on the part of the energy town representatives. There is some ambivalence when it comes to the main speech act and the simultaneous construal of relation to the energy town representatives; C-Julia initially asks about possible former actions by the energy town representatives ('if you have done'), then reiterates this as a question about the existence of something ('do you have some sort, is there some sort of'), and finally characterises her contribution as *just a suggestion*. She thus moves between requesting more knowledge and, in a hedged form, asking the energy town representatives to provide this knowledge. Whether for information or for action, her request is clearly argued, an argument that can be reconstructed as 'since there are so many similar initiatives in Denmark, it would be obvious to bring in experience from those'.

In his answer, the energy town representative treats C-Julia's turn solely as a request for information, and more narrowly as being about the existence of a *central register*. He explicitly aligns with her (*exactly as you say*), though thematically the alignment only covers the precondition for her question (that many municipalities work in this area). The suggestion part of C-Julia's contribution, however, is left unanswered, and E-Peter ends his turn by construing the information issue as a question of '*just [...] using the internet*', that is, as something that does not require further collective action or planning.

The exchange could have ended here, but the citizen comes back and reiterates the question, or rather she leaves out the ambivalence and reformulates it as a request, calling on the energy town representatives to gather information about other similar initiatives. Though the deontic elements of the request is mitigated through modality ('*I would perhaps like to call on you*'), it is nevertheless a way of (interpersonally) challenging the authority of the energy town representative as well as (ideationally) challenging their understanding of how to proceed in the group. As such, it represents a *critical discourse moment*.

In the response from E-Peter, the request is turned down implicitly by a comprehensive description of the energy town representatives' intentions with the citizen group. These intentions are described by drawing heavily on a *discourse of participatory democracy* ('*practise democracy*', not '*dictate anything*', '*autonomous group*'), in which the agency of the citizen participants is foregrounded. Moreover, this discourse is also used *rhetorically*; it does not only represent a state of affairs, but is also used in a situated action. More specifically, the discourse of participatory democracy is used as defensive rhetoric (Potter 1996) – that is, as an argumentative move to counter another position, *in casu* to counter the request put forward by the citizen. Thus, the citizen's request to provide more information about experiences made by other similar municipalities is assumed, in the interactional realisation of the discourse of participatory democracy, to be in contrast with the ideal of participatory democracy. The initial negation that '*we wouldn't come and dictate anything*' establishes the following depiction of the participatory ideal as being in contrast to a point of view that must logically be associated with the preceding citizen request. Paradoxically then, the discourse of participatory democracy is used as defensive rhetoric in response to a participating citizen, with the implicit argument that the requested information would limit her and the citizen group's ability to participate democratically.

After this turn, the discussion moves on to other topics put forward by other participants, and the issue seems to be closed. But approximately nine minutes later, the same citizen (C-Julia) brings it up again. As another citizen reports on a simple energy saving practice that he has heard about on the radio, C-Julia relates to it as '*something like that I was calling for*' and then reiterates the call for gathering '*some sort of knowledge*' on similar initiatives. This exchange triggers a response from a third energy town representative (E-Brian), and the following exchange, involving also another citizen, C-Hans, takes place:

E-Brian: well I think that is a really good eh how to put it task for for this group to
            work on to try to investigate (.) what sort of experience has been made
            elsewhere (.) I really think that is a good idea to pursue () eh because it it
            we put you know very much weight on the principle that it is up to you

<table>
<tr><td></td><td>to kind of 'accept the challenge' and and try to go for some of these eh different initiatives and experience made elsewhere (.) so I think it is a brilliant [suggestion to work on].</td></tr>
<tr><td>C-Julia:</td><td>[well just offhand] (.) if you work with it kind of permanently (.) right (.) I mean you probably have some channels or something (.) that you can sort of gather these things (.) eh that you have the access to the knowledge you must be in some fora (.) around (.) right (.) where one knows about those things.</td></tr>
<tr><td>E-Ann:</td><td>it is just that it is so complex because it is (.) you know (.) tools within all kinds of (.) genres I imagine (.) right (.) what one could do in such a group here (.) and there are so many places to gather it (.) you know (.) because we are constantly (.) well eh [inaudible] we see different things one does elsewhere right (.) of course we could go out to (.) we could (.) you know (.) go out and do it now (.) right (.) because we just pass it on but eh (.) it would require very much work.</td></tr>
<tr><td>C-Hans:</td><td>one could say that if we split into groups then we could you know within the group maybe find out maybe with a little help from you if needed [and then] try to (.) start to google</td></tr>
<tr><td>E-Ann:</td><td>[exactly]</td></tr>
</table>

In his response to C-Julia, E-Brian highly praises her suggestion ('*good idea*', '*brilliant suggestion*'), yet he thereby implicitly reinterprets the suggestion as being about a task for the *group*, not for the energy town representatives. This reinterpretation also allows him to justify the praise with reference to the representatives' understanding of the group as a citizen-driven space, which is in line with the already mentioned contribution from E-Peter. However, C-Julia comes back again, leaps into E-Brian's praise, and recasts her suggestion. This is not done by repeating or reformulating the suggestion, but by casting the energy town representatives as being more capable of taking action. C-Julia points to several ways in which the energy town representatives, repeatedly addressed with a plural *you*, allegedly have advanced knowledge positions in comparison with the citizens ('*work with it kind of permanently*', '*have some channels*', '*have the access to the knowledge*', '*must be in some fora*'). C-Julia's recast of her suggestion is clearly understood and oriented to by yet another energy town representative E-Ann in the turn that follows. She refers in different and rather vague terms to the complexity of the task ('*so complex*', '*all kinds of (..) genres*', '*so many places*'), which builds up to the final claim that the task '*would require very much work*'. The delivery is heavily loaded with markers that take for granted, or appeal to, a shared understanding ('*you know*', '*right*', '*of course*'). E-Ann acknowledges C-Julia's suggestion as a possibility in principle ('*of course we could*'), but turns it down due to lack of resources. This pragmatic response may indeed be more difficult to challenge, and with the mediating assistance of another citizen, C-Hans, it settles the issue and the negotiation of the critical discourse moment. C-Hans offers a new suggestion which incorporates elements from both the energy town representatives' and, to a lower degree, C-Julia's contributions. C-Hans refers back to a previously introduced idea of splitting into groups and adds the suggestion that the energy town representatives could assist the groups, formulated in a downgraded form ('*maybe*', '*a little*') that is consistent with E-Ann's preceding reference to lack of resources. E-Ann immediately applauds C-Hans's suggestion ('*exactly*'), and in the further interaction this understanding is no longer challenged. In that sense, the negotiation of the critical discourse moment introduced by C-Julia ends at this point. In the remaining part of the meeting, the suggestion to split into groups and investigate in the groups about former experiences in similar municipalities is treated by the participants as a decision, but at the later meetings in the series it is in fact not picked up again, perhaps due to lack of resemiotisation devices such as written minutes.[7] The issue raised by C-Julia is thus left behind by the participants in the later process.

How do these exchanges and negotiations of a critical discourse moment relate to tensions in the integration of citizen voices and, in particular, to tensions between bottom-up and top-down approaches? For one thing, the energy town representatives' initial open and unrestrained call for citizen suggestions for organising the process further is responded to by a citizen who challenges the hitherto framing of the process. Interestingly, the challenge does not consist in asking for more citizen participation and fewer constraints on citizens' options to act, but in a call for a well-founded knowledge to guide the participation process. Furthermore, the citizen implies that it is the responsibility of the energy town representatives to provide this knowledge. Instead of asking for more citizen participation, she *questions the preconditions* for a sensible involvement and calls on the municipal organisers to establish a knowledge-based, and hence an improved, frame for the participation process. The citizen contribution is clearly an enactment of citizen participation, whereas at the same time it calls for a stronger *governing*, in the sense of management or guidance, of the citizen participation. It could thus be described as a bottom-up action that calls for a top-down initiative. In this sense, a tension is played out between bottom-up and top-down approaches to public engagement, but perhaps in a less straightforward way than might first have been expected.

If this challenge from the citizen represents a paradoxical combination of a bottom-up enactment and a call for top-down guidance, so does the response from the energy town representative in the first sequence. The energy town representative answers the call from the citizen by drawing on a discourse of participatory democracy, and furthermore treats the citizen's suggestion as being in contrast with the ideals of open and unrestrained citizen participation. The citizen's bottom-up call for a top-down initiative is thus turned down by the energy town representative on the grounds that it conflicts with the organisers' bottom-up ideals. The energy town representative's response can be seen as a reversal of the tension between *representing* and *acting* bottom-up or top-down approaches, observed in the citizen's contribution. The energy town representative *represents* the process in the citizen meeting as ideally bottom-up, but at the same time *acts* with this representation to resist a bottom-up initiative from a citizen.

Thirdly, the tension between bottom-up and top-down approaches takes on a new form in the last sequence analysed. When the citizen finds an occasion to reiterate and insist on her suggestion, an energy town representative responds to the citizen's suggestion with reference to the complexity of the task and the lack of resources. In contrast to the response in the earlier sequence, this new response does not resist the citizen's suggestion normatively, but pragmatically. The tension played out here is thus not between conflicting ideals, but between those ideals and the capacity to carry them out in reality. The bottom-up approach realised by the citizen's enactment is thus constrained by the energy town representative with reference to the organisers' *lack of power* in terms of their inadequate capacity to take on the governing task suggested by the citizen. Again, this may seem paradoxical, in the sense that the formally more powerful energy town representative turns down a request for governing from a formally less powerful citizen with reference to their lack of power to govern the process.

Forming strategies and discourse coalitions

Among the ideas generated in the first brainstorming meeting, some seemed to gain increasing prominence in that they were taken up again and addressed in subsequent meetings. We will offer examples of topics that transgress boundaries of meetings, considering their role in the formation of discourse coalitions and how the discursive construal of more persistent ideas may point to a tension between top-down and bottom-up processes. A topic that was raised at an early stage in the series of meetings was the problem that citizens in Frederikshavn cannot freely choose a heating source; instead they have to be members of the local district heating plant (Frederikshavn Energy Utility), which entails a very inflexible taxation system in terms of a flat rate that every member has to pay. Besides, some citizens find that the energy bills are not sufficiently transparent. A consequence of this is that there seems to be no incentive to invest in the environmentally sustainable renovation or modernisation of houses as long as the Energy Utility does not reward citizens for reducing energy consumption. The corollary of this is that citizens feel demotivated when it comes to engaging in climate mitigation efforts, which might eventually prevent the energy town project from accomplishing its goals. These issues were being seriously discussed and negotiated in the citizen meetings. Some of the participants suggested introducing a smiley system, while others found it more expedient to write a letter to the editor of a local newspaper in order to complain about constraints imposed by various rules and regulations. As a compromise between these positions, a suggestion was made to invite the Energy Utility to a meeting as shown in the following excerpt:

C-John: rather than spending time on writing a letter to the editors (.) would it not be a better idea to invite representatives from the Energy Utility who would have knowledge about these things? Somebody who knows

	something about how the flat rate tax is calculated (.)and somebody who is not afraid of facing (.) maybe (.) a small group of activist citizens with district heating?
E-Laila:	we could do that for our next meeting [...]
C-Jane:	I would like to suggest something else (.) an alternative thing (.) that we wrote the letter to the editor and then invited the man [the Energy Utility] to a meeting (.) in the letter to the editor. [...]
C-Nick:	but could we suggest a slight change of perspective (.) in order to encourage dialogue (.) to say (.) well (.) how about one of us contacting the Utility (.) to say well (.) how is it that these things are organized (.) what are the rules and what are the possibilities of changing things (.) to reward people who take initiatives to increase their use of sustainable energy? and then describe THAT in a letter to the editor (.) what the real challenge is?
E-Laila:	that would be a good idea.
C-Nick:	we could contribute to changing these things.
E-Ann:	then it would also be more factual (.) wouldn't it?
C-John:	perhaps you are right (.) perhaps that would be the best way of avoiding conflict.
C-Tom:	we HAVE TO avoid a conflict (.) we do not want to have them as our adversaries.
C-Nick:	I mean (.) if only we CAN get a dialogue going.

In the excerpt, the idea of inviting the Energy Utility is introduced as an alternative to writing a letter to the editor. Ideationally, the idea suggested by C-John is supported on grounds of *knowledge* ('*somebody who would have knowledge about these things*') and, interpersonally, on grounds of *tenacity* ('*somebody who is not afraid of facing citizens*'). The proposition is partly rebutted by C-Jane who defends a position advocated in an earlier meeting when there was consensus about writing a letter to the editor. However, in the recontextualised version, C-Jane partly aligns with C-John's suggestion by suggesting that the invitation to the Energy Utility should instead be included in the letter to the editor, unlike what she had suggested in an earlier meeting. Perhaps sensing a threat of emerging conflict, a third citizen voices a suggestion for a compromise ('*a slight change of perspective*'), namely that the letter to the editor should be postponed till after the meeting with the Energy Utility. The grounds that support this third proposition are partly interpersonal ('*in order to encourage dialogue*') and partly ideational, addressing a need for more knowledge of the rules of the game ('*what are the rules and what are the possibilities for changing things*'). It is worth noticing that as the voices of C-John and C-Nick take over, C-Jane, who had argued in favour of writing a letter to the editor before a meeting with the Energy Utility, remains quiet in the dialogue following the overruling of her proposition.

In the excerpt, we see the early stages of the formation of discourse coalitions – that is, attempts to discursively construe common projects and enroll new members. These seem to happen at different stages and at different levels in a hierarchy. First, as C-Nick proposes *'a slight change of perspective'*, the participants seem to view this as a way of compromising earlier propositions, and C-John, C-Nick and C-Tom rally around C-Nick's idea, even if it incorporates C-Jane's idea of writing a letter to the editor – albeit at a later stage – and partly challenges C-John's idea of not spending time on writing a letter. In the formation of a discourse coalition, the role of the Energy Secretariat should not be ignored. Both representatives seem very supportive of ideas from the citizens; however, while only E-Laila supports the proposition for writing a letter to the editor, both E-Laila and E-Ann support the *'slight change of perspective'* suggested by C-Nick. According to E-Laila *'that would be a good idea'* and E-Ann repeats the exclamation, backing it by an additional reference to the idea of writing a letter to the editor: *'then it would also be more factual, wouldn't it?'* The strong support by E-Laila and E-Ann might be an important aspect in the formation of a discourse coalition across the citizens and the secretariat, which includes both C-Jane and C-John, who started out challenging C-Jane's original idea. Interestingly, C-John contributes to the discourse coalition by construing the Energy Utility as an external enemy (*'the best way of avoiding conflict'*), and he might thus contribute to building consensus among all the participants. In this new discourse coalition, the citizens align with the representatives from the energy town secretariat for a common purpose, namely that of convincing the Energy Utility that some procedures have to be changed, if the goals of the energy town project are to be accomplished. The tension that we noticed earlier between the energy town secretariat and some of the citizens has now taken on a new form where some of the citizen voices and secretariat voices have aligned to form a discourse coalition posed against the Energy Utility.

This impression is further nourished by signs of animosity between the energy town project and the Energy Utility. In the planning meeting that preceded the meeting with the Energy Utility, E-Laila gives an account of her experience of trying to cooperate with the Energy Utility. This may be substantiated through a recent encounter in which the *enemy* image, painted by C-John above, seems to be reinforced:

E-Laila: well (.) the suggestions about smileys (.) I sent them to the Utility right away (.) and I am a little sad that I have to tell you (.) but I HAVE to be honest (.) You see (.) they were actually rather annoyed with us (.) because we took the liberty to sort of criticize their professional expertise (.) you know (..) but I said that they should look at it from a positive perspective as an indication that we would like to co-operate with them about this issue (.)

By construing the Energy Utility people as *'being annoyed with us'* and as being critical of the energy town project taking *'the liberty to criticise their professional expertise'*, E-Laila does not pave the way for dialogue with the Utility. In a similar vein, one of the citizens voices a critique against the energy bill produced by the Utility suggesting that 'we are confused about how it is all organized – I mean – that they [the Utility people] ought to improve their communication'. While one of the purposes of meeting the Utility was to engage in dialogue to achieve a common goal, the newly established discourse coalition of citizens and secretariat seems to be taking a different and confrontational course.

Enacting strategies

In the planning meeting leading up to a meeting with a representative from the Energy Utility (EUR-Dorrit), the 'activist citizens' had been very enthusiastic about the idea that the Utility should offer smileys to citizens who significantly reduced their energy consumption. And although E-Laila had pre-empted the Utility's negative reaction to suggestions about a smiley system, one of the citizens uses the topic as a point of entry into a discussion in the meeting with the Energy Utility about possible ways of motivating people to engage in climate-friendly behaviour:

C-Kurt:	that thing about a smiley (.) that was a way of having something that could motivate people (.) then one might consider that (.) say (.) we know the consumption over the past years (.) then we could say one could perhaps cut 10% off the electricity consumption and then receive a smiley for that year (.) and then if one could retain it (.) then one would also get a smiley in 2011 and 2012.
EUR-Dorrit:	but then just to provoke you (.) now you say that you are below average (.) that means that you would never get a smiley…
C-Kurt:	But I would (.) I do not get close to the 4300 m3 for four people (.) I can still save 10% on what I do today.
EUR-Dorrit:	no, no, but you would not be able to go on reducing (.) it would be much easier if…
C-Dan:	It is in such a case where we have Energy Town Frederikshavn (.) and we have to sort of reduce (.) we have to both reduce [energy consumption] but also find some alternative energy sources (..) this is where we could make the campaign and say that […] if you save 10% (.) then you will get a smiley (.) and then we would have reduced by 10%.

As predicted by E-Laila, EUR-Dorrit was not favourably disposed towards a smiley system, and in the example she rebuts C-Kurt's claim twice on grounds that it is not possible to reduce consumption beyond a certain minimum level, which would then prevent the citizen from obtaining smileys in the long run. C-Kurt counters EUR-Dorrit's rebuttal by backing his first claim, and EUR-Dorrit repeats her rebuttal, but only to be interrupted by C-Dan, who supports C-Kurt's claim that a smiley system would motivate people. In backing C-Kurt's claim, C-Dan appeals to EUR-Dorrit's sense of solidarity with the energy town project, by referring to the need to 'sort of reduce' and the need to 'find some alternative *energy sources'.* By referring to the smiley system as a campaign, C-Dan invites EUR-Dorrit to become a member of the discourse coalition that the citizens have formed with the Secretariat. EUR-Dorrit, however, does not accept the invitation. This interpretation is substantiated through numerous dialogical encounters observed throughout the meeting of the activist citizens and EUR-Dorrit. The citizens ask questions such as *'how do we manage to have a reduced tax rate on heating?', 'How do we bring it [flat rate tax] down?', 'where can I read about this?'* or *'what is the tax money spent on?'* However, EUR-Dorrit provides very brief answers such as *'Actually, the flat rate tax does not constitute such a big percentage'* or *'money cannot just be shifted around from one account to another',* answers that seem to indicate that the Utility is not prepared to remove the structural barriers that present an obstacle to reaching the goals set by the energy town project.

The relationship between the citizens and the secretariat, on the one hand, and the formation of an energy town project discourse coalition posed against the Utility, on the other, seems to vary between top-down and bottom-up approaches. The way in which the citizens organise and prepare themselves for meeting the Utility carries elements of empowerment in a genuine bottom-up process; at the same time, the interaction between citizens and the energy town representatives has elements of a top-down process in that the citizens expect the energy town representatives to provide the knowledge needed for the citizens to be able to engage in the project. The energy town representatives are construed by the citizens as having the power to decide which initiatives are feasible and which ones are less so, due to their assumed access to and knowledge about the municipal framework and structural barriers. Moreover, the process is highly influenced by what is represented as insurmountable structural constraints by the Utility representative who takes the air out of the citizens' bottom-up strategy for persuading the Utility to remove some of the structural constraints.

Conclusion

This chapter has presented a case study of public participation in the context of a local sustainability initiative. In line with Irwin (2006) and Phillips (2011), we have carried out an empirical study of the practice of public participation, in order to explore tensions between top-down and bottom-up strategies from a discourse analytical and dialogical point of view. Our analyses have focused on the ways in which public participation is discursively and interactionally enacted and negotiated in critical discourse moments in a public engagement process as part of the energy town project. In the invitation letter, the citizens were, paradoxically, called upon to act as 'activists' in a new, yet unspecified, sense of the word. While the oppositional bottom-up identity of the activist was not explicitly drawn upon in the citizens' repositioning, some of the citizens challenged the organisation of the engagement process, as shown in our first example. These citizen initiatives were not blocked in an overtly top-down way, but were met with discursive strategies that foregrounded citizen participation and downplayed the agency capacity of the energy town organisers, but which nevertheless came to limit the participatory potential of the citizen contributions. New tensions between bottom-up and top-down approaches thereby emerged, as seen in the insisting citizen's call for governing initiatives and the municipal authorities' refusal of the call with reference to both participatory ideals and lack of resources.

In their continuous quest for strategies to accomplish energy town goals, the citizen voices aligned with energy town representatives in a process of translating diverging opinions into a unified voice that seemed prepared to form a discourse coalition with the local Energy Utility. In this process, positions held by some citizens were challenged by others, and representatives from the energy town secretariat seemed to play a role in reaching consensus about how to approach the Utility as they were able to draw on inside knowledge about the Utility. The tension between bottom-up and top-down approaches was thus temporarily brought to a standstill in the relationship between the citizens and the secretariat as voices aligned to prepare for the formation of a discourse coalition with the EUR. As we have seen, however, this turned out to be futile, as suggestions about introducing a smiley system and changing the fixed tax on heating bills were overruled by the powerful voice of the Energy Utility representative.

On the one hand, our analyses thus point to a need for greater preparation and organisation of the public engagement process on behalf of the organisers, not as opposed to citizen participation, but as a way of enabling and facilitating it. On the other hand, the analysis points to a need for continuous interactional reflection on the management of the participation process, as an integral part of that very process. In this interactional reflection, as shown in the case, the use of a participatory discourse does not necessarily imply a participatory practice. The double need for organising and reflecting may not least be a challenge for local (municipal) organisations with little experience with public engagement and little support from other municipal bodies, who may view the public engagement process more instrumentally as a way of gathering public support or implementing already made decisions more effectively. Finally, our analyses have indicated that genuine public participation in a local community addressing the complex issue of climate change mitigation is perhaps an even bigger challenge than what we have seen in studies of public engagement with science in other fields, such as nanotechnology, not least because the successful outcome of a process depends on the capability of a wide variety of social actors to re-negotiate well-established institutional practices

Acknowledgements

We would like to thank the Danish Council for Independent Research in Humanities for financial support of the project and the editors of the book for valuable comments on earlier versions of this chapter.

References

Allum, N., Boy, D. and Bauer, M. W., 'Eurepean Regions and the Knowledge Deficit Model'. In M. W. Bauer and G. Gaskell (eds), *Biotechnology: The Making of a Global Controversy*. Cambridge: University press, 2002, pp. 224–243.

Bakhtin, M. M., *Speech Genres & Other Late Essays*. Austin: University of Texas Press, 1986.

Bauer, M. W. and Gaskell, G. (eds), *Biotechnology: The Making of a Global Controversy*. Cambridge: Cambridge University Press, 2002.

Bernstein, B., *The Structuring of Pedagogic Discourse*. London: Routledge, 1990.

Bäckstrand, K. and Lövbrand, E., 'Climate Governance beyond 2010: Competing Discourses of Green Governmentality, Ecological Modernization, and Civic Environmentalism'. In M. E. Pettenger (ed.), *The Social Construction of Climate Change: Power, Knowledge, Norms, Discourses*. Farnham: Ashgate, 2007, pp. 123–146.

Callon, M., 'Some Elements of a Sociology of Translation: Domestication of the Scallops and the Fishermen of St Brieuc Bay'. In J. Law (ed.), *Power, Action and Belief: A New Sociology of Knowledge*. London: Routledge, 1986, pp. 196–233.

Carvalho, A., 'Ideological Cultures and Media Discourses on Scientific Knowledge: Re-reading News on Climate Change'. *Public Understanding of Science*, 16 (2007), pp. 223–243.

Chilton, P., 'Metaphor, Euphemism, and the Militarization of Language'. *Current Research on Peace and Violence*, 10 (1987), pp. 7–19.

Chouliaraki, L. and Fairclough, N., *Discourse in Late Modernity: Rethinking Critical Discourse Analysis*. Edinburgh: Edinburgh University Press, 1999.

Cottle, S., *Global Crisis Reporting: Journalism in the Global Age*. Maidenhead: Open University Press, 2009.

Delgado, A., Kjølberg, K. L. and Wickson, F., 'Public Engagement Coming of Age: From Theory to Practice in STS Encounters with Nanotechnology'. *Public Understanding of Science*, (2010), pp. 1–20.

Dietz, T. and Stern, P. (eds), *Public Participation in Environmental Assessment and Decision Making*. Washington, DC: The National Academies Press, 2008.

Doyle, J., *Mediating Climate Change*. Farnham: Ashgate, 2011.

Fairclough, N., *Analysing Discourse: Textual Analysis for Social Research*. London: Routledge, 2003.

Foucault, M., 'Society Must Be Defended'. *Lectures at the College de France, 1975–76*. Picador, 2003.

Felt, U. and Fochler, M., 'Machineries for Making Publics: Inscribing and De-scribing Publics in Public Engagement'. *Minerva*, 48 (2010), pp. 219–238.

Gamson, W., *Talking Politics*. UK: Cambridge, University Press, 1992.

Garfinkel, H., *Studies in Ethnomethodology*. Englewood Cliffs, NJ: Prentice-Hall, 1967.

Giddens, A., *The Politics of Climate Change*. Cambridge: Polity Press, 2009.

Hajer, M. A., *The Politics of Environmental Discourse: Ecological Modernization and the Policy Process*. Oxford: Clarendon Press, 1995.

Hopkins, R., *The Transition Companion: Making Your Community More Resilient in Uncertain Times*. Totnes: Green Books, 2011.

Kurath, M. and Gisler, P., 'Informing, Involving or Engaging? Science Communication, in the Ages of Atom-, Bio- and Nanotechnology'. *Public Understanding of Science*, 18:5 (2009), pp. 559–573.

Irwin, A., 'The Politics of Talk: Coming to Terms with the "New" Scientific Governance'. *Social Studies of Science*, 36:2 (2006), pp. 299–320.

Lassen, I., Horsbøl, A., Bonnen, K. and Pedersen, A. G. J., 'Climate Change Discourses and Citizen Participation: A Case Study of the Discursive Construction of Citizenship in Two Public Events'. *Environmental Communication*, 5:4 (2011), pp. 411–427.

Latour, B., *Reassembling the Social: An Introduction to Actor-Network-Theory*. Oxford: Oxford University Press, 2005.

Lemke, J. L., 'Across the Scales of Time: Artifacts, Activities and Meanings in Ecosocial Systems'. *Mind, Culture, and Activity*, 7:4, (2000), pp. 273–290.

Linell, P. and Marková, I., 'Acts in Discourse: From Monological Speech Acts to Dialogical Inter-Acts'. *Journal for the Theory of Social Behavior*, 23:2 (1993), pp. 173–195.

Mejlgaard, N., 'Scientific Citizenship: Conceptualisation, Contextualisation and Measurement'. Ph.D. thesis, Aarhus, Dansk Center for Forskningsanalyse, 2007.

Mejlgaard, N. and Stares, S., 'Participation and Competence as Joint Components in a Cross-National Analysis of Scientific Citizenship'. *Public Understanding of Science* 19:5 (2010), pp. 545–561.

Norgaard, K. M., *Living in Denial: Climate Change, Emotions, and Everyday Life*. Cambridge, MA and London: MIT Press, 2011.

Phillips, L., *The Promise of Dialogue: The Dialogic Turn in the Production and Communication of Knowledge*. Amsterdam/Philadelphia: John Benjamins, 2011.

Potter, J., *Representing Reality: Discourse, Rhetoric and Social Construction*. London: Sage, 1996.

Royal Society of London, *The Public Understanding of Science*. London: Royal Society, 1985.

van Leeuwen, T., 'Discourse as the Recontextualization of Social Practice: A Guide'. In R. Wodak and M. Meyer (eds), *Methods of Critical Discourse Analysis*. London: Sage, 2009, pp. 144–161.

Wodak, R., 'From Conflict to Consensus? The Co-construction of a Policy Paper'. In P. Muntigel, G. Weiss and R. Wodak (eds), *European Union Discourses on Un/Employment: An Interdisciplinary Approach to Employment Policy-Making and Organizational Change*. Amsterdam: John Benjamins, 2000, pp. 73–114.

Wolf, J., 'Ecological Citizenship as Public Engagement with Climate Change'. In L. Whitmarsh, S. O'Neill and I. Lorenzoni (eds), *Engaging the Public with Climate Change: Behaviour Change and Communication*. London and Washington, DC: Earthscan, 2010, pp. 120–137.

Wynne, B., 'Public Engagement as a Means of Restoring Public Trust in Science: Hitting the Notes, but Missing the Music?' *Community Genetics*, 9:3 (2006), pp. 211–220.

——— 'Public Participation in Science and Technology: Performing and Obscuring a Political-Conceptual Category Mistake'. *East Asian Science, Technology, and Society: An International Journal*, 1:1 (2007), pp. 1–13.

Website

www.energycity.dk [Accessed on 11 June 2012].

Notes

1   The most recent count published on Denmark's Naturfredningsforenings website. Since February 2010, the number of Climate Municipalities with a declared goal of CO_2 reduction has increased from 58 to 70. Available: http://www.dn.dk/klimakommuner [Accessed on 12 October 2011].

2   The Danish Model. www.energycity.dk [accessed on 12 June 2012].

3   In this article Energy Town Frederikshavn (in capital letters) is used as a proper name, while we use lower case letters when referring to the energy town project as a generic name.

4   The research reported in this article was funded by the Danish Research Council for Culture and Communication.

5   The names do not correspond to the real names of the participants. 'C' before a name refers to *citizen,* whereas 'E' refers to *energy town representative.*

6   The excerpts shown in the analysis are translated versions. The original transcripts in Danish, which formed the basis of our analysis, are available from the authors. A note on transcription notation: Pauses are indicated by (.), omitted passages by [...], and overlapping talk by [talk]. Feedback signaling is not represented in the transcript.

7   Minutes were introduced later in the process, seemingly at the initiative of the energy town representatives.

Chapter 9

The Stem Cell NetWork: Communicating Social Science through a Spatial Installation

Maja Horst

During 2004–2007 the Danish research Project 'Creating Science: Crafting Stem Cell Research in a Moral Landscape' investigated the cultural, social and ethical aspects of stem cell research. It was funded by the Danish Social Science Research Council. Empirically, the project was inspired by the legalisation of embryonic stem cell research, which was decided upon by the Danish Parliament in 2003 following scientific pressure and intense public discussion. Internationally, huge expectations had been connected to stem cell research, which was seen to be a possible way to generate medical cures for diabetes, Parkinson's, spinal cord injuries and a number of other serious diseases, but the high expectations had also been coupled with wide-scale ethical discussions. A crucial issue in this regard was the fact that embryonic stem cell research was conducted on fertilised human eggs and that the eggs were destroyed in the process (Holland et al. 2001; Gottweis 2002; Holm 2002; Lee 2001; Hauskeller 2004; Nisbet 2005). The Danish research project, however, took as a starting point that there were a number of other social and cultural issues that could be objects for discussion in connection with the introduction of stem cell research. These issues included questions of resource priorities, intellectual property rights, patient involvement and expectations management. Theoretically, the research project therefore started from a conviction that stem cell research does not fall from the sky as a fixed and ready-made entity, but is shaped by – and shapes – the social context in which it emerges. The project consisted of a number of different cross-disciplinary sub-projects which focused on the various aspects of the making of stem cell research. One of these sub-projects concentrated on the creation of the public acceptability of embryonic stem cell research. It was conceived within the framework of critical Public Understanding of Science (PUS) and its focus on the need for democratic dialogue about scientific and technical change (Irwin 1995; Irwin and Wynne 1996). The inspiration from this literature, however, also led the entire project group to consider its own contribution to public debate about emerging science in general and stem cell research in particular. In an effort to include more engaging and involving forms of research communication, the project group therefore chose to collaborate with a spatial designer, Birte Dalsgaard, to create an installation that would experiment with novel ways of communicating the research conducted within the framework of the project. The installation was created in 2005 as *The Stem Cell NetWork – a Social Science Lab*.

This chapter tells the story of this installation and reflects on how it engaged non-researchers in dialogue about research. First, it discusses the theoretical inspiration and conceptual background for the installation. These included an effort to communicate research problematics rather than facts, a focus on meaning-making rather than the comprehension of ready-made scientific knowledge, and the creation of curiosity and engagement through an open invitation to participation. Inspired by critical PUS, our aim was to find ways of engaging in dialogue with audiences about our research, since we expected this to be beneficial for both our audiences and ourselves. On the one hand, we thought the dialogical engagement would contribute to a democratic dialogue about emerging science and allow publics a new form of 'voice' in relation to science and technology. On the other hand, we also expected that we, as researchers, would learn from the engagement with non-researchers. Following the account of the conceptual framework underpinning the installation as an experiment in public engagement, the next section of the chapter outlines the process by which we designed the installation. The subsequent two sections describe the installation and the visitors' reactions to it. The concluding section discusses the lessons learned in relation to public participation in science communication. In particular, it focuses on what it means to do dialogic science communication.

A starting point for the chapter is the premise that public sense-making about emerging science and technology is a process of negotiation and deliberation in a shifting landscape of statements and opinions (Horst 2008). The creation of technical innovations and emerging scientific fields is not independent of this process, as public acceptability is one of many resources needed for an innovation to be successful. In the research project we studied these processes of meaning-making, but, through the creation of the installation, we also actively invited citizens to take part in the process. In this way, we sought to 'open up' (Stirling 2008) the processes of opinion formation and invite citizens to take active part in these processes, at the same time as we were also studying the processes.

Conceptual framework for the installation

Theoretically, the idea to create an installation grew out of an increasing sense of unease with the gap between the theoretical insights of the tradition of critical PUS and the practice of communicating those insights. Until the mid-1990s, science communication was primarily understood as a question of disseminating knowledge from experts to lay people within the terms of traditional PUS. Public scepticism towards science and technology was interpreted as a result of a deficit in public knowledge of, for instance, the facts about genetically modified organisms, nuclear power and mad cow disease (for an influential example, see Bodmer 1985). The publication of *Misunderstanding Science?* (Irwin and Wynne 1996), and related papers, changed the scholarly field of PUS. It moved the focus towards understanding the ways in which various publics make sense of science by drawing upon their own experiences, and also towards how science can benefit from a constructive dialogue with these various publics. Subsequently, there has been a strong promotion of dialogic forms of science communication and experimentation with different forms of public engagement in the scholarly community of PUS (see for example Durant 1999; Einsiedel and Eastlick 2000; Michael 2001; Wilsdon and Willis 2004), and there has also been a proliferation of dialogue-based public engagement practices – particularly around emerging science and technology. However, when it comes to PUS knowledge itself, research communication has tended to use very monological formats, such as written or oral presentations of arguments in the medium of language. This had also been a personal experience before I engaged with this installation as I had very often found myself giving talks to non-PUS-researchers in which I (to my own distress) was talking about dialogue, but practising monologue. In this way, scholars of PUS have seemed to find it difficult to 'take their own medicine' and experiment with novel ways of entering into dialogue with their stakeholders about their own knowledge production.

On this basis, the collaboration between the spatial designer and the research group was born as an ambition to experiment with spatial and interactive communication. The collaboration was not guided by well-defined goals and success criteria. Rather, the ambition was to allow the experiment to develop in an explorative way that also had the potential to surprise the participants. We therefore agreed on a set of 'rules of engagement', which would serve as guiding principles for our ambitions (see also Horst and Michael 2011) and were based on insights and discussions within the academic discussions taking place in the field of PUS and the study of science communication more broadly (see also Cheng et al. 2008):

- The installation should *make the communication dialogic and interactive and this should be the prime focus*. The effort was to begin with dialogue, rather than treat it as an optional add-on to the dissemination of scientific knowledge. In many research communication efforts, there is an expectation that publics should first let themselves be 'informed by the facts' before they are able to take part in a dialogue (for a criticism of this model, see Irwin 2001). In the context of the installation, we aimed at avoiding this kind of entry barrier and make the invitation to engagement as unconditional of research-based knowledge as possible.

- The installation should seek to *communicate research-based problematics, rather than ready-made 'packages of knowledge'*. This ambition was based on the idea that it can be difficult to create dialogue and participation around a discussion of stable and uncontroversial facts. When a phenomenon is conceived of as a 'fact', it has become stabilised (Latour and Woolgar 1979) in a way that might close off dialogue rather than open it up. If the objective is to engage researchers and their publics in dialogue with the aim that both parties learn from the encounter, the debate has to be focused on issues where researchers are open to input and suggestions, for instance research problems and questions. The project group consisted of eight researchers from different social scientific disciplines, each of which examined a social/cultural aspect of stem cell research in Denmark. The ambition with the installation was to focus on the central research problem of each of these aspects. It was crucial that the research communication was *not* conducted *after* the research process or viewed as an add-on appendage, but rather fully integrated in the research practice.

- The installation should *create engagement, irritation or curiosity rather than just understanding*. A central concern within the discussions of public engagement with science is whether dialogue is just another way of trying to get the public to consent to traditional scientific development (Hagendijk and Irwin 2006; Levidow and Marris 2001; Wynne 2005). This specific installation was based on social science about stem cell research, and although we would try to enable visitors to understand different aspects of the issue of stem cell research, the primary aim was not to create a cognitive understanding of the social science forming the basis of the installation. The idea with this specific exercise was to accept that publics should not always be guided towards a specific goal. Rather, the installation should be an open invitation to engage and interact in ways that seemed meaningful to the visitors themselves.
- The installation should be developed as an effort to *communicate with more than words*. Language is a medium with which most researchers and scientists are very comfortable, but this comfort is not universally shared in society. As mentioned above, social science, in particular, is haunted by an almost exclusive focus upon words as the medium of communication. In contrast to this, the format of a spatial installation would allow spatial, kinaesthetic and tactile forms of communication, and the expectation was that these forms of communication would inspire visitors and invite them to participate in other ways than the traditional use of language.
- The experiment should try to *engage the visitors both cognitively and emotionally*. The ambition was to create a form of research communication that acknowledged multiple intelligences and approaches other than the purely intellectual and linguistic form. This was based on an assumption that such an alternative form could appeal to a wider audience at the same time as overcoming some of the limitations connected to traditional forms of one-way research communication – both regarding what is communicated and to whom it is communicated.

Based upon these rules of engagement, the objective was to create a spatial installation that would communicate central points from the work of the research project on social and ethical aspects of stem cell research. Inspired by the work on the social construction of technology (Bijker and Law 2000; Bijker et al. 1986), the fundamental axiomatic assumption was that emerging science and technology, such as stem cell research, is developed in a complex social process in which it both shapes and is shaped by the contexts. Furthermore, it is assumed that it is a dynamic and continuing process which can be influenced by actors who have an interest in doing so. The objective was therefore to create an interactive installation, where visitors would be asked to participate in meaning-making and opinion formation (Habermas 1991) in relation to stem cell research, hereby simulating the social and cultural shaping processes of making stem cell research into reality.

A second important assumption of the research project was that any given phenomenon is configured differently in different contexts (Star and Griesemer 1989). In the research project, each of the researchers worked with different cultural and social contexts for the understanding of stem cell research and these differences in contextualisation were crucial to the organisation and outcome of the interdisciplinary research group. It therefore became an objective to design the installation as a set of different spatial confinements, each of which could symbolise a particular aspect or problem in the research projects. By using the spatial setting to create different contextualisations of stem cell research, the idea was to let visitors experience the multi-contextuality of the subject.

The assumption that the social shaping process is dynamic and affected by material as well as social influences was inspired by the work of Bruno Latour and the wider framework of Actor-Network-Theory (see for instance Callon 1986; Latour 1987, 1996; Law and Hassard 1999). It has been discussed elsewhere how the political debate about emerging technologies can be understood as a 'Laboratory of Public Opinion' (Horst 2008). In this 'public laboratory', different actors propose various statements that are linked to each other in ways that, over time, make some statements appear more unavoidable and other statements less unavoidable. As the process evolves, these links serve as the basis for decisions about the (il)legitimacy of new technologies. In the same way, the objective of the installation was to let visitors experience this dynamic process of opinion formation by engaging them in decisions about a number of issues related to stem cell research. Furthermore, visitors' decisions should involve making a physical mark such as writing a comment or casting a vote, which would leave traces for the subsequent visitors to see. The idea was that the installation would take shape from the decisions made by the visitors, so that the installation itself would represent the outcome of the debate taking place in it.

Design of the installation

Due to financial restrictions, it was impossible to create an installation that could have been placed in the public sphere as we originally had imagined. We therefore had to settle for an 80 m² test model, which would allow us to try out some basic ideas about spatial research communication and the creation of interaction according to the rules of engagement mentioned above. The test model was built in a basement at Copenhagen Business School where I worked at the time (for pictures and more information about the installation, see www.stamcellenetvaerket.dk). The conceptual work was done during the autumn of 2004 and the construction took place during January–March 2005. The actual construction work was done by a group of four people who usually work with art, theatre settings and other types of creative built environments. As mentioned, the funding for the creation of the installation was very limited, but with the help of these creative builders, its finish and aesthetics were acceptable for a test model. Our specific objectives for the creation of the installation were to investigate the following questions:

- Can the visitors make sense of the installation?
- Will the visitors choose to participate and engage with the installation?
- How will visitors make sense of the installation?

Crucial for Actor-Network-Theory is the concept of translation which implies that a shift from one medium to another is never simply the same statement in a different form (Latour 1987: 108–121). Rather, any translation is always productive because it creates different or additional meanings. In making the installation, we were aware of this and sought to use it productively by engaging the researchers of the project group in conversations about their research and how it could be conceptualised in a way that could be translated into a physical installation (research results have been published in Danish, see Koch and Høyer 2007). For this purpose, the designer developed a number of visual brainstorming tools which could be used in meetings about the installation and its content. During a series of such meetings in Autumn 2004 and with the designer's visual and spatial interpretations of these meetings, the conceptual model for the installation slowly took shape.

It was decided to design the installation as a three-dimensional 'gaming board', where visitors could move between a series of small rooms. Each of these rooms was designed to illustrate an aspect, such as a central insight, axiom or problem from the work of researchers in the research project. Together, the rooms illustrated the multi-contextuality of stem cell research and the point that it can be endowed with different meanings in different contexts (spaces). In each of the rooms, the topic of stem cell research was shaped in a particular way, which demonstrated certain problems and led to certain questions and forms of interaction. The rooms covered many contexts, such as the medical clinic for IVF (where the fertilised eggs used for stem cell research came from), the stem cell laboratory, legislation, economic markets, patients' everyday life, history, expectations about the future, moral

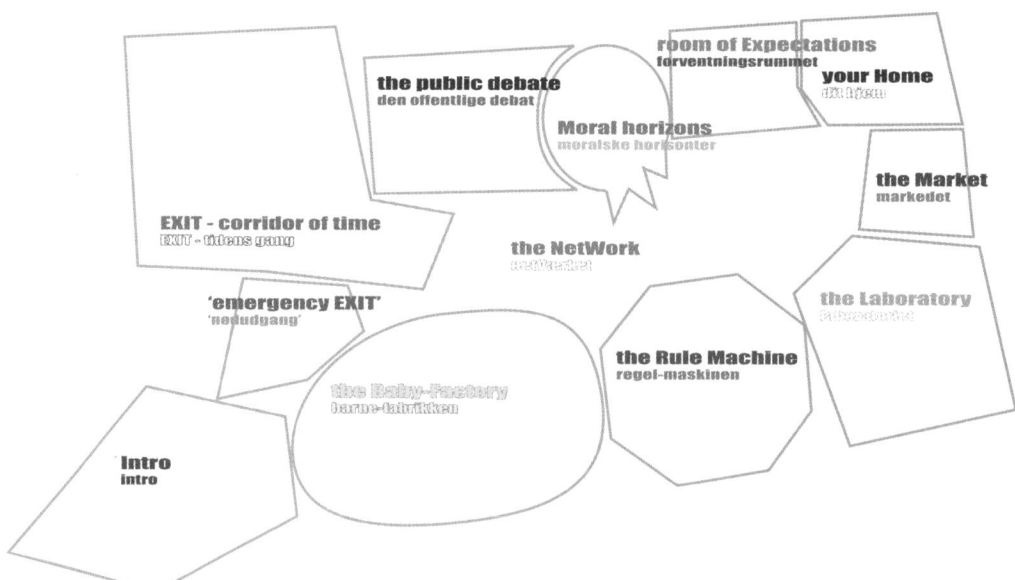

Figure 9.1: Map of installation.

horizons and public debate. Visitors could pass through these rooms in different, but not completely random, sequences (Figure 9.1).

Visitors could think of themselves as their own gaming piece in this three-dimensional gaming board. Throughout the installation, they were confronted with a number of different problematics and encountered different types of choices through physical meetings with different scenarios. They had to mark their choices or priorities in different physical ways which would change the appearance of the installation accordingly. As mentioned above, this represented an effort to demonstrate how the landscape of opinion formation changes character when people interact. If all visitors made choices that favoured the prohibition of embryonic stem cell research, then the appearance of the installation would make this visible, and subsequent visitors would meet this particular expression of preferences within the installation. More generally, the changing nature of the appearance of the installation also served to illustrate that social problems are dealt within and shaped by social contexts. The installation was therefore not just a site for individual reflection and opinion formation, it also served to make it visible that opinion formation takes place in a social setting.

A tour of the installation

As can be seen on the map of the installation, visitors entered the installation through an introductory room where the walls were covered in pictures and explanations of the nature of stem cell research and the scientific expectations associated with it. When leaving this room, visitors entered a bright yellow room, which we called 'the Baby Factory'. The first thing that happened in this room was that visitors were told that they needed to spit twice into a plastic jug, and subsequently they were allowed to take a number of '*embryo nuggets*' out of a hole in a purple box. Visitors were given one to three of these nuggets, which were peach-coloured, scone-sized lumps. The nuggets were a central artefact in the installation, basic to the ways in which visitors were asked to engage with the installation. Conceptually, they were based on the observation that the fertilised eggs created as part of IVF-treatment are a crucial material part of stem cell research. The hole in the purple box was covered with slime, which made it a bit awkward to get the nuggets out. The conceptual idea behind the spitting and the slime was that women in fertility clinics undergo a rather unpleasant and painful bodily experience when they are having IVF-treatment (Svendsen 2007), and we wanted to convey some of this experience to the visitors. Additionally, we expected that the nuggets would be seen to be more valuable to visitors when the process of acquiring them was connected to a certain 'cost' in the form of unpleasantness. Again, this was thought to reproduce some of the emotions experienced by people undergoing fertility treatment. For couples desperately trying to conceive a baby, a fertilised egg is very valuable and the fact that their creation is connected to bodily pain and unpleasantness serves to increase this sense of value.

Before leaving the room, visitors were asked to decide whether they wanted to donate one of more of their nuggets for stem cell research and sign in a book if they wanted to donate. Subsequently, visitors who chose to donate were asked to leave the room through a blue door and visitors who chose not to donate were asked to use a red door. Both doors were open but whereas the blue door was normal size, the red door was small and narrow, so that visitors had to squeeze to get through. The idea behind this feature was taken from the social scientific description of the donation process in the IVF clinic. The personnel in these clinics are seen as being very professional and ask for donations in a way that leaves it up to the couples to decide freely – a process that is also strictly regulated by law – but the nature of the question of donation is such that the infertile couples most often feel that somehow it is easier to donate than not to do it.

Both doors, however, led to the next room which we called 'the Rule Machine'. This room was designed on the basis of research on the legislation and regulation of stem cell research and the use of fertilised eggs (Hartlev 2007). The room was chequered in red and blue and had a column in the middle. On the column it was explained that visitors had to decide what kind of protection they wanted for their embryo nugget. There were five different options for protective suits which visitors could wrap their nugget in:

- a garbage bag symbolising that the nugget could be used for everything including, for instance, soap production;
- a gym suit symbolising that the nugget could be used for disease prevention but also things like research on human enhancement etc;
- a builder's suit symbolising that the nugget could be used for research on disease prevention;
- a suit of armour symbolising that the nugget could only be used for research on some forms of serious diseases;
- a cage with a lock which symbolised that the nugget could not be used for anything (Figure 9.2).

Each of the suits corresponded to one of five differently coloured exit doors and visitors were asked to choose the appropriate door. However, only one of these doors was a real door. When visitors opened the other doors, they were met by a wall and a sign that read: 'Sorry, you cannot choose this form of protection for your nugget. Our society has already decided how the nuggets should be protected – please use the yellow door where nuggets are allowed to be used for research on disease prevention.' The conceptual idea behind this room was to let visitors consider regulation as an opportunity to 'protect' a phenomenon which might be considered valuable. We wanted them, on the one hand, to think about how they would like the regulation to be, but, on the other hand, they should experience that regulation is not an individual matter. Once a society has decided upon a certain form of regulation, all citizens have to comply with that.

Figure 9.2: Rule machine.

The next room that visitors would enter was white and called 'the Laboratory'. Upon entering this room, visitors were asked to take separate routes depending on whether they had chosen to donate their nuggets. The ones who had chosen not to donate were asked to proceed into the next part of the installation, whereas the ones who had chosen to donate were let into the laboratory room. This room was devised on the basis of our interactions with stem cell researchers in Denmark and the idea was to convey that research is not a straightforward linear process whereby the donation of fertilised eggs automatically leads to the production of new cures for serious diseases. From the laboratory, visitors were led to the central room of the installation which we called 'the Network'. From this room visitors could enter five other rooms which were designed in order to display various features of the social contexts of stem cell research.

One of the next rooms was called 'your Home', and here visitors were asked to enter on their own. The central feature in this room was a hospital bed next to a wall painting of a homely setting. Visitors were asked to turn an hour-glass standing next to the bed and then lie down. When lying on the bed, visitors would naturally look up at the ceiling where they would see a sign saying: 'You are now incurably ill. Take a moment to consider how it feels ... Your only hope is that someone else will come in and hereby save you before it is too late.' Being too late referred to the fact that the hour-glass might run out before someone else entered the room, and the idea was to convey the mixed sense of hope and dependency in relation to medical research which is experienced by patients suffering from serious diseases such as Parkinson's disease and spinal cord injuries. The room was inspired by research on the hopes and expectations of patients and their rationales for participating in clinical trials (Huniche 2007).

From the central Network room, visitors could also enter 'the Room of Expectations'. Here they were asked to write their hopes for the future on little green pieces of paper, and their fears on similar red ones, and then fasten these paper notes with pegs on green bamboo sticks coming out of the floor. The effect was that the room came to have a little 'wood' of red and green expectations through which visitors had to move in order to get in. This room was inspired by a central and shared assumption in the research group which has been formulated as a 'sociology of expectations' (Brown et al. 2000; Van Lente 1993). Its central feature is to understand expectations as socially performative in the present: rather than primarily being occupied with whether expectations are justified in the future, the sociology of expectations focuses on the way in which various expectations influence the possibilities of acting and thinking in the present. By letting visitors formulate their own hopes and fears and making them visible among others' expectations, the idea was to make visitors aware that they were moving in a landscape of expectations, which could be both red (characterised by fear) and green (characterised by hope).

In the room called 'the Public Debate', visitors were given a little cube symbolising 100 million Danish Crowns (approximately 13 million Euro), and told they had to decide whether to spend it on cancer treatment, hip operations, malaria prevention, obesity research or stem cell research. On one of the walls each of these five options had a column and the black cubes could be stacked on top of each other, so that the wall came to resemble a column diagram depicting resources spent on each of these areas, depending on how visitors chose to place their cube. On the remaining three walls and the floor, the surface consisted of black and white squares, 20 cm wide, on which visitors were asked to write statements arguing for their choices. There was also a set of grey mats, which could be fastened on top of these squares. Hereby visitors could cover arguments left by previous visitors if they disagreed with them, or they could uncover arguments previously hidden. The conceptual idea was to let the room display the dynamic process of public debate in which statements are made with reference to each other, but where subsequent participants always have the option of connecting to some statements and forgetting other ones (Horst 2008). Simultaneously, the room was designed to demonstrate how public resources have to be prioritised between a number of worthy causes – and that this prioritisation takes place under the influence of public debate and statements about what is preferable and acceptable.

Visitors' reactions to the installation

As mentioned previously, the installation was built in a basement in Copenhagen Business School in Spring 2005. Sadly, the basement room had to be used for different purposes immediately after the construction, so the installation only existed for five days after it was finished. We did, however, document the work with the installation on the website www.stamcellenetvaerket.dk and also on a DVD. It should also be mentioned that we subsequently received funding to do a second installation which was presented to different types of publics (Horst and Michael 2011). During the five days, we presented the installation to as many interested stakeholders as possible and also interviewed visitors in four focus groups. The focus groups were composed differently in order to explore reactions from different types of visitors:

- Adult stakeholders working with science communication, some of whom knew each other;
- Students from a high-school class, aged 17–18, well known to each other;
- Second-year students from the programme in business and communication, well-known to each other;
- Master-level students from CBS and Copenhagen University, not familiar with each other.

It should be noted that we had to conduct the focus group interviews ourselves and this naturally may have resulted in certain biases in the answers from participants. We did, however, also document their interaction with the installation with the help of a professional filmmaker/video-artist. In particular, he put up a number of surveillance cameras, which made it possible to follow the movements and discussions of the visitors inside the installation without being visibly present, although of course we had told the visitors about this before they entered.

The following discussion is therefore based on the surveillance video from inside the installation, recordings of the focus group discussions and individual answers to a small questionnaire that was distributed before the focus group discussion. The analysis of this material was made with the main aim of answering the three above-mentioned questions, which summarised the core objective of our work with the installation. Can visitors make sense of the installation? Will they choose to participate and engage? And will they grasp some of the overall points about the social shaping of new technologies? Viewed in hindsight, our analysis of reception in the focus groups can be said to be slightly biased towards the more traditional PUS practice, where the objective is centred on whether audiences understand/comprehend messages rather than how they make sense of something. This was probably an outcome of an explicit obligation to the funding agency and a wish to demonstrate that such an experiment with spatial social science communication would be valuable and productive. Nevertheless, it should be remembered that the creation of the installation was done as a playful experiment and the presentation to focus groups and other audiences was not primarily done with the aim of testing specific hypotheses.

Before moving on to a discussion of the outcomes and learning points from these different activities, it should also be noted that valuable experience came from the actual work of creating the installation. This learning occurred continuously and was experienced by the designer labouring to create a spatial installation and the research group aiming at translating complex social scientific knowledge into simple concepts which could be communicated to a larger audience in an unfamiliar way (Horst 2012).

The first of our objectives was to investigate whether and how visitors could make sense of the installation. To start with, it can be noted that we received a lot of positive comments about the installation. All visitors thought it was a fun and interesting way of engaging with social science. Obviously, they knew we were the ones who had created the installation, and in so far as they may have had more negative thoughts about the installation, they may have chosen not to share them with us. However, from the surveillance tapes it is obvious that people were engaging in a lot of different ways with most elements.

In the focus group discussions, a number of specific elements were discussed because some visitors had found them a bit difficult to understand, but the general impression was that visitors had made sense of the overall content of the installation as well as most of the specific interactive elements. The focus group discussions also included a general discussion of the issue of stem cell research and most participants had a very nuanced and many-facetted understanding of the social, cultural and ethical implications of stem cell research. We cannot claim that this was solely the outcome of the installation, but visitors made many references to features in the installation when they talked about the issues, and it can be assumed that the installation contributed to visitors' meaning-making about these issues. In all focus groups most visitors agreed that the installation had helped them see nuances that they had not thought about before, but there were pronounced differences in the way visitors would present their own thinking on stem cell research. Some visitors had very clear ideas about the way stem cell research should be conducted and regulated, whereas most visitors said that the installation had made it more difficult for them to have a clear-cut opinion about the issues. We regarded it as a positive outcome that the installation gave visitors a more nuanced picture of the social, cultural and ethical aspects of stem cell research, because in general this would serve to improve the quality of the public discussions of such issues.

Our second objective was to make visitors interact with the installation, and we can safely say that there was a lot of interaction in and around the installation. Apart from a few of the high-school students, visitors took a long time working their way through the installation and they interacted with almost all elements. In addition, there was quite a lot of interaction among the visitors inside the installation. It might be expected that people who knew each other would talk, but from the surveillance tapes we can see that also people who did not know each other would quickly fall into discussing the features of each room. Typically, they would first engage in a meta-discussion about how to 'read' the room and what they were expected to do. Although we had tried to make the rooms and interactions speak for themselves, we did have to leave instructions in the rooms explaining what visitors were supposed to do. We deliberatively formulated the instructions in the imperative in order to make them as simple as possible ('spit twice in the jug', 'lie down on the bed', 'write your arguments here'). At the same time, some rooms, particularly the Baby Factory and the Rule Machine, had rather a lot of this meta-text, and visitors spent a good deal of time orienting themselves and making sense of these instructions. This orientation time seemed to decrease as visitors moved through the installation, an observation that led us to conclude that visitors gradually got used to the conceptual form of the installation and found it easier to understand the intentions of the design as they moved along (Figure 9.3).

The negative aspect of the amount of meta-text in the first rooms became obvious while talking to the visitors in the focus groups. Many of them said that they thought that we, as designers of the installation, were in favour of embryonic stem cell research. Since this was not the case – rather, as a research group we had aimed to be more descriptive than normative – we inquired into this impression. We found that almost all of the visitors felt very emotionally moved by the experience of visiting the room called 'your Home', where they were put in the situation of people suffering from serious diseases and hoping that, for instance, stem cell research would result in future treatments. In our conceptual design, this room was thought to correspond in an opposite way to the room called 'the Baby Factory',

Figure 9.3: Stem cell laboratory.

where we had tried to make visitors experience the hopes and fears of people in fertility treatment and the way in which the fertilised egg symbolises something very valuable, which perhaps should *not* be used for stem cell research. Visitors, however, did not have the same strong emotional experience when engaging with this room, and, reflecting on this, we thought that the emotional engagement was hindered by the amount of cognitive work necessary for visitors to orient themselves in this room. From this observation we would suggest that there is a potential conflict between cognitive and emotional influences in this form of communication, or at least that it is important to balance these different influences, bearing in mind that emotional appeals may lead to greater engagement with the issue in focus.

After having decoded the meta-communication of each of the rooms, visitors would typically engage in discussions about the issue and their different preferences. Sometimes this would lead to a joint decision and at other times they would stop the conversation and start acting or reflecting individually again. Many of the discussions would lead to questions among the visitors about issues that the installation itself did not present any answers to. In the focus groups, a couple of visitors said that they would have preferred if more knowledge had been made available in the installation. They were all very clear that they did not want any of the existing elements removed or the general design changed, but they would 'just have liked an option to seek more knowledge' about the issues as they moved along. In the light of this, we concluded that it would probably have been preferable to include a feature where visitors could look in a specific place for more facts or explanation. We would suggest, however, that this feature should be made available on demand so that visitors actively had to seek this out because this would also convey the notion that knowledge is not always readily available; rather it is something people actively have to pursue if they experience a need for this. It was quite clear from the focus group discussions that there were differences between people in terms of how much they enjoyed and preferred the cognitive vis-à-vis the emotional elements of the installation. These differences were particularly pronounced in the group of adult stakeholders working with science communication, where some visitors clearly thought that the installation needed more 'facts', whereas others thought that the absence of 'facts' was the best feature of the installation.

It should be mentioned in this context that when visitors asked for more facts and knowledge, they did not mean social scientific knowledge but rather knowledge about the science of stem cell research. In addition, most visitors did not really catch on to the idea that the installation was an effort to communicate social science. One explanation for this is probably that science communication is a widely known phenomenon and research communication is not often taken to mean the communication of social sciences or humanities. When asked to visit an installation about stem cell research, people naturally would think that the science embedded in the installation is connected to this topic and not to social scientific studies of the social, cultural and ethical aspects of this phenomenon, despite our efforts to explain this. We would, however, argue that visitors did in fact *experience* social science embedded in the installation, although they may not have been cognitively aware of this. Simply by their act of engaging with the installation, they were enacting the social scientific point about opinion formation as a process in a social setting.

In relation to this point, it should be stressed that the focus group methodology suffered from the bias that experiences had to be converted into language in order to be made visible in the discussions. We expected that this would give precedence to cognitive experiences and reflections. In order to inquire into visitors' emotional experiences of the installation, we posed two questions to focus group participants individually and asked them to answer by choosing one out of a set of four pictures, and subsequently write a few words about why they had chosen that particular picture. The first question was about their image of the installation and the two sets of pictures showed four different chairs and four different flowers. Visitors chose rather differently, but a large number of the answers revolve around an experience of diversity, many layers and a sense of 'simple, yet complex'. The second question was about how the visitors felt when inside the installation, and the pictures accompanying this question were animals and cakes. These answers were also diverse but a majority of them mention a sense of insecurity and confusion in the face of 'big questions'. Despite the fact that visitors generally expressed a rather positive evaluation of the installation as a communicative form, these answers point to the fact that they did not necessarily feel comfortable when engaging with the installation. In the focus group discussions, this was discussed as a productive tension and considered very valuable. Many of the visitors would stress the feeling of 'being confused at a higher level', and we would interpret these statements as an indicator that visitors did grasp some of the complexity connected to the social shaping of stem cell research.

Despite these considerations we would conclude that the third of our objectives – to convey research-based points about the social shaping of new technologies – was only partly met because it is hard to say that visitors came to understand the social science embedded in the installation through their visit. However, in the focus groups people were very happy about discussing the social shaping of stem cell research and some of them made connections to, or asked for explanations of, various elements in the installation. These experiences suggest that the most valuable way of using such an installation for the communication of research is by combining the visit to the installation with a subsequent discussion with researchers or communicators about its content and how it relates to social science. This also underscores the general ambition of the installation: to stimulate dialogue and invite people to interact, contribute and make sense, according to their own preferences and backgrounds. While the installation does not necessarily convey very precise 'understandings', it is excellent as an artefact that allows audiences to explore meaning-making in collaboration with the researchers. Despite the fact that the focus groups were designed to answer more narrow questions about whether the visitors could make sense of the installation and succeed in getting them to engage, the actual focus group discussions also served to explore meaning-making in relation to the issues in a highly dialogic fashion.

Conclusion

Working with this installation was a valuable experience. First of all, it was challenging and stimulating to try to translate complex social scientific knowledge into concepts that were so simple that they could be communicated spatially. Secondly, it was fun to see the installation built and to use it to communicate with non-social scientists in ways that were both engaging and informative. Thirdly, we take the various outcomes to indicate that it is also a success in terms of pointing to spatial research communication as a new and valuable form of research communication when it comes to social science, in general, and research-based knowledge about the public acceptability of emerging science and technology, in particular.

The last of these points should not be interpreted to mean that all research communication should now be done in similar ways. Rather, alternative forms and media should be seen as an addition to more traditional forms of communication, and they should be used for particular efforts where they have a specific advantage. One such advantage might be that they can tap into emotional registers and let visitors experience and become co-creators of meanings produced through their engagement in the installations rather than being told what the message is. Precisely for this reason, however, our work with the installation demonstrates that these experiences should not stand alone. Many visitors clearly wanted to consider the issues in a more traditional form of deliberation as we did in the focus group discussions. It is reasonable to suggest that the curiosity created by the experience of (the message of) complexity and multi-contextuality in the installation was a very fertile ground for the subsequent discussions about the social, cultural and ethical aspects of stem cell research in the focus groups. By invoking curiosity, confusion and a sense of complexity through the engagement with the installation, visitors' thoughts may have been opened up in a way that was very productive for the subsequent discussion of the issues.

However, as the work with the installation has demonstrated, it can be difficult to find ways of evaluating the effects of emotional influences and the creation of engagement through the stimulation of curiosity and confusion. This is particularly a problem if effects are conceived in the manner of traditional PUS as a question of understanding/comprehension. Although the creation of this installation was done from a framework that stresses interpretation, dialogue and meaning-making, we were also under obligation from the funders to investigate the effects of the installation more traditionally. This led our focus group analysis to focus less on the complex ways in which visitors made sense of the installation and more on whether they understood the communication format of the installation itself. A conclusion could be that although we cannot use this type of experiment with spatial installations to argue that emotional influences are better at creating engagement than cognitive inputs, it would be valuable to keep experimenting with these different influences. Furthermore, the installation serves as a particular proposition about the future debate about stem cell research, and in this way it has been part of the public debate about science (albeit to a limited audience), much in the same way as newspaper articles and other public statements about science.

The work with the installation demonstrated that it is important for any kind of dialogue between science and the rest of society that research communicators think about the kinds of messages they put forward. In order for visitors to be able to engage with the installation, It needs to have a particular set of messages for visitors to interact with. To strive for dialogic research communication is therefore not a question of not having messages but rather of allowing your communication partners to disagree and formulate their own responses to the messages put forward. The installation was an invitation for visitors to engage – it presented a number of different statements in either words, images or spatial arrangements, but it subsequently allowed visitors to act on the basis of their own preferences, experiences and interpretative frameworks. In this way, the 'messages' of the installation represented an invitation to discussion and shared meaning-making, hereby demonstrating that public sense-making about emerging science and technology is a process of negotiation and deliberation in a shifting landscape of statements and opinions.

In a similar vein, it should also be stressed that there is a need for the further development of frameworks for science/research communication that focus on how to engage citizens in dialogue about emerging science and technology. Rather than focusing primarily on the communication of natural science which is the focus in the many science centres and most other science engagement exercises, it should be acknowledged that social science has valuable input and that this ought to be integrated in the efforts to do 'research communication'. Based on our experiences with the stem cell network, it can be argued that a fruitful social dialogue about science and technology is based on as many inputs as possible and conducted with respect for the ways in which different actors react and express themselves. It is by being open to other formats, expressions and opinions than our own that we really learn about the life we live in common in our joint society.

References

Bijker ,W. E. and Law, J. (eds), *Shaping Technology/Building Society*. Cambridge: The MIT Press, 2000.

Bijker, W. E., Hughes, T. P. and Pinch, T. J., (eds), *The Social Construction of Technological Systems*. Cambridge: The MIT Press, 1986.

Bodmer, W., *The Public Understanding of Science*. London: The Royal Society, 1985.

Brown, N., Rappert, B. and Webster, A. (eds), *Contested Futures: A Sociology of Prospective Techno-Science*. Aldershot: Ashgate, 2000.

Callon, M., 'Some Elements of a Sociology of Translation: Domestication of the Scallops and the Fishermen of St. Brieuc Bay'. In J. Law (ed.), *Power, Action and Belief*. London: Routledge, 1986, pp. 196–233.

Cheng, D., Claessens, M., Gascoigne, T., Metcalfe, J., Schiele, B., Shi, S.,(eds), *Communicating Science in Social Contexts*. Springer, 2008.

Durant, J., 'Participatory Technology Assessment and the Democratic Model of the Public Understanding of Science'. *Science and Public Policy*, 26:5 (1999), pp. 313–319.

Einsiedel, E. F. and Eastlick, D. L., 'Consensus Conferences as Deliberative Democracy'. *Science Communication*, 21:4 (2000), pp. 323–343.

Gottweis, H., 'Stem Cell Policies in the United States and in Germany: Between Bioethics and Regulation'. *Policy Studies Journal*, 30:4 (2002), pp. 444–469.

Habermas, J., *The Structural Transformation of the Public Sphere – An Inquiry into a Category of Bourgeois Society.* Cambridge: The MIT Press, 1991.

Hagendijk, R. and Irwin, A., 'Public Deliberation and Governance: Engaging with Science and Technology in Contemporary Europe'. *Minerva*, 44:2 (2006), pp. 167–184.

Hartlev, M., 'Legitemering af stamcelleforskning. Samspil mellem lovgivning og teknologi'. In L. Koch and K. Høyer (eds), *Håbets Teknologi: Samfundsvidenskabelige perspektiver på stamcelleforskning i Danmark.* Copenhagen: Munksgaard, 2007, pp. 45–66.

Hauskeller, C., 'How Traditions of Ethical Reasoning and Institutional Processes Shape Stem Cell Research in Britain'. *Journal of Medicine and Philosophy*, 29:5 (2004), pp. 509–532.

Holland, S., Lebacqz, K. and Zoloth, L. (eds), *The Human Embryonic Stem Cell Debate: Science, Ethics, and Public Policy.* Cambridge: The MIT Press, 2001.

Holm, S., 'Going to the Roots of the Stem Cell Controversy'. *Bioethics*, 16:6 (2002), pp. 493–507.

Horst, M., 'The Laboratory of Public Debate: Understanding the Acceptability of Stem Cell Research'. *Science and Public Policy*, 35:3 (2008), pp. 197–205.

——— 'Caring for Discomfort: Science Communication Experiments between Diffusion, Dialogue and Emergence'. In L. Phillips, M. Kristiansen, M. Vehviläinen and E.Gunnarsson (ed.), *Knowledge and Power in Collaborative Research: A Reflexive Approach.* London: Routledge, 2013.

Horst, M. and Michael, M., 'On the Shoulders of Idiots: Re-thinking Science Communication as "Event"'. *Science as Culture*, 20:3 (2011), pp. 283–306.

Høyer, K., 'Hvem ejer cellerne? Etisk kategorisering, rettigheder og patent'. In L. Koch and K. Høyer (eds), *Håbets Teknologi: Samfundsvidenskabelige perspektiver på stamcelleforskning i Danmark.* Copenhagen: Munksgaard, 2007, pp. 93–108.

Huniche, L., 'Med livet i hænderne. Kroniske hjertepatienters perspektiver på eksperimentel stamcellebehandling'. In L. Koch and K. Høyer (eds), *Håbets Teknologi: Samfundsvidenskabelige perspektiver på stamcelleforskning i Danmark.* Copenhagen: Munksgaard, 2007, pp. 225–248.

Irwin, A., Citizen science. A study of people, expertise and sustainable development. London: Routledge, 1995.

——— 'Constructing the Scientific Citizen: Science and Democracy in the Biosciences'. *Public Understanding of Science*, 10:1 (2001), pp. 1–18.

Irwin, A. and Wynne, B. (eds), *Misunderstanding Science?* Cambridge: Press Syndicate of the University of Cambridge, 1996.

Koch, L. and Høyer, K. (eds), *Håbets Teknologi: Samfundsvidenskabelige perspektiver på stamcelleforskning i Danmark.* Copenhagen: Munksgaard, 2007.

Langstrup, H., 'Celler til hvem? Stamcelleforskningen og de hypotetiske brugere'. In L. Koch and K. Høyer (eds), *Håbets Teknologi: Samfundsvidenskabelige perspektiver på stamcelleforskning i Danmark.* Copenhagen: Munksgaard, 2007, pp. 133–155.

Latour, B., *Science in Action.* Cambridge: Harvard University Press, 1987.

——— *Aramis or the Love of Technology.* Cambridge: Harvard University Press, 1996.

Latour, B. and Woolgar, S., *Laboratory Life: The Construction of Scientific Facts*. New Jersey: Princeton University Press, 1979.

Law, J. and Hassard, J. (eds), *Actor Network Theory and After*. Oxford: Blackwell Publishers, 1999.

Lee, D. A., 'Embryonic Stem Cells: Scientific Possibilities, Ethical Considerations, and Regulation in the UK'. *Interdisciplinary Science Reviews*, 26:2 (2001), pp. 112–124.

Levidow, L. and Marris, C., 'Science and Governance in Europe: Lessons from the Case of Agricultural Biotechnology'. *Science and Public Policy*, 28:5 (2001), pp. 345–360.

Michael, M., 'Comprehension, Apprehension, Prehension: Heterogeneity and the Public Understanding of Science'. *Science, Technology, & Human Values*, 27:3 (2001), pp. 357–378.

Nisbet, M. C., 'The Competition for Worldviews: Values, Information, and Public Support for Stem Cell Research'. *International Journal of Public Opinion Research*, 17:1 (2005), pp. 90–112.

Sommerlund, J. and Horst, M., 'Markedsdannelse og stamceller: Konstruktionen af køber, sælger og vare'. In L. Koch and K. Høyer (eds), *Håbets Teknologi: Samfundsvidenskabelige perspektiver på stamcelleforskning i Danmark*. Copenhagen: Munksgaard, 2007, pp. 111–132.

Star, S. L. and Griesemer, J. R., 'Institutional Ecology, "Translation" and Boundary Objects: Amateurs and Professionals in Berkley's Museum of Vertebrate Zoology, 1907–39'. *Social Studies of Science*, 19:3 (1989), pp. 387–420.

Stirling, A. '"Opening up" and "Closing down": Power, Participation, and Pluralism in the Social Appraisal of Technology'. *Science, Technology & Human Values*, 33:2 (2008), pp. 262–294.

Svendsen, M. N., 'Mellem reproduktiv og regenerativ medicin. Donation som handlerum i fertilitetsklinikken'. In L. Koch and K. Høyer (eds), *Håbets Teknologi: Samfundsvidenskabelige perspektiver på stamcelleforskning i Danmark*. Copenhagen: Munksgaard, 2007, pp. 181–204.

Svendsen, M. N. and Koch L., 'Det overskydende æg: kategoriseringsprocesser i et moralsk landskab'. In L. Koch and K. Høyer (eds), *Håbets Teknologi: Samfundsvidenskabelige perspektiver på stamcelleforskning i Danmark*. Copenhagen: Munksgaard, 2007, pp. 207–222.

Van Lente, H., 'Promising Technology: The Dynamics of Expectations in Technological Developments'. Thesis in science and technology studies, University of Twente, 1993.

Wilsdon, J. and Willis, R., *See-through Science – Why Public Engagement Needs to Move Upstream*. London: Demos, 2004.

Wynne, B., 'Risk as Globalizing "democratic" discourse? Framing Subjects and Citizens'. In M. Leach, I. Scoones and B. Wynne (eds), *Science and Citizens*. London: Zed Books, 2005, pp. 66–82.

Note

A version of this chapter has previously been published in French in the journal *Questions de Communication*, vol 17 (2010).

Chapter 10

Issue-centred Exploration with a Citizen Panel: Knowledge Communication and ICTs in Participatory City Governance

Pauliina Lehtonen and Jarkko Bamberg

The involvement of citizens in urban planning and neighbourhood development is intimately tied to questions of knowledge. In the international literature on urban planning, citizens' first-hand knowledge on the qualities of places, the environment and the social processes of particular neighbourhoods has long been recognised as important. For instance, the seminal book by Jacobs (1961) argued against planning based entirely on technical-rational information and outlined the significance of inductive reasoning for the development of cities. At least since then, the field of urban planning has recognised the value of involving different forms of knowledge and engaged in developing methods for doing so.

The acknowledgement of different forms of knowledge in urban planning represents an example of the more general shift towards participatory governance. Participatory governance has been described as an attempt to reconfigure the relations between authorities, experts and citizens as a counter-reaction to practising top-down decision-making (see Pierre 2000; Hajer and Wagenaar 2003); from the perspective of participatory governance, contemporary decision-making is seen to build increasingly upon network-like environments with a plurality of voices instead of hierarchical procedures that exclude citizens from decision-making. In consequence, one of the central concerns of urban planning and participatory governance is to provide settings that foster meaningful interaction between actors relying on different types of knowledge, such as local experiential knowledge of everyday life or technical-rational knowledge on regional socio-economic processes (e.g. Fischer 2000).

During recent decades, the Internet and spatial technologies have been proposed as offering the potential to enable and enhance the inclusion of different forms of knowledge in spatial policymaking and planning (see Kingston 2007; Jankowski 2009). It is difficult, however, to establish participatory settings that work. Engineering democracy, as Blaug (2002) puts it, can produce undemocratic outcomes. One of the problems relates to the ways in which knowledge is intertwined with practice (Cook and Yanow 1993). When knowledge is detached from the practice and original site of its production, some kind of translation is necessary. For instance, as Yanow (2004) has pointed out, some of the available knowledge remains often non-utilised in organisations because it is situated on the periphery from the viewpoint of management. Similarly, residents' experiential knowledge is not easily assimilated in the institutions of city governance and urban planning.

The knowledge translation problem cannot be overcome by applying some general and inevitably abstract principles derived from, for example, the theories underpinning deliberative democracy. Taking account of the complexity of social processes, the methods of participation should be adapted to the particular contexts and issues that are being dealt with. This complexity also implies that participatory processes should be flexible and they should make room for emergent, ongoing changes and adjustments (Gomart and Hajer 2003). But how is it possible to carry on practising participation in the face of emergent contingencies? Should we rely (only) on ad-hoc methods that are generated in each case anew? In this chapter, our answer to the last question is 'not necessarily'.

In this chapter we aim to show that a research strategy that we call *issue-centred exploration* can be utilised to discover dimensions of information technology, which may aid the development of participatory methods that take different types of knowledge into account. As an example of issue-centred exploration, we present an account of a research project in which a citizen panel was set up in order (1) to address issues relating to the local environment and (2) to discuss the potential of the Internet and spatial technologies to enhance participatory methods. This twofold aim is crucial for the present discussion. We aim to show that the issues raised by residents provide a useful basis for exploring the elements of communication technology that facilitate the inclusion of different forms of knowledge in urban planning and neighbourhood development. So the purpose of participation in this case is not solely about co-producing knowledge about issues or providing solutions to them; in addition, the articulation of citizen voices is used to trigger further discussion among the panel about the elements of Information and Communication Technologies (ICTs) that could help in interaction with authorities and knowledge translation between actors relying on different ways of knowing.

The chapter is based on an empirical case study that we carried out in the city of Tampere, Finland.[1] The University of Tampere and the City of Tampere organised a research and development project in the local neighbourhood of Tesoma. We worked collaboratively with civil servants and inhabitants in this project. A citizen panel was initiated to discuss local neighbourhood matters. The research design treated issue formation as a pivotal theme in developing communication and interaction between citizens and institutions.

We start by presenting the conceptual framework on which our research approach is based. Then we introduce our case, a citizen panel that was initiated in Tesoma neighbourhood, and describe the working methods of the panel. We move on to show how the panel's knowledge base was actively shaped and supported in the process. The panel was provided with various institutional data, such as information about the city's practices in relation to the maintenance of green areas. This information provided input to discussions in which the panel also drew on its own existing, more experiential and first-hand knowledge. Panel members were able to reflect upon the technical-rational information from their own perspectives.

The authors studied the ways in which the panel discussed and used the institutional data in its activities. The analysis of this process leads us to describe how the discussions of the citizen panel helped to recognise aspects of the problem of knowledge translation. This in turn helped us as researchers to identify three dimensions of knowledge communication through which ICTs can facilitate the communication of knowledge between residents and administration: (1) access and retrieval, (2) tracking and interpretation, and (3) production and sharing of information (Bamberg and Lehtonen 2011). These dimensions enhance the knowledge translation and communication between citizens and the city administration and thus further processes of participatory governance. The first dimension relates to the way in which information on the various aspects of the city and local environment is organised and made available (e.g. different aspects of user interface on the Web that affords information to be retrieved in particular ways). The second dimension relates to the way in which technical-rational information is translated for residents so that they can extend their knowledge base (e.g. visualising spatio-temporal processes by means of interactive maps). The third dimension relates to the way in which local experiential knowledge is translated into the domain of planning and public administration (e.g. using different semiotic resources, such as maps, photographs and written comments to communicate).

Attention to all of these dimensions is important, as they help to increase people's access to knowledge resources and interaction between different actors which are crucial prerequisites for political participation (Carpentier 2011: 28). Here we consider participation beyond the traditional political institutions to mean continuous, if fluctuating, interaction between citizens and institutional actors in order to make decisions about public matters (Wagenaar 2007; cf. Carpentier 2011).

In addition, we also identified spatial tools, such as interactive maps and visualisations, which supported these dimensions. The chapter highlights that the work of the panel with the issues that it considered important was crucial in identifying the three dimensions that facilitate knowledge communication. We label the process in which the dimensions were identified *issue-centred exploration*.

Conceptual framework for issue-centred exploration

Why establish a citizen panel to discuss the potential features of ICTs to facilitate participation while the panel is at the same time given the task of deliberating on neighbourhood matters? Why not leave the design of ICT applications to professional web designers? Our conceptual framework draws on literature in the field of science and technology studies (STS). STS warns against falling into the trap of technological determinism in which technological tools are developed and believed to work in a specific, predefined way and for specific purposes (e.g. Bijker and Law 1992; Akrich 1992). Instead, technology is defined and its functions determined through meaning-making processes and the performance of different entities (see Grint and Woolgar 1997; Law and Singleton 2000). Design processes, it is argued, should always take the user into account. If, however, one pays attention to the performativity of technology (see Law and Singleton 2000: 775), a further specification regarding the users has to be made; users and their tasks are not predetermined, they are discovered in the process of addressing issues.

There is now a well-established tradition of participatory or user-centred design seeking to involve the user in the design process (e.g. Schuler and Namioka 1993). Our approach has similarities, but there are two differences that we would like to point out. First, the aim of our approach is to explore the potential of ICTs for public participation. The exploration takes place in practice and seeks conceptual insight to facilitate later developments of participatory ICT instruments. Hence the main goal is not to produce (or design) particular applications. Second, instead of the user or 'use situation' (Bødker, Grønbæk and Kyng 1993), our approach takes 'issues' as its core element. Here we lean particularly on Marres (2007), who argues that issues are central for the way in which 'the public' comes into being (see also Dahlgren 2009; Dayan 2006): particular issues engage some people and not others, which means that issues can be conceived as 'an organising principle of the public' (Marres 2007: 769). Marres builds her argument on Dewey's (1927/1991) thinking that the public emerges and takes shape through recognising problems that the institutions of governance are not capable of dealing with. From this perspective, the public is never a general public, but a constituency formed around a particular issue.

Hajer (2003) has argued that citizens are political activists on 'stand-by'; often policymaking on certain issues triggers active citizenship. This means also that the procedures of public participation should be tied to particular issues. But issues have to be constructed. They have to be defined, framed and articulated. The publics and their issues perform themselves into being, and for this activity the publics with their constituent issues need settings for communication (Bamberg 2012). Thus the articulation of citizen voices builds upon the dynamics between particular issues, people who are 'drawn to' these issues, and particular communicative settings that trigger the public to emerge and allow it to perform and to ascribe meanings to particular issues (Bamberg 2012; cf. Felt and Fochler 2010). We assume that an organised citizen panel can provide a communicative setting of this kind.

The citizen panel can be viewed as a type of 'mini-public', which are 'designs in which small groups of people deliberate together' (Goodin and Dryzek 2006: 221). The citizen panel worked as a focus group that is typically distinguished as a semi-structured group discussion method (Lunt and Livingstone 1996). In this case, this way of working enabled us as researchers to gain in-depth knowledge of the intertwining processes of neighbourhood participation and local knowledge production. The approach allowed us to see how issues were articulated and what participatory methods were found useful from the residents' point of view and why. A central goal of our research was the development of democratic practices within (local) communities. Knowledge production is understood as a collaborative process in which local community members participate as co-researchers (e.g. Reason and Bradbury 2008; Flicker et al. 2008). It should be stressed, though, that the idea of discussing the potential of ICTs for participation did not emerge bottom-up from the citizen panel, but was central to the research aim formulated by the university researchers prior to carrying out the citizen panel.

The citizen panel

The citizen panel was started as a joint project of the University of Tampere and the City of Tampere. The researchers[2] from the university and the civil servants[3] from Tampere planned and implemented the project together. The aim of the research project was to study the potential of ICTs to improve participatory methods in city governance. The central assumption behind this aim was that the ICTs have the potential for facilitating citizen participation by encouraging (knowledge) interaction between actors that are members of different social worlds. Both for the researchers and the civil servants the idea underpinning the establishment of the citizen panel with respect to local community development was to give residents an opportunity to have a greater voice in the development process of their living environment. The remit of the panel was to discuss local issues related to the living environment and to come up with suggestions for solutions to problems.

The panel's action was connected to the preparation of a general development plan that the Regional Development Centre, our project partner in the city organisation, was working on. In Finland, the general development plan gives guidelines for future development and land-use of specific areas, such as neighbourhoods. For the Regional Development Centre one aim of this project was to gather local knowledge on the issues that residents regard as significant in their living environment. This knowledge was gathered to be used as background information for the Regional Development Centre in developing the general development plan of Tesoma.

The city of Tampere is located in southern Finland and has a population of circa 210, 000. The neighbourhood of Tesoma is located 8–10 kilometres from the city centre and has a population of circa 15, 000. Tesoma represents a typical Finnish neighbourhood that was built during the rapid urbanisation of Finland during the 1960s and 1970s. The population movement demanded city housing for increasing numbers of residents. Since then, the image of these neighbourhoods has suffered from negative effects of suburbanisation such as increased unemployment and crime rates.

The project ran from 2002 to 2003. At this time, Finnish society was undergoing three developments that underpinned the establishment of the citizen panel. First, there was a drive to revitalise suburban neighbourhoods, which involved renewing local infrastructure and coping with social problems related to, for example, increased unemployment. Second, there were attempts to encourage the diffusion of ICTs in society. These attempts were part of the increasing national attention paid to advancing the Finnish information society. Third, efforts were made to further practices of citizen participation in governance as part of a turn to participatory governance in Finland.

Local residents were informed about the panel with invitations delivered to some 2600 households in the area. The invitation, written together by the university researchers and the civil servant from the Regional Development Centre, provided the details of the project and its aims, such as information about the project partners, funders and the citizen panel as a method of participation. This information was based on the project design that the researchers and the city had formulated together. Three principles were emphasised in the invitation: (1) the panel is a way to increase local democracy, (2) participants of the panel create new knowledge and (3) the panel's work is public.

The panel was open for all residents of Tesoma. There was no selection of who could participate. This was a conscious choice of the researchers and the civil servant, as they saw it important to give residents of the neighbourhood an equal chance to take part. On the basis of the invitation, approximately 30 residents were interested in joining the panel. However, when the panel started, the number of volunteer residents who came to the first meeting was 12. The number of the participants stayed rather stable throughout the project. Occasionally there were a few more residents participating in the panel's meetings (up to 15). The majority of the participants were male; there were only three female participants. Their ages varied between approximately 35 and 65 years, and their vocational backgrounds were diverse. The panel included a driving school teacher, a photographer, an office worker, a priest, a maintenance man for public facilities, an electrical engineer and an IT engineer. Some of the participants were retired.

Some of the participants were actively involved in local activities such as the parents' association of the local school or the board of their tenant-owner's association. During the work with the panel, we noticed that several of the participants had considerable experience and knowledge in relation to certain topics. This experience derived either from their professional career or from knowledge developed, for instance, through their hobbies. One participant was passionately involved in the maintenance of local forests and green areas which was partly based on this person's private interest in these issues. Another saw the local youth as an important topic to talk about which derived from the person's active engagement in the parents' association of the school.

The panel was in operation for over a year (February 2002–April 2003) and held two-hour meetings every two weeks. In the meetings the researchers and the civil servant from the Regional Development Centre chaired the panel's discussions and worked as a secretary who documented the meetings. The civil servant and the researchers wanted the work of the panel to be based on the residents' experiences. They wanted the panel to identify what the residents regarded as problematic issues in their neighbourhood, and together formulate suggestions for how fix them. These issues were closely connected to the practice of daily life. The participants listed as key problems, for example, traffic conditions, the visual appearance and character of the shopping mall in the area and its surroundings (this area was regarded as the centre of the neighbourhood), maintenance of the recreational areas and spaces for leisure activities, and the lack of social spaces for the youth.

The active shaping of the panel's knowledge base

Early on, a typical way to work with the panel was developed in the panel's meetings collectively with the residents, the researchers and the civil servant. At every meeting the residents picked a theme they wanted to discuss. The panel discussed the same theme over two or three meetings. The researchers believed that this form of working would help panel members to reflect on and formulate solutions to problems and acquire relevant information and knowledge to support their arguments. In the meetings the panel collectively with the researchers and the civil servant refined its arguments into development proposals that were delivered with the help of the civil servant to the city administration. For instance, in the meetings the civil servant or the researchers wrote down the panel's ideas on a PowerPoint slide that was simultaneously projected on the wall. This way everybody could comment on and suggest improvements to the development proposals. When the panel members raised an issue in the meetings, the researchers and the civil servant also actively chaired the discussions by asking further questions, such as how to proceed with the issue and how to find solutions to it. In addition, they tried to invite more quiet persons to join the discussion.

At the first meeting, the researchers and the civil servant asked the residents to bring up issues they wanted to discuss. The issues that came up related to the state of the neighbourhood and the participants considered several development suggestions. The suggestions were developed in the panel's discussion and based on arguments and views that the panel members brought up. For instance, they were generally worried about the security of the neighbourhood. They emphasised concerns about how to keep the neighbourhood environment pleasant. In their view, these issues were not taken into account enough in the city administration. One of the residents condensed their experiences like this:

If something breaks, nothing is done to it.

Already at the first meeting the panel discussed improvements, such as fixing street lighting and the general appearance of the area and finding ways to limit driving speeds that were experienced to be too high in the neighbourhood. The panel, for instance, had noticed that some of the changes that the city had made were not supporting the residents' daily life. One resident noted that:

It is difficult to cross Tesomankatu street because the pedestrian crossing was moved to a worse location.

Quite soon in its discussions the panel recognised together with the researchers and the civil servant that to be taken seriously in the eyes of the city administration, it needed to have a grasp of knowledge based on technical-scientific information. The panel members supposed that their proposals should be based on something else than their experiences or 'how they feel about it' in order to be taken into account in the administration. This is a stamp that is often given to residents' first-hand knowledge (cf. Irwin and Wynne 1996). The panel's finding led to the need to acquire technical-scientific information to back up its discussions (see Heikkilä and Lehtonen 2004). This meant that the residents, for instance, acquired background material from the city. This material, such as statistics or maps, built upon the kinds of knowledge different from the experiential knowledge that the panel members had regarding their neighbourhood.

In general, the panel's discussions were supported with information that related to different aspects of the neighbourhood. For instance, the panel was provided with documentation on the history and current situation of the area's spatial development. Additionally, the panel received information regarding future land use plans. To widen their local knowledge base, the panel members also acquired experiential knowledge from their fellow residents of the neighbourhood; they asked how people had experienced a certain problem and tried to gather feedback on the panel's proposals and development suggestions.

The participation of the city organisation brought a rare chance for residents to access and analyse GIS (Geographic Information System) data, such as demographic data of their neighbourhood. They used this technical-scientific data as a resource to co-construct and reflect on views that were forwarded to city government to make residents' views visible (see Heikkilä and Lehtonen 2003). Traditionally, the GIS data have not been accessible to residents. Recently, the potential of visualising spatial information to enhance dialogical methods of participation has been studied (see Sieber 2006).

Usually a few panel members were willing to prepare a certain topic for the next discussion. In the meetings the members of the panel typically introduced the material and the information they had been able to acquire beforehand. These materials were used as inspiration and as background for the panel's proposals for problem solutions. Often the group came up with a first solution to a question at hand. However, when it discussed this solution in the following meeting, it often noticed that the solution needs improvement; the panel abandoned its first solution and created another one that the panel members felt was more appropriate and reasonable. After the panel formulated its views, the civil servant helped to forward the proposals and comments to the city administration.

The panel tried to encourage dialogue with the city by asking for responses to its proposals and inviting different civil servants to discuss face-to-face with the panel. These requests had variable degrees of success; sometimes the panel did not get any reaction from the city. However, sometimes the panel's proposals succeeded in raising dialogic encounters with the civil servants. For example, civil servants who were responsible for the maintenance of the recreational and green areas in the city visited the panel's meetings a couple of times. During these visits, the panel organised walking tours with these civil servants. These encounters supported the interaction and translation between different types of knowledge as the residents were able to show the civil servants the problematic places in the neighbourhood and explain why they were experienced as problems.

In the encounters with the residents the civil servants also got the chance to discuss the grounds for their decisions which otherwise often remain invisible to inhabitants. For example, in a walking tour the residents and the civil servants visited the shores of a lake that is in the neighbourhood. The residents wanted to illustrate in real life that the paths near the shore get wet during spring and autumn. The civil servant replied that it is possible to improve the paths, for instance, by transporting some gravel. However, she explained that she could not promise when this would happen because of the expenses; the paths were inaccessible by a lorry, which meant that it would be more expensive to bring the gravel. During these face-to-face encounters, the actors were able to see different ways of approaching issues. The civil servants saw the problem-ridden places with their own eyes, and the panel got responses to its questions.

Dimensions through which ICTs facilitate knowledge communication

After the panel had established its working methods in a later phase of the project, the researchers started a discussion regarding the possibilities that ICTs could offer for residents in their interaction with the city administration. The researchers raised this idea because studying the potential of ICTs to improve participatory methods in city governance was our main research objective. At the same time, the members of the panel were keen on improving conditions in their area. This interest in the neighbourhood encouraged the panel to start to think about designing digital forms of public participation that would increase residents' opportunities to participate in public discussion, and also would enhance their possibilities to follow the preparation processes of issues in decision-making.

The issue of the communication and the articulation of knowledge between different actors, such as the example above about transporting gravel to damp paths, repeatedly arose in the group's activities. In what follows, we will illustrate this issue with more examples. Through following the practices of the panel, we identified three dimensions related to knowledge translation (see Bamberg and Lehtonen 2011). The first dimension relates to the way in which information is organised and made available. This relates to the form of information and the type of access to information. The second dimension relates to the way in which technical-rational information is translated for residents so that they can extend their knowledge base. The third dimension relates to the way in which local experiential knowledge is translated into the domain of planning and public administration. In what follows, we discuss how the panel deliberations on the issues of the neighbourhood and the issue-centred exploration facilitated the identification and explication of these dimensions. We demonstrate that attention to these dimensions advances the development of participatory instruments.

The organisation of information

The cooperation between the residents and the civil servants made visible the different ways to approach and organise information. Local residents approach issues from their grassroots perspective. Following this, the panel argued that the neighbourhood is a concept around which public information services of administration, such as online municipal services, should be aggregated. They saw a gap in the perspectives through which residents and city government approach issues as one reason that can be a source for tensions and ambiguity in public engagement.

The different logic of actors came up, for instance, when the panel was talking about the online services that the city of Tampere provided for its residents. The panel emphasised that useful online information services would serve residents in their daily activities. Information that could be useful in these activities would include, for example, web services that would entail various information, such as contact details of local authorities, leisure facilities, parking lots, recreation areas and meeting spaces in the neighbourhood. This information would need to be arranged in a way that would be easy to find and use. Thus, the panel had faced difficulties when it searched for information about its neighbourhood on the city's website. The website was built on the governmental way of knowing which did not match the ways residents wanted to access information. The panel experienced the city's website as difficult to use and cumbersome because of the differences between ways of knowing. This is illustrated in the following opinion of one of the panel members:

> *The search engine on the City website does not work as it should. The user has to click too many times when searching for information and one does not necessarily find the piece of information one is searching for even then. One cannot find the right search words if the user does not know thoroughly the city administration and the concepts it uses.*

The panel's experiences illustrated that if residents want to easily find information from the city's website, they were supposed to be able to understand bureaucratic processes and the logic of administration. This logic is based on divisions, sectors and duties which guide how information is organised (Heikkilä and Lehtonen 2004: 251–252). However, from a resident's point of view, information is presented in a fragmented way on the city's website. For residents, gathering spatial information in one place on the city's website would better serve residents. Then, information would be easy to spot and retrieve. This would make the website more user-friendly. In addition, the panel believed that organising information this way could support more effective governance. The panel argued that contacts from citizens to civil servants would possibly decrease if information would be more easily and accurately accessible online.

The transparency of governmental information

The discussions of the panel frequently addressed the issue that it was difficult for residents to gain access to the kind of information that the city governance uses in decision-making. The panel members referred, for instance, to databases of the city government that include specific information for local neighbourhoods. The residents also pointed out that they often lack the knowledge that the institutional actors use to make decisions; the decisions are made at a distance from residents and communicated to the public in a top-down fashion. The information that has been used to back up decision-making is not necessarily accessible to residents. One of the panel members addressed this as follows:

We have just recently heard that they are closing down groups in the nursery of Tesoma. They have said that the reason is that the amount of children is decreasing in the area. It would be good to be able to check this information on an online map. Now we just have to trust that the grounds [for the decision] are okay.

The panel argued that residents should be given access to the information and knowledge that public decision-making utilises. This was seen as a move that would encourage people's understanding of their neighbourhood, as one panel member proposed:

Residents already have a lot of information about their neighbourhood or home town. Information that would be made available on the net can, however, help to check if one's own impressions are correct or not.

If residents were provided with information that is used as the grounds for decision-making, they would also become more aware of the kind of information that city governance values. Revealing information would help to make governmental processes more transparent, and help the residents to become more aware of what is going on in their city.

Opening the privileged information of city governance up for citizens would serve the aims of participatory democracy. Moreover, it has been noted that keeping decision-making or decision implementation at an administrative or privatised level often fuels the opposition of citizen groups or administrative inertia (Wagenaar 2007: 21). We think that the interests of residents in political affairs and policymaking could be encouraged with a strategy based on furthering the transparency of governmental information. In our view the translation and communication of information that has served as a basis of decision-making might reduce the tensions and ambiguities that result when there is no shared meaning across different social worlds.

Online services supporting the interpretation of information could equip residents with diverse data. In general, this kind of data could enhance residents' capabilities to participate in public discussion and to evaluate local socio-economic and political processes. This type of information would, according to the citizen panel's view, help with understanding and interpreting governmental decisions and their grounds. This can be anticipated to cultivate the quality of reciprocal interaction between residents and city administration. For example, information about local spatial development and the trajectories of current socio-spatial processes is the kind of information that citizens usually have no access to.

The panel considered that interactive spatial simulations could illustrate long-term spatial–temporal information, simultaneously binding it to neighbourhood localities. For example, one panel member suggested that one could locate on a map where families with children live. There could also be a feature that overlays the development of population change on the map. According to this panel member, this would aid residents' deliberation when the city has an intention to locate a nursery. So representing temporal changes with visual and spatial tools can be illustrative and this may help residents to take an active, informed stance in relation to governmental decisions. The citizen panel emphasised the need for temporal information to equip citizens with competences to evaluate, for example, long-term policies affecting spatial developments. These kinds of matters could touch upon, for instance, municipal decisions on closing down day care or decreasing the amounts of pupils in schools. This information would encompass a wider view of an issue at hand than just that of an individual resident's. However, the panel also recognised the need for information that would aid residents in arranging their everyday life. These requirements were linked to situations in which spatial-temporal information of one's living environment would clarify city-governmental decisions, be it vast future policies or specific planning proposals.

Shared ways of communicating knowledge

In addition to dimensions relating to the organisation of information and the transparency of governmental information, we also identified a dimension relating to ways in which residents' informal knowledge on their neighbourhood could be translated and communicated to the city administration. This dimension is a prerequisite for the participation of citizens in decision-making, which is central to participatory governance.

A starting point in the project was to consider residents as local experts. Traditionally the kinds of knowledge and expertise that have been recognised as relevant in urban planning have been defined as rational, technical-scientific planning knowledge. Nevertheless this knowledge is viewed as insufficient in situations where agents and forms of knowledge meet (Irwin and Wynne 1996; Fischer 2000; Hajer and Wagenaar 2003). As noted in Chapter 1 of this book, proponents of participatory governance argue, often on the basis of models of deliberative democracy, that public participation in decision-making about science and technology leads to better and more accountable decisions.

The question of finding commonly shared means for communicating knowledge emerged when the panel acknowledged that it is sometimes difficult to express one's ideas, questions and other messages in a simple format, such as written text. However, the textual form seems often to be the primary means that the city administration offers for sending citizens' feedback. The panel came up with an idea that would expand the means of knowledge communication, particularly equipping citizens with possibilities to illustrate and visualise their messages with photos, pictures or marking places on an online map. As one member of the panel summarised:

One picture tells more than thousand words.

The residents believed that it would be easier for city administrators to interpret residents' experiential knowledge if residents could attach some visual or other explanatory elements to their messages. This kind of service could support the communication of citizens' messages and knowledge to civil servants. In addition, the panel was certain that it would help mediate comments in a way that would be clearer from the perspective of city government. Relating to this, the panel got an idea to combine written and visual messages when contacting civil servants. For example, the panel suggested that the city could produce a map of the surroundings of Tesomajärvi Lake which is in the neighbourhood. The panel members envisioned that by marking places on the map, residents could plan routes for new walking paths or could show places that would need better lighting around the lake. The panel also suggested that it would be useful to be able to attach photos of the area to the map. The photos could illustrate matters more concretely.

The panel imagined that the use of various communicative means could prevent misunderstandings that might occur when city administrators interpreted citizens' experiential knowledge. Often the reasons for misunderstandings emerge from the communicative tools that do not serve the interaction of different knowledge forms. These misunderstandings relate to the different logics of actors.

Often the citizens' first-hand knowledge might not necessarily reach administration. For instance, the administration might not be aware of local-level issues: things that would need instant repairing or maintenance but might be too local to be detected in a vast city organisation, such as broken streetlights. This is because the city organisation is based and functions on a different kind of knowledge system. Finding commonly shared means of presenting knowledge with communication technology would help provide city government with neighbourhood-level experiential information.

The panel's discussions of the local green areas serve as an example of the differences between the types of knowledge used by residents and city administration. When the panel discussed the maintenance of the recreation and green areas in Tesoma, it gained access to information that was categorised by the city organisation for the general maintenance of green areas. The citizen panel then evaluated the data against its experiential understanding of the green areas in the neighbourhood. The residents observed the classifications and categorisations both on a map and in nature with civil servants. They compared the technical-scientific information provided by the city of Tampere to their own knowledge. After this, the panel created its proposal on how to develop the maintenance and use of recreational areas. It visualised its arguments with a map by attaching a brief explanatory comment on specific places that were experienced as meaningful and important, or that had problems.

Some of the ideas that the panel brought up can now be identified in recent local online participatory tools. One recent example which was developed by using the outcomes of the citizen panel was a forum of geographically referenced public discussion. It was used in a land use planning process in the city of Tampere. This participatory online tool used aerial photographs as an interface. The tool allowed users to mediate their knowledge by moving and attaching graphic icons to the aerial photos. They could also make conjoined written commentaries with icons. Users could access earlier statements of other users and articulate their opinions and counterarguments. The comments eventually formed geographically referenced threads of public discussion. This application was used in an early planning phase to initiate discussion of the 'character' of the neighbourhood. The discussion was then produced to develop a vision for the area (Bamberg 2010). This example demonstrates that while working with the panel, we were able to identify crucial aspects relating to the problems of knowledge translation.

Another recent local initiative represents the use of ICTs in a way that furthers the participation of citizens in local governance. The city of Tampere has set up an online service for residents which allows users to inform the administration about broken streetlights by giving a spatial interface with a map to point out the exact location where the light has gone out. A similar service has been designed in Manchester where Environment-on-Call (EoC) system lets users inform the local government of defects in neighbourhoods (see Kingston 2007). [4] These services facilitate interaction between citizens and the city, relating to problems of daily life. Taken at face value, these services may look trivial from a citizen participation perspective. However, in addition to taking care of the quality of neighbourhoods, they serve an important function by maintaining at least a certain level of interaction between residents and institutional actors of the city. Maintaining a high level of interaction between different actors is beneficial to participatory city governance (Wagenaar 2007).

Spatial visualisations supporting the dimensions that facilitate knowledge communication

The use of visual tools, such as drawings, photos or maps became common to the ways in which the panel tried to articulate its local knowledge to city administration. Especially, the use of spatial visualisations, such as interactive maps, was recognised in the panel to work well when interacting with the civil servants. The residents, the researchers and the civil servant together understood that when forwarding the panel's proposals to the city government, the proposals needed to be clearly formulated and articulated.

Here, the spatial visualisations were considered useful. For example, maps fit the bureaucratic approach to administration because they offer a general overview of spatial entities, such as neighbourhoods. And while places in maps are viewed from above, from the citizens' point of view, they still provide means to point out specific details in them and thus a possibility to capture local particularities. Online spatial visualisations seem to provide a way to situate larger issues in the neighbourhood and anchor them to the particular and vice versa, thus taking different scales into account. Our results with the panel show that the residents were able to present their ideas on wider scales and combine different knowledge resources as they discussed issues that mattered to them (see also Waterton and Wynne 1999).

However, while maps were found to be useful tools for communicating citizens' voices, it should be remembered that maps always construct reality from a certain point of view. Things are framed in particular ways in maps which entails that the use of maps is not free of power (Monmonier 1991; Pickles 1995). Hence maps have implications for citizen participation in science communication. Maps simplify complex reality into clearly defined entities and provide a view from above, making this perspective useful for governing (Scott 1998; Latour & Hermant 1998). Actually it is quite likely that one of the reasons for the citizen panel to use maps was that the panel understood how powerful representations they are in the context of city governance. However, one should not be blinded by the power of maps and reduce articulation of issues to map presentations. They allow only certain things and their spatial dispersion to be seen over a selected area. This differs from the usual resident's perspective that relies on the street-level view of everyday practices. This street-level view also needs other ways of articulating issues, such as narratives.

On the construction of the citizen panel for issue-centred exploration

The citizen panel was established top-down by our research project, which shaped the panel and its outcomes. The panel can be viewed as a typical mini-public, which was established top-down by particular kind of experts, 'who claim to hold the expertise on how to create forums that give voice to publics' (Felt and Fochler 2010: 220; see also Rose 1999). This kind of approach to participation has been criticised in science communication where recent research has identified ways in which people are expected to participate and ways in which the participatory methods seek to construct 'the public' (see e.g. Goodin and Dryzek 2006; Lezaun and Soneryd 2007; Michael 2009; Braun and Schultz 2010; Felt and Fochler 2010). So close attention has to be paid to 'how publics construct themselves and are constructed' (Felt and Fochler 2010: 224) within a particular political and cultural context. Crucially, if the formation of the public is dependent on issues as Marres (2007) argues, one has to pay close attention to the issues as well.

Regarding the citizen panel in Tesoma, we want to address two aspects relating to the construction of the public and the role of the issues in this construction. First, the issues related to neighbourhood development and urban planning are more closely tied to specific places and certain geographical scales than what is commonly addressed in participatory exercises of science communication which are often established around issues whose definitions are spatially more vague, such as GMOs or climate change. Second, in the case at hand, the question is framed around familiar everyday issues, such as the qualities of a neighbourhood, whereas usually the issues of science communication are driven by 'hard science'.

These aspects are central to the way in which the mini-public, that is, the citizen panel, was constructed and appropriated its role within the process. From the outset it was residents' expertise that was called for to provide knowledge about the qualities of their neighbourhood. The citizen panel was not about handling issues that can be characterised primarily as complex or scientific; it was more about giving insight on the aspects of Tesoma neighbourhood that institutions of government were not aware of.

As the issue of neighbourhood development was confined to the Tesoma area, the panel was open for the residents of the neighbourhood. Participants did not represent a random sample which is one option in these kinds of participatory exercises (Goodin and Dryzek 2006). The invitation was sent to the households of Tesoma that were included in the neighbourhood renewal programme; this way the group of potential participants was defined spatially. One of the important questions relating to the use of mini-publics concerns political representativeness. Mini-publics consist of a small number of people and thus they rarely represent the wide spectrum of views of larger population. In the case at hand, however, the framing of the issue allowed the invitation to be sent to every household of Tesoma that was included in the neighbourhood renewal programme. The size of the panel was not predetermined and everyone interested in the issues of their neighbourhood was allowed to take part in the panel. In this sense, the issues helped to organise the mini-public (cf. Marres 2007).

Of course, this did not ensure that all social characteristics are present in the panel. People's decision to join the panel 'implies the ability to position oneself as a citizen able to contribute to the respective participation design and topic' (Felt and Fochler 2010: 227). So we must recognise that the panel as a participatory method and the way of inviting residents to the panel affected the composition of its participants. For example, no unemployed people joined the panel. In addition, ethnic minorities were missing from the panel. Therefore, whilst the citizen panel consisted of residents who were interested in taking part by means of this participatory exercise and willing to work with the city administration and the university, they were also able to do so due to their particular social position.

Concluding remarks about issue-centred exploration

In this chapter we have discussed a case study of citizen participation in science and environment communication in relation to city governance. The participation practices were developed in a collaborative process with local actors, particularly the residents, the researchers and the city administration. We have illustrated how dimensions of knowledge translation can be supported by ICTs, which create sites for interaction between different actors.

The panel's experiences demonstrate how the use of technology does not take place in a void but is constantly interactively constructed (cf. Bijker and Law 1992). With an approach based on issue-centred exploration, we were able to address the question of how communication technology can enhance the interpretation, communication and interaction of different types of knowledge that come together in city governance. With our interventionist research approach (see Mesman 2007), we gained the opportunity to experiment with and consider the use of communication technology for participation in a specific context, in a context where the meaning-making took place through socio-material practices. This is important, as the cultural context always has an impact on how different methods are appropriated and applied (Felt and Fochler 2010).

The process of issue-centred exploration takes the user into account but focuses on the articulation of issues that are considered important. We want to emphasise how, for instance, the development process of technological tools can happen through the research process; sometimes it can be fruitful to cultivate ideas in an analytical research process instead of starting to develop a concrete application.

In our case, citizen voices were articulated through issue formulation. Although the researchers and the civil servant managed the process, the issues that the panel took up in discussions emerged from bottom-up processes. For example, traffic was an issue that was introduced into the discussion by the panel members. The importance of this topic was that it was based on experiential knowledge acquired in everyday life. When this issue was discussed in the panel, the panel identified (interactive) maps and photos as useful technological tools for helping to articulate and communicate residents' knowledge about this issue.

In this chapter we have not discussed how the issues that the panel took up were handled in the city administration. We have wanted to illustrate the approach of issue-centred exploration for studying ICTs' potential for participation, not to argue how the citizen panel's proposals on the neighbourhood issues were received in administration. Another straightforward reason is the institutional inertia of city administration; neighbourhood development processes take a long time to move on.

It is important to stress that the identified dimensions were not utilised within the citizen panel to produce concrete applications or instruments of participation. It will be left to a separate process, to further research and design, to test how the dimensions are configured in particular applications and concrete cases of participatory governance. Nevertheless, spatial visualisations were considered to support the execution of the dimensions in practice. Examples of participatory instruments that are similar to the suggestions of the citizen panel can be found around the world (for example the aforementioned Environment-on-Call in Manchester, England; see Kingston 2007). Thus we can argue that issue-centred exploration can be used to further understand the potential of communication technologies that are developing continuously. Of course, this does not guarantee more democratic practices of city governance, but at least this kind of approach can direct our gaze to the dimensions that are key to the development of new participatory instruments.

Drawing on Dewey (1991/1927), we consider that issues can trigger citizens' participation; the issues raised by the panel provided the triggers that the residents needed to start to consider solutions to problems. We have paid attention to issue formulation and shown how the focus on issues helped to identify the ICT-related dimensions of knowledge translation that can support the communication of different forms of knowledge. The approach that we have called issue-centred exploration can provide a new way to develop instruments of participation, by paying attention both to users of the instruments and particularly to the issues that the users articulate. In our view, issue-centred exploration, as a dialogical research approach (see Phillips 2011), helped citizen panel members to acknowledge the boundaries of certain types of knowledge and find forms of communicating knowledge that are feasible from residents' standpoints.

References

Akrich, M., 'The De-scription of Technical Objects'. In M. Bijker and J. Law (eds), *Shaping Technology/Building Society: Studies in Sociotechnical Change*. Cambridge, MA: MIT Press, 1992, pp. 205–224.

Bamberg, J., 'Ambiguities in Knowledge Production: Multimodal Analysis of Discourse and Dramaturgy in Public Participation GIS Experiments'. *Environment and Planning B: Planning and Design*, 37:5 (2010), pp. 895–910.

———— 'Shaping Places Online: Exploring the Potential of the Internet for Spatial Local Governance'. *Acta Universitatis Tamperensis 1717*, Tampere: Tampere University Press, 2012.

Bamberg, J. and Lehtonen, P., 'Facilitating Knowledge Sharing in E-Governance: Online Spatial Displays as Translating Devices'. In A. Manoharan and M. Holzer (eds), *E-Governance and Civic Engagement: Factors and Determinants of E-Democracy*, US: IGI Global, 2011, pp. 149–172.

Bijker, W. and Law, J. (eds), *Shaping Technology/Building Society: Studies in Sociotechnical Change*. Cambridge, MA: MIT Press, 1992.

Blaug, R., 'Engineering Democracy'. *Political Studies*, 50 (2002), pp. 102–116.

Bødker, S., Grønbæk, K. and Kyng, M., 'Cooperative Design: Techniques and Experiences from the Scandinavian Scene'. In D. Schuler and A. Namioka (eds), *Participatory Design: Principles and Practices*. Hillsdale, NJ: Lawrence Erlbaum, 1993, pp. 157–176.

Braun, K. and Schultz, S., '"…a certain amount of engineering involved": Constructing the Public in Participatory Governance Arrangements'. *Public Understanding of Science*, 19:4 (2010), pp. 403–419.

Carpentier, N., 'The Concept of Participation. If They Have Access and Interact, Do They Really Participate?' *Communication Management Quarterly*, 21 (2011), pp. 13–36.

Cook, S. and Yanow, D., 'Culture and Organizational Learning'. *Journal of Management Inquiry*, 2:4 (1993), pp. 373–390.

Dahlgren, P., *Media and Political Engagement: Citizens, Communication and Democracy*. Cambridge: Cambridge University Press, 2009.

Dayan, D., 'Mothers, Midwives and Abortionists: Genealogy, Obstetrics, Audiences and Publics'. In S. Livingstone (ed.), *Audiences and Publics: When Cultural Engagement Matters for the Public Sphere*. Changing Media, Changing Europe, volume 2. Bristol, Portland: Intellect, 2006, pp. 43–76.

Dewey, J., *The Public and its Problems*. Chicago: Swallow Press, 1991/1927.

Felt, U. and Fochler, M., 'Machineries for Making Publics: Inscribing and De-scribing Publics in Public Engagement'. *Minerva*, 48 (2010), pp. 219–238.

Fischer, F., *Citizens, Experts, and the Environment: Politics of Local Knowledge*. Durham and London: Duke University Press, 2000.

Flicker, S., Maley, O., Ridgley, A., Biscope, S., Lombardo, C. and Skinner, H. A., 'e-PAR: Using Technology and Participatory Action Research to Engage Youth in Health Promotion'. *Action Research*, 6:3 (2008), pp. 285–303.

Gomart, E. and Hajer, M., 'Is *That* Politics? For an Inquiry into Forms in Contemporary Politics'. In B. Joerges and H. Nowotny (eds), *Social Studies of Science and Technology: Looking Back, Ahead*. Dordrecht, Boston: Kluwer Academic Publishers, 2003, pp. 33–61.

Goodin, R. and Dryzek, J., 'Deliberative Impacts: The Macro-Political Uptake of Mini-Publics'. *Politics & Society*, 34:2 (2006), pp. 219–244.

Grint, K. and Woolgar, S., *The Machine at Work: Technology, Work and Organization*. Cambridge: Polity Press, 1997.

Hajer, M., 'A Frame in the Fields: Policymaking and the Reinvention of Politics'. In M. Hajer and H. Wagenaar (eds), *Deliberative Policy Analysis: Understanding Governance in the Network Society*. Cambridge: Cambridge University Press, 2003, pp. 88–112.

Hajer, M. and Wagenaar, H. (eds), *Deliberative Policy Analysis: Understanding Governance in the Network Society*. Cambridge: Cambridge University Press, 2003.

Heikkilä, H. and Lehtonen, P., 'Between a Rock and a Hard Place: Boundaries of Public Spaces for Citizen Deliberation'. *Communications: The European Journal of Communication Research*, 28:2 (2003), pp. 157–172.

———— 'Social Navigation: A Tool for Citizenship. Residents Formulating Ideas for Participatory Online Services'. In E. Sirkkunen and S. Kotilainen (eds), *Towards Active Citizenship on the Net: Possibilities of Citizen Oriented Communication. Case Studies from Finland*. Tampere: Journalism Research and Development Centre, Department of Journalism and Mass Communication, Publications, series C37, 2004, pp. 243–272.

Irwin, A. and Wynne, B. (eds), *Misunderstanding Science?: The Public Reconstruction of Science and Technology*. Cambridge: Cambridge University Press, 1996.

Jacobs, J., *The Death and Life of Great American Cities*. New York: Random House, 1961.

Jankowski, P., 'Towards Participatory Geographic Information Systems for Community-Based Environmental Decision Making'. *Journal of Environmental Management*, 90 (2009), pp. 1966–1971.

Kingston, R., 'Public Participation in Local Policy Decision-Making: The Role of Web-Based Mapping'. *The Cartographic Journal*, 44:2 (2007), pp. 138–144.

Latour, B. and Hermant, E., *Paris, Ville Invisible*. Paris: La Découverte-Les Empêcheurs de penser en rond, 1998. Available: http://www.bruno-latour.fr/sites/default/files/downloads/PARIS-INVISIBLE-GB.pdf [Accessed on 30 November 2012].

Law, J. and Singleton, V., 'Technology's Stories: On Social Constructivism, Performance, and Performativity'. *Technology and Culture*, 41:4, (2000), pp. 765–775.

Lezaun, J. and Soneryd, L., 'Consulting Citizens: Technologies of Elicitation and the Mobility of Publics'. *Public Understanding of Science*, 16 (2007), pp. 279–297.

Lunt, P. and Livingstone, S., 'Rethinking the Focus Group in Media and Communication Research'. *Journal of Communication*, 46:2 (1996), pp. 79–98.

Marres, N., 'The Issues Deserve More Credit: Pragmatist Contributions to the Study of Public Involvement in Controversy'. *Social Studies of Science*, 37:5 (2007), pp. 759–780.

Mesman, J., 'Disturbing Observations as a Basis for Collaborative Research'. *Science as Culture*, 16:3 (2007), pp. 281–295.

Michael, M., 'Publics Performing Publics Of PiGs, PiPs and Politics'. *Public Understanding of Science*, 18:5 (2009), pp. 617–631.

Monmonier, M., *How to Lie with Maps*, second edition. Chicago: University of Chicago Press, 1996.

Phillips, L., 'Analysing the Dialogic Turn in the Communication of Research-Based Knowledge: An Exploration of the Tensions in Collaborative Research'. *Public Understanding of Science*, 20:1 (2011), pp. 80–100, originally published online 18 August 2009.

Pickles, J., *The Ground Truth: The Social Implications of Geographic Information Systems*. New York and London: The Guilford Press, 1995.

Pierre, J. (ed.), *Debating Governance: Authority, Steering, and Democracy*. New York: Oxford University Press, 2000.

Rose, N., *Powers of Freedom: Reframing Political Thought*. Cambridge: Cambridge University Press, 1999.

Reason, P. and Bradbury, H. (eds), *The Sage Handbook of Action Research: Participative Inquiry and Practice*, second edition. Los Angeles and London: Sage, 2008.

Schuler, D. and Namioka, A. (eds), *Participatory Design: Principles and Practices*. Hillsdale, NJ: Lawrence Erlbaum, 1993.

Scott, J., *Seeing Like a State: How Certain Schemes to Improve the Human Condition Have Failed*. New Haven: Yale University Press, 1998.

Sieber, R., 'Public Participation Geographic Information Systems: A Literature Review and Framework'. *Annals of the Association of American Geographers*, 96:3 (2006), pp. 491–507.

Wagenaar, H., 'Governance, Complexity, and Democratic Participation: How Citizens and Public Officials Harness the Complexities of Neighbourhood Decline'. *The American Review of Public Administration*, 37:17 (2007), pp. 17–50.

Waterton, C. and Wynne, B., 'Can Focus Groups Access Community Views?' In R. Barbour and J. Kitzinger (eds), *Developing Focus Group Research: Politics, Theory and Practice*. London: Sage, 1999, pp. 127–143.

Yanow, D., 'Translating Local Knowledge at Organizational Peripheries'. *British Journal of Management*, 15:S1 (2004), pp. 9–25.

Notes

1   Both authors of this chapter worked on the research project. The project was led by Ph.D. Heikki Heikkilä from the University of Tampere. Pauliina Lehtonen (University of Tampere) worked as a full-time researcher and Jarkko Bamberg (University of Tampere) as a part-time researcher on the project.

2   The authors of the chapter and Heikki Heikkilä.

3   The Regional Development Centre of the City of Tampere was our partner in this project. The Centre has now ceased to exist, but at the time of the project the Centre focused on environmental and spatial planning issues. One of the civil servants from the Centre, a planner, collaborated closely with the researchers on the project.

4   See also a service called 'Fix My Street' (http://www.fixmystreet.com/, accessed on 10 January 2012), which also lets users report local problems.